# MICROSOFT® WORKS 4.0 FOR WINDOWS® 95

**WILLIAM R. PASEWARK, SR., PH.D.**
*Professor Emeritus, Texas Tech University*
*Office Management Consultant*

**WILLIAM R. PASEWARK, JR., PH.D., C.P.A.**
*University of Houston*

Quick torial™

**JOIN US ON THE INTERNET**
WWW: http://www.thomson.com
EMAIL: findit@kiosk.thomson.com

A service of I(T)P®

SOUTH WESTERN EDUCATIONAL PUBLISHING

I(T)P® An International Thomson Publishing Company

Cincinnati • Albany • Bonn • Boston • Detroit • London • Madrid • Melbourne • Mexico City • New York
Philadelphia • Pacific Grove • Paris • San Francisco • Singapore • Tokyo • Toronto • Washington

Copyright © 1997

by **SOUTH-WESTERN EDUCATIONAL PUBLISHING**

Cincinnati, Ohio

**ALL RIGHTS RESERVED**

The text of this publication, or any part thereof, may not be reproduced or transmitted in any form or by any means, electronic or mechanical, including photocopying, recording, storage in an information retrieval system or otherwise, without the prior written permission of the publisher.

I(T)P™

**International Thomson Publishing**

South-Western Educational Publishing is a division of International Thomson Publishing, Inc. The ITP trademark is used under license.

ISBN: 0-538-71475-1

1 2 3 4 5 6 PR 00 99 98 97 96

Printed in the United States of America

## Credits

| | |
|---|---|
| Editor in Chief: | Bob First |
| Managing Editor: | Janie F. Schwark |
| Developmental Editor: | Angela C. McDonald |
| Production: | Custom Editorial Productions, Inc. |
| Art Director: | John Robb |
| Consulting Editor: | Custom Editorial Productions, Inc. |

Microsoft® and Windows® 95 are registered trademarks of Microsoft Corporation.

## To the Student

Microsoft Works for Windows is an *integrated* software program because it combines word processing, spreadsheet, and database tools. These tools can be used for letter writing (the word processor), recording income and expenses (the spreadsheet), and making lists of names and addresses (the database). You can easily exchange and combine documents and information among the tools. Integrated software is used in personal, academic, career, and business settings to complete tasks quickly and accurately.

You may have no experience with computers, you may have experience using Microsoft Works, or experience using other word processor, spreadsheet, or database programs. In any case, *Microsoft Works 4.0 for Windows 95: QuickTorial*™ will help you learn about computers or achieve a higher level of computer competency.

The authors planned this book to provide a realistic, complete, and successful learning experience for you. Objectives listed at the beginning of each lesson give you an overview of the lesson. Short segments of text explain new infomation and tell why it is important. Then, bulleted steps help guide you through the computer operation exercises. These exercises give you a chance to practice the concepts you have just learned. The book includes many illustrations and exercises to simplify complex concepts and operations. Activity questions and review exercises help you review the lessons.

## To the Teacher

Students enter computer courses with widely varying levels of skill and knowledge. Some may already know several software programs; others may have limited computer experience. *Microsoft Works 4.0 for Windows 95: QuickTorial*™ is designed to help all students develop computer competency using an integrated software package.

This book is appropriate for students in a variety of educational settings, including high school, community college, continuing education, vocational technical school, career college, weekend courses, adult education programs, and personal instruction. Estimated completion times are included in each lesson but will vary depending on the student's ability and previous computer experience. An average completion time for the book is 12–15 hours.

Microsoft Works 4.0 for Windows 95 has the following system requirements:

- Microsoft Windows 95 operating system or Microsoft Windows NT Workstation version 3.51 or later
- 386DX or higher processor (486 recommended)
- 6 MB of memory for Windows 95 (8 MB recommended); 12 MB of memory for Windows NT Workstation
- 3.5" high- or low-density disk drive
- 5 MB of free space on hard disk to install; 20 MB for complete installation

- VGA or higher-resolution video adapter (Super VGA-256 color recommended)
- To print, any Windows-compatible printer will operate with Works
- Mouse or other pointing device
- To communicate, a 2400 or higher baud modem (9600 baud modem recommended)

The *student's book* is organized around the following features:

- *Learning objectives* at the beginning of each lesson give students an overview of the lesson.
- *Enumerated step-by-step instructions* for specific operations allow students to progress independently.
- *Computer exercises* immediately following the presentation of new concepts and instructions give students the opportunity to apply what they have just learned.
- The *integration lesson* teaches students how to merge the word processing, spreadsheet, and database tools.
- *Illustrations* explain complex concepts and serve as reference points as students complete exercises.
- *Activity questions* and *review exercises* follow lessons to gauge student understanding of the lesson's concepts and operations.
- A comprehensive index supplies quick and easy accessibility to specific parts of the book.

The *teacher's manual* includes the following features designed to ensure a successful and enjoyable teaching experience:

- *General teaching suggestions* that are strategies for effective instruction with a minimum of stress.
- *Specific teaching suggestions* for each lesson.
- *Time estimates* for the completion of each lesson.
- *Reproducible short-answer and production tests* and solutions.
- *Evaluation of learning* by students using the Review Exercise Progress Record and the teacher using the realistic grading system.
- The *template disk* contains pre-keyed text for exercises and review exercises and may be copied for students. This disk allows students to use class time learning computer operations rather than keying text into the computer. The *solutions disk* contains solutions to exercises, review exercises, and production tests so that you can check students' work.

## Acknowledgments

The authors thank Todd Knowlton and Dawna Walls for their dedicated and effective contributions to this publication.

Many professional South-Western sales representatives make educationally sound presentations to teachers about our books. The authors know of and appreciate very much a sales representative's valuable function as "bridge" between the author and the teacher.

## Some Other Books by the Authors

### TRANSFER OF LEARNING AMONG MICROSOFT PROGRAMS

Screens, commands, and operations for Microsoft Office programs are similar to, and sometimes identical with, those for many versions of other Microsoft products, such as Works. Therefore, students who learn any Microsoft program will benefit from the enormous amount of *transfer of learning* that occurs when they use other Microsoft programs.

The Microsoft Windows books listed below are available exclusively from South-Western Educational Publishing. Also available are Macintosh and DOS versions of Microsoft Works books, as well as a ClarisWorks tutorial.

### WINDOWS 3.0, 3.1 AND 3.11

**Tutorial and Applications Series**

*Microsoft Works for Windows 2.0: Tutorial and Applications (High School)*

*Microsoft Works for Windows 2.0: A Practical Approach (College)*

*Microsoft Works for Windows 3.0: Tutorial and Applications*

*Microsoft Office Professional 4.3: Tutorial and Applications*

**Quick Course Series**

*Microsoft Works for Windows 3.0: Quick Course*

**Applications for Reinforcement Series**

*Microsoft Works 2.0/3.0 for Windows: Applications for Reinforcement*

### WINDOWS 95

**Tutorial and Applications Series**

*Microsoft Works 4.0 for Windows 95: Tutorial and Applications*

*Microsoft Office 7.0 for Windows 95: Tutorial and Applications*

**QuickTorial™ Series**

*Microsoft Works 4.0 for Windows 95: QuickTorial™*

*Microsoft Office for Windows 95: QuickTorial™*

**Applications for Reinforcement**

*Microsoft Works 4.0 for Windows 95: Applications for Reinforcement*

Desktop publishing books include Aldus PageMaker, Express Publisher, PFS: First Publisher, and Publish It!

The Pasewarks and South-Western Educational Publishing won the Textbook and Academic Authors Association *Texty Award* for the best computer book in 1994.

**iii Preface**

**1 Getting Started with Works**

Objectives, 1; Introduction, 1; Starting Works, 1; Dialog Boxes, 3; The Works Screen, 4; Opening Documents, 5; Scrolling, 7; Closing Documents, 8; Exiting Works, 8; Activities, 9; Review, 10

**11 Lesson 1: Creating and Saving a Document**

Objectives, 11; Creating New Documents, 11; The Document Window, 13; Entering Text, 13; Saving Your Work, 14; Activities, 17; Review, 18

**19 Lesson 2: Editing Text and Printing**

Objectives, 19; Moving the Cursor, 19; Highlighting Text, 20; Inserting Text, 20; Moving Text, 21; Copying Text, 22; Drag and Drop, 23; Previewing Your Document, 24; Printing Your Document, 25; Activities, 27; Review, 28

**31 Lesson 3: Margins, Indents, Spacing, and Alignment**

Objectives, 31; Margins, 31; Indenting, 32; Spacing, 35; Alignment, 35; Activities, 37; Review, 38

**39 Lesson 4: Fonts and Checking Spelling**

Objectives, 39; Fonts, 39; Using the Spelling Checker, 41; Activities, 43; Review, 44

**45 Lesson 5: Tabs, Page Breaks, and Search and Replace**

Objectives, 45; Tabs, 45; Page Breaks, 48; Find, 49; Replace, 50; Activities, 51; Review, 52

**55 Lesson 6: Advanced Copying, Headers, and Footers**

Objectives, 55; Copying Text Between Documents, 55; Copying Format and Style, 55; Special Characters, 56; View All Characters, 57; Headers and Footers, 58; Activities, 60; Review, 61

# contents

**65 Lesson 7: Moving the Highlight, Entering Data, and Saving**

*Objectives, 65; Creating and Opening Spreadsheets, 65; Parts of a Spreadsheet, 65; Moving the Highlight in a Spreadsheet, 66; Entering Data into a Cell, 68; Adjusting Column Width, 69; Changing Data in a Cell, 70; Saving a Spreadsheet, 71; Activities, 72; Review, 73*

**75 Lesson 8: Cell Appearance and Inserting and Deleting Rows and Columns**

*Objectives, 75; Selecting a Group of Cells, 75; Changing Cell Appearance, 75; Inserting and Deleting Rows and Columns, 79; Activities, 81; Review, 82*

**83 Lesson 9: Copying and Moving Data and Printing**

*Objectives, 83; Copying Data, 83; Moving Data, 86; Freezing Titles, 87; Printing a Spreadsheet, 88; Activities, 89; Review, 90*

**93 Lesson 10: Using Formulas**

*Objectives, 93; What are Formulas?, 93; Entering and Editing Formulas, 94; Using the Highlight to Create Formulas, 95; The Autosum Command, 96; Formula Helpers, 97; Activities, 99; Review, 100*

**103 Lesson 11: Cell References and Function Formulas**

*Objectives, 103; Cell References, 103; Function Formulas, 105; Activities, 110; Review, 111*

**115 Lesson 12: Charts**

*Objectives, 115; Types of Spreadsheet Charts, 115; Creating a Chart from a Spreadsheet, 115; Saving a Chart, 119; Changing the Type of Chart, 120; Printing Charts, 120; Activities, 121; Review, 122*

**125 Lesson 13: Databases: Opening a Database and Switching Views**

*Objectives, 125; Parts of a Database, 126; Viewing a Database, 127; Moving the Highlight in the Database, 129; Activities, 132; Review, 133*

**135 Lesson 14: Adding and Deleting Records and Printing**

*Objectives, 135; Adding and Deleting Records, 135; Saving a Document, 136; Copying Data, 137; Inserting a Record, 138; Moving Data, 139; Printing a Database, 139; Activities, 141; Review, 142*

**143 Lesson 15: Creating a Database and Designing Fields**

*Objectives, 143; Creating a New Database, 143; Creating Fields, 144; Inserting Fields in an Existing Database, 145; Adjusting Field Size, 147; Moving a Field in Form Design View, 147; Field Alignment, 148; Font, Style, and Size, 149; Activities, 150; Review, 151*

**153 Lesson 16: Formatting Database Fields and Calculating in the Database**

*Objectives, 153; Field Formats, 153; Calculating in the Database, 157; Activities, 159; Review, 160*

**163 Lesson 17: Hiding Fields, Hiding Records, and Searching**

*Objectives, 163; Hiding Fields and Field Names, 163; Hiding Records, 165; Searching a Database, 165; Activities, 169; Review, 170*

**171 Lesson 18: Sorting and Using Filters**

*Objectives, 171; Sorting a Database, 171; Using Filters, 173; Activities, 177; Review, 178*

# contents

**183  Lesson 19: Database Reporting**

*Objectives, 183; Database Reports, 183; Using the ReportCreator, 183; Giving a Title to a Report, 184; Specifying Fields for a Report, 185; Sorting and Grouping a Report, 185; Changing the Appearance of a Report, 188; Saving Reports in a Database, 191; Printing a Database Report, 191; Activities, 192; Review, 193*

**197  Lesson 20: Integration Basics**

*Objectives, 197; Introduction to Integration, 197; Moving and Copying Data Between Documents, 197; Linking, 199; Updating a Linked Document, 200; Form Letters, 200; Creating a Form Letter, 201; Printing Form Letters, 202; Activities, 204; Review, 205*

**207  Index**

# Getting Started with Works

## ❖ OBJECTIVES

Upon completion of this lesson, you will be able to:

1. Describe an integrated software package.
2. Start Works.
3. Use dialog boxes.
4. Open and close documents.
5. Exit Works.

**Estimated Time:** 1 hour

## ❖ INTRODUCTION

Microsoft Works is an integrated software package that combines several computer tools into one program. Works consists of a word processor tool, a spreadsheet tool, a database tool, and a communications tool in one program. Because Works is an integrated program, the tools can be used together. For example, numbers from a spreadsheet can be included in a document created in the word processor.

## ❖ STARTING WORKS

Works is started from the Start menu in Windows. To start Works, click the Start button on the taskbar, click Programs, click Microsoft Works 4.0, and click Microsoft Works 4.0 in the menu which appears, as shown in Figure GS–1.

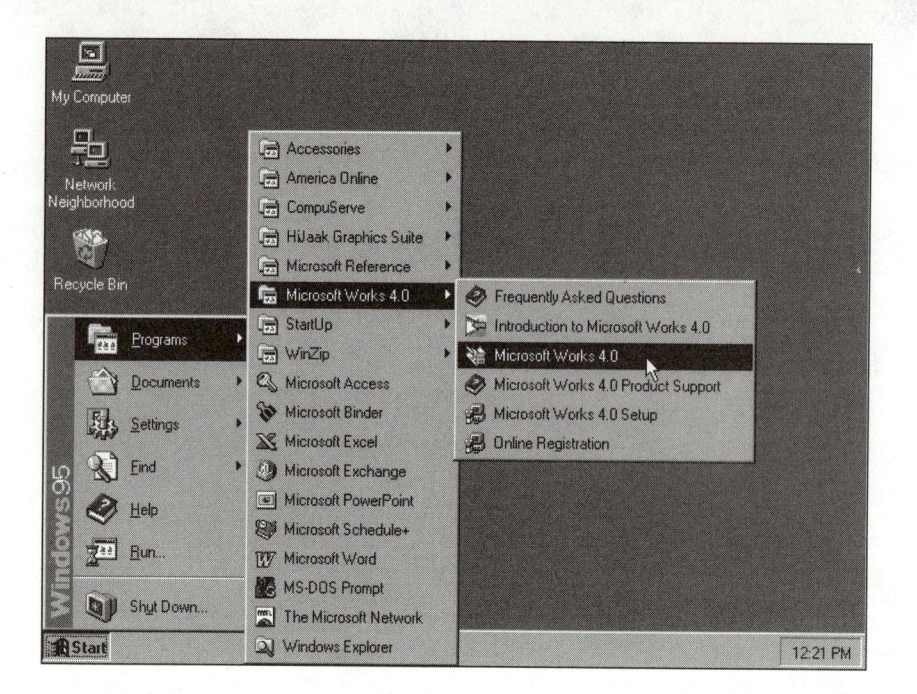

**Figure GS–1**
The Start menu allows you to start Works.

# Exercise GS-1

This exercise assumes that Windows 95 is already running on your computer.

1. Click the **Start** button. The Start menu appears.

2. Click the **Programs** item in the **Start** menu. The Programs menu appears.

3. Click the **Microsoft Works 4.0** item in the **Programs** menu. Another menu appears.

4. Click the **Microsoft Works 4.0** item. Works starts. The Works Task Launcher appears (see Figure GS–2).

5. Leave the Works Task Launcher on the screen for the next activity.

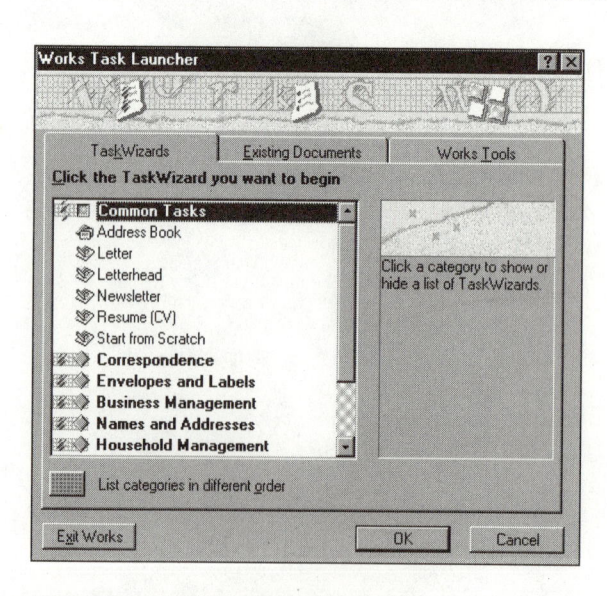

**Figure GS–2**
The Works Task Launcher appears after you start Works.

2   *Microsoft Works 4.0 for Windows 95: QuickTorial*™

## ❖ DIALOG BOXES

The Works Task Launcher is an example of a dialog box. A dialog box is a window that requests additional information so the computer can complete an operation. Dialog boxes have buttons, lists, and/or option groups to simplify operations to be performed.

Some dialog boxes, like the Works Task Launcher, are divided into sections that are accessed by clicking tabs. To switch to another section of the dialog box, click the appropriate tab.

To choose a button in a dialog box:

- Position the pointer over the button you want to choose.
- Click the mouse.

In addition to buttons, dialog boxes can include lists and option groups. You will learn more about lists later. There are two types of option groups. If there is a bullet (•) next to one of the options in the group, then only one option at a time can be chosen. If there are check boxes next to options in the group, you can choose as many of the options as you want, or none at all.

To choose an option:

- Click an option in the option group.
- Click the **OK** button to accept the options and close the dialog box.

> **note**
> Pressing and then quickly releasing the mouse button is called *clicking*. Clicking twice rapidly is called *double-clicking*.

## Exercise GS-2

In this exercise, you will use the Works Task Launcher dialog box to open a word processing file.

1. Click the **Works Tools** tab.
2. Click the **Word Processor** button. A new word processing file appears, as shown in Figure GS–3.

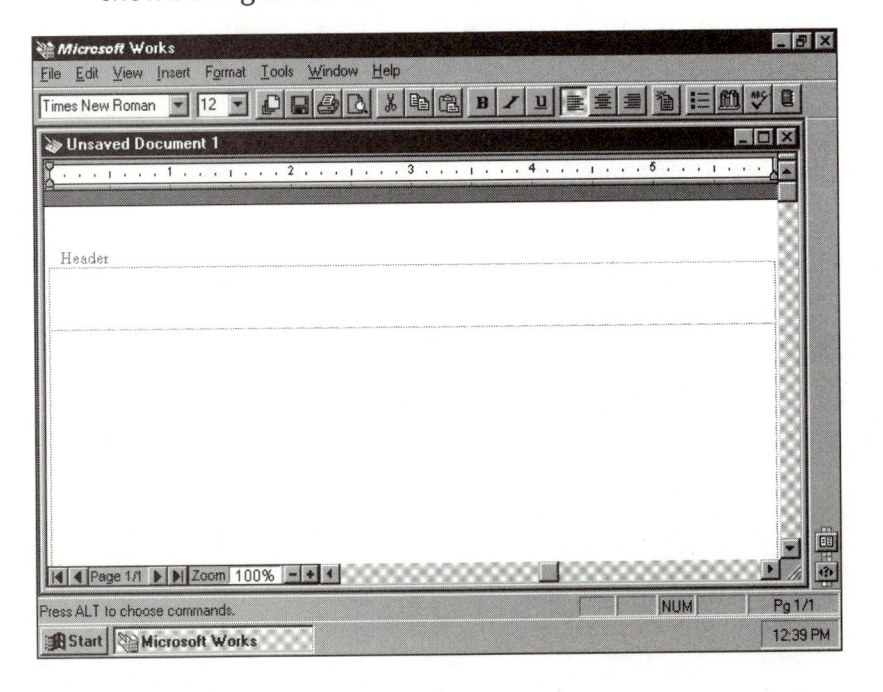

**Figure GS–3**
You can open a new file from the Works Task Launcher.

Getting Started with Works 3

### ❖ THE WORKS SCREEN

The Works screen consists of windows, menus, a toolbar, and a status bar.

#### WINDOWS

Almost everything is in a window. All of these windows share some common features that allow you to change their shapes, sizes, and locations. Figure GS–4 shows a window and its controls.

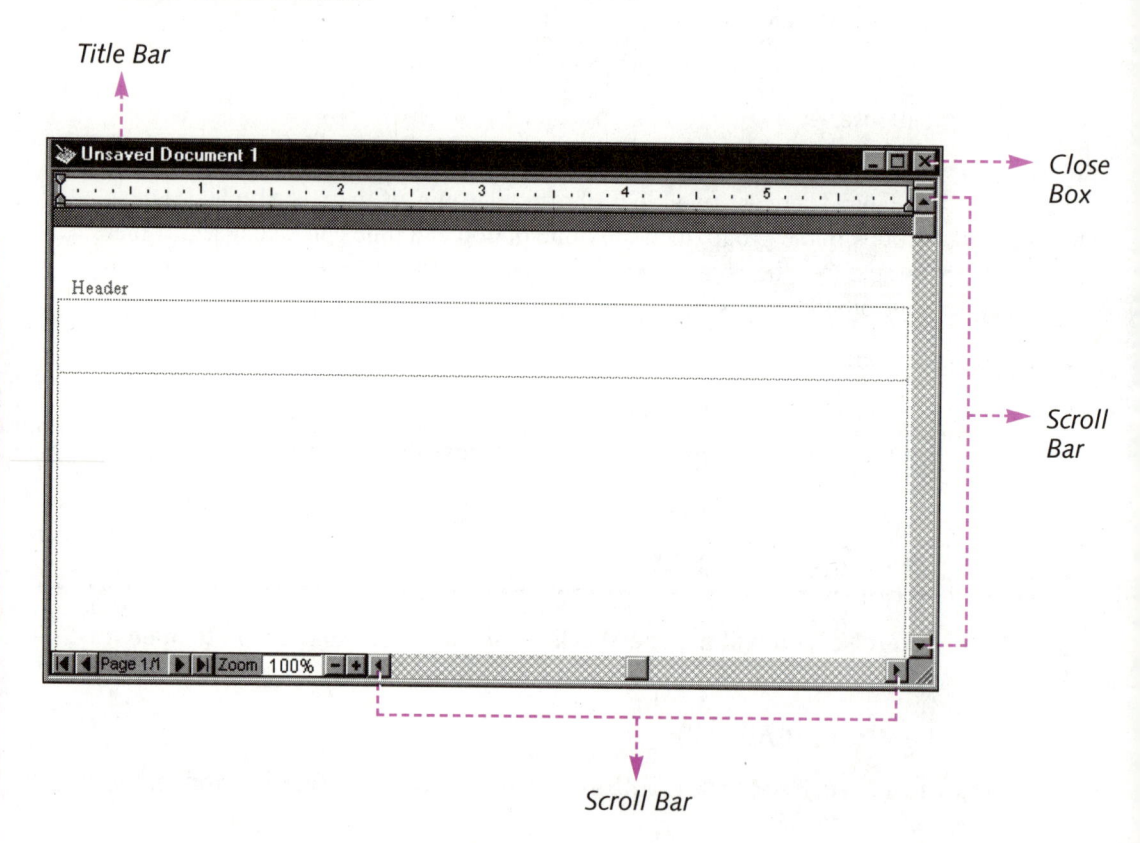

**Figure GS–4**
**A window is a box that allows you to view a document.**

*Title Bar*, *Close Box*, *Scroll Bar*, *Scroll Bar*

The close box allows you to close the window. Closing a window makes the window disappear from the screen. The title bar shows the name of the window. In most cases, this will be the name of the document you are viewing in the window. Scroll bars are used when the file contains more information than the window can display. You will learn about scroll bars later in this lesson.

#### THE TOOLBAR

The toolbar, shown in Figure GS–5, provides shortcuts that can be accessed with the mouse. The shortcuts in the toolbar change with each of the Works tools.

To choose a command from the toolbar:

- ❖ If necessary for the command, highlight the data to which the command will apply.

- ❖ Point to the toolbar button and click.

#### MENUS

The menu bar lists the names of the currently available menus. Some of the menus are available in every Works tool, but each tool has unique menus.

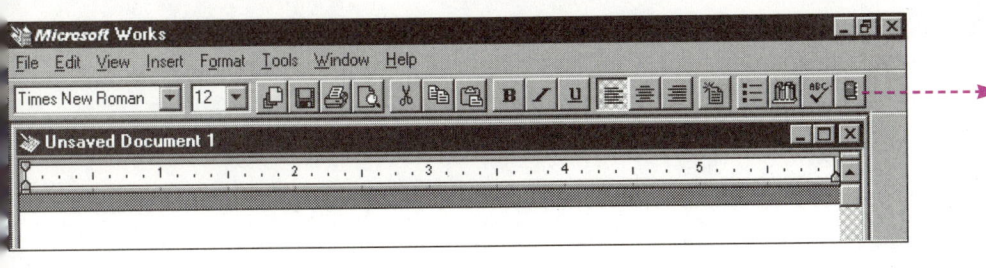

*[Screenshot of Microsoft Works window with toolbar labeled]* → Toolbar

**Figure GS–5**
**The toolbar provides shortcuts for each of the Works tools.**

To access a menu:

- Point to the menu name and click. A menu will drop down from the name, displaying the choices available.
- Click the command you want to use.

# Exercise GS-3

**In this exercise, you will practice using menus.**

1. Practice pulling down menus.
2. Choose **Close** from the **File** menu. The word processor document created in the last exercise closes. The Works Task Launcher appears.

## THE STATUS BAR

The status bar will alert you to information important to the tool you are using. For example, in the word processor, the status bar will tell you what page of your document the cursor is on. The status bar also gives a description of the highlighted command.

## ❖ OPENING DOCUMENTS

The process of opening and closing documents is the same for each tool in Works. The Open dialog box opens documents from any of the Works tools. It also allows access to various disk drives. Figure GS–6 shows the Open dialog box. The Open dialog box enables you to open a file from any available disk and directory. The Look in box, near the top of the dialog box, is where you select the disk drive that contains the file you want

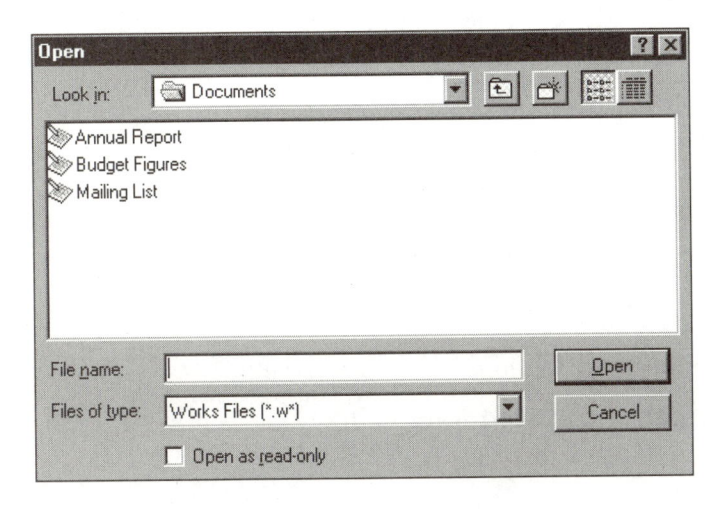

*[Screenshot of Open dialog box showing Annual Report, Budget Figures, Mailing List]*

**Figure GS–6**
**Using the Open dialog box, you can open a file from any available disk and directory.**

*Getting Started with Works* 5

to open. The Directories box shows you what directories are on the disk using pictures of folders. A folder is an appropriate way to show a directory or subdirectory graphically, because, like a folder, a directory groups files that have something in common.

To open a document:

❖ Choose **New** from the **File** menu.

- or -

Click the **Existing Documents** tab in the Works Task Launcher and click the **Open a document not listed here** option. The Open dialog box appears.

❖ If you want to open a document from a floppy disk, insert the disk.

❖ If the document you want is not displayed, click the down arrow in the Look in box to display a scrolling list of folders and disk drives, as shown in Figure GS–7.

*Up One Level Button*

**Figure GS–7**
The Open dialog box allows you to navigate through drives and folders to find the document you need.

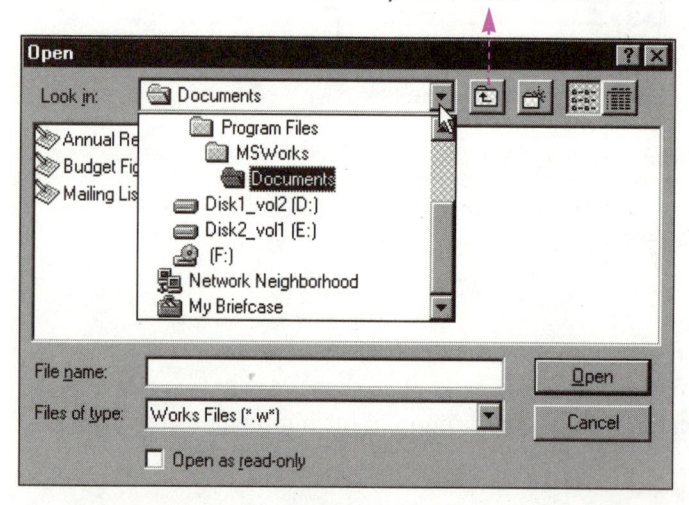

❖ Click the appropriate drive.

❖ If the document is in a directory on the disk, double-click the directory's folder in the scrolling window in the dialog box. This step can be repeated, if necessary, to change into another directory. If you go too deep into folders, click the Up One Level button to back up to the previous folder.

❖ When you locate the correct folder, click the name of the document. The filename appears in the File name box.

❖ Click **Open.** The document opens.

**note**

If your template files are not on a floppy disk, ask your instructor for directions that apply to you.

## Exercise GS-4

In this exercise, you will practice navigating through directories.

1. Click the **Existing Documents** tab in the Works Task Launcher.
2. Click the **Open document not listed here** button.
3. Insert your template disk in the floppy disk drive.

4. Choose the appropriate drive for the Look in scrolling list.
5. Open the *Letters* folder.
6. Open the *Gabriel* folder, which is in the *Letters* folder.
7. Open *Ski Cost,* and leave the document open for the next exercise.

To work on more than one document at a time, choose Open from the File menu and open another document. To make one of the documents the active document, choose its name from the Window menu.

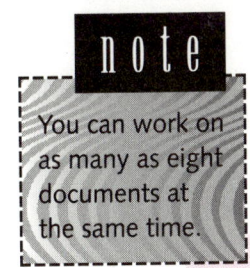

> **note**
> You can work on as many as eight documents at the same time.

## Exercise GS-5

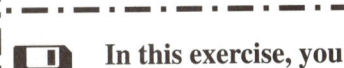

**In this exercise, you will practice opening more than one document.**

1. While *Ski Cost* is still on the screen, open *Ski Trip Letter* from the same directory.
2. Use the Window menu to make *Ski Cost* the active document.
3. Leave both documents open for the next exercise.

## ❖ SCROLLING

When your document is longer than a single page, you need an easy way to move from page to page. Scrolling is the process of moving through a document. You can easily scroll through your document using a mouse, but there are also a number of keys that allow you to move your cursor in the document.

The scroll bars are illustrated in Figure GS–8. Click on the scroll arrows to move one line. Click above or below the scroll box to move one window. The scroll box indicates your approximate position in the document. You can also drag the scroll box to move quickly to a specific part of a document.

> **note**
> Dragging is accomplished by holding down the mouse button and moving the pointer.

Scroll Arrow    Scroll Box                    Scroll Bar            Scroll Arrow

**Figure GS–8**
The scroll bars, scroll boxes, and scroll arrows provide ways to move through a document quickly.

*Getting Started with Works* 7

## ❖ CLOSING DOCUMENTS

Closing a document removes the document from the screen and closes the file on the disk.

To close a document:

❖ Choose **Close** from the **File** menu.

- or -

Click the close box of the window.

## ❖ EXITING WORKS

End your Works session by choosing Exit Works from the File menu or clicking the Exit Works button in the Works Task Launcher. When you choose Exit Works, several operations occur. First, documents close. If you did not save one or more documents, you get the chance to save them at this point. Second, the Works program closes.

## Exercise GS-6

**In this exercise, you will practice scrolling using the mouse, closing documents, and exiting Works.**

1. Switch to *Ski Trip Letter* and practice scrolling through it using the mouse.
2. Close both of the windows on your screen. The Works Task Launcher appears.
3. Click the **Exit Works** button to close the program.

# activities

## ❖ TRUE/FALSE

In the blank space before each sentence, place a **T** if the statement is true and an **F** if it is false.

__F__ 1. An integrated software package combines common word processors into one program.

__F__ 2. Works is started from the Accessories menu.

__T__ 3. Closing a document removes the document from the screen.

__T__ 4. More than one document can be on the screen at the same time.

__F__ 5. To exit Works, choose Stop from the File menu.

## ❖ COMPLETION

Answer the questions below in the space provided.

1. List four tools included in Works.

    *Word processor, spreadsheet, Database, Communications*

2. What parts of the screen allow you to move to different parts of a document?

    *Scroll box, Scroll bar, cursor,*

3. What is the purpose of the toolbar?

    *• shortcuts using mouse.*

4. What command allows you to load a document without closing the current document?

    *file, open*

5. What are the two ways to close a document?

    *file - close*
    *close box*

# review

## Review Exercise GS-1

**In this exercise, you will start Works, access the Open dialog box, and open a folder.**

1. Start Works and access the Open dialog box.
2. Open the *Letters* folder.
3. Open the *Gabriel* folder.
4. Use the Up One Level button to return to the *Letters* directory.
5. Leave the Open dialog box on the screen for the next review exercise.

## Review Exercise GS-2

**In this exercise, you will open three documents from the Open dialog box.**

1. Open the *Britney* folder in the *Letters* folder.
2. Open the document named *Vacation*.
3. From the *Gabriel* folder in the *Letters* folder, open *Ski Cost* and *Ski Trip Letter*.
4. Use the Window menu to make *Vacation* the active window.
5. Close all documents.
6. Exit Works.

# lesson 1

# Creating and Saving a Document

## ❖ OBJECTIVES

Upon completion of this lesson, you will be able to:

1. Start the word processor and create new documents.
2. Key text into the word processor.
3. Save a document.

**Estimated Time:** 1/2 hour

## ❖ CREATING NEW DOCUMENTS

You have already seen that when you start Works, you can choose which tool to work with, choose to open an existing file, or use a TaskWizard. No matter which of the tools you decide to use, the process of starting Works and creating a new file is the same.

To create a new document when Works is running:

- Choose **New** from the **File** menu. The Works Task Launcher will appear, as shown in Figure 1–1.
- Click the **Works Tools** tab of the Works Task Launcher.
- Click the **Word Processor** button.

Works displays the new document on top of the document that is already open. The new document window becomes the active window. You can determine this because the title bar of the active window is a different color or intensity than the title bar of the inactive window.

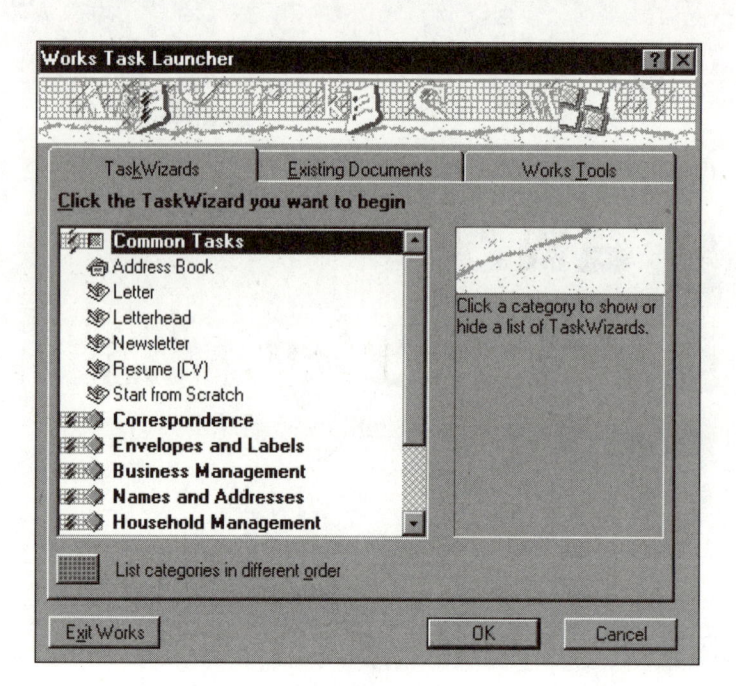

**Figure 1–1**
The **Works Task Launcher** is used to open a new document while Works is running.

## Exercise 1-1

**In this exercise, you will start Works and create a new document.**

1. Start Works and create a new word processor document.
2. Create another blank word processor document using the **New** command.
3. Leave the blank documents open for the next exercise.

Recall how to move back and forth between documents by choosing the document you want to become active from the Window menu. You can only enter text in an active window.

## Exercise 1-2

**In this exercise, you will practice switching between two documents using the Window menu.**

1. Practice switching between the two blank documents using the **Window** menu.
2. While *Unsaved Document 2* is active, choose **Close** from the **File** menu to close the document.
3. Leave *Unsaved Document 1* open for the next exercise.

## ❖ THE DOCUMENT WINDOW

The document window is the window where you will actually do your work. The windows in every tool share some features that will make your work easier, as shown in Figure 1–2.

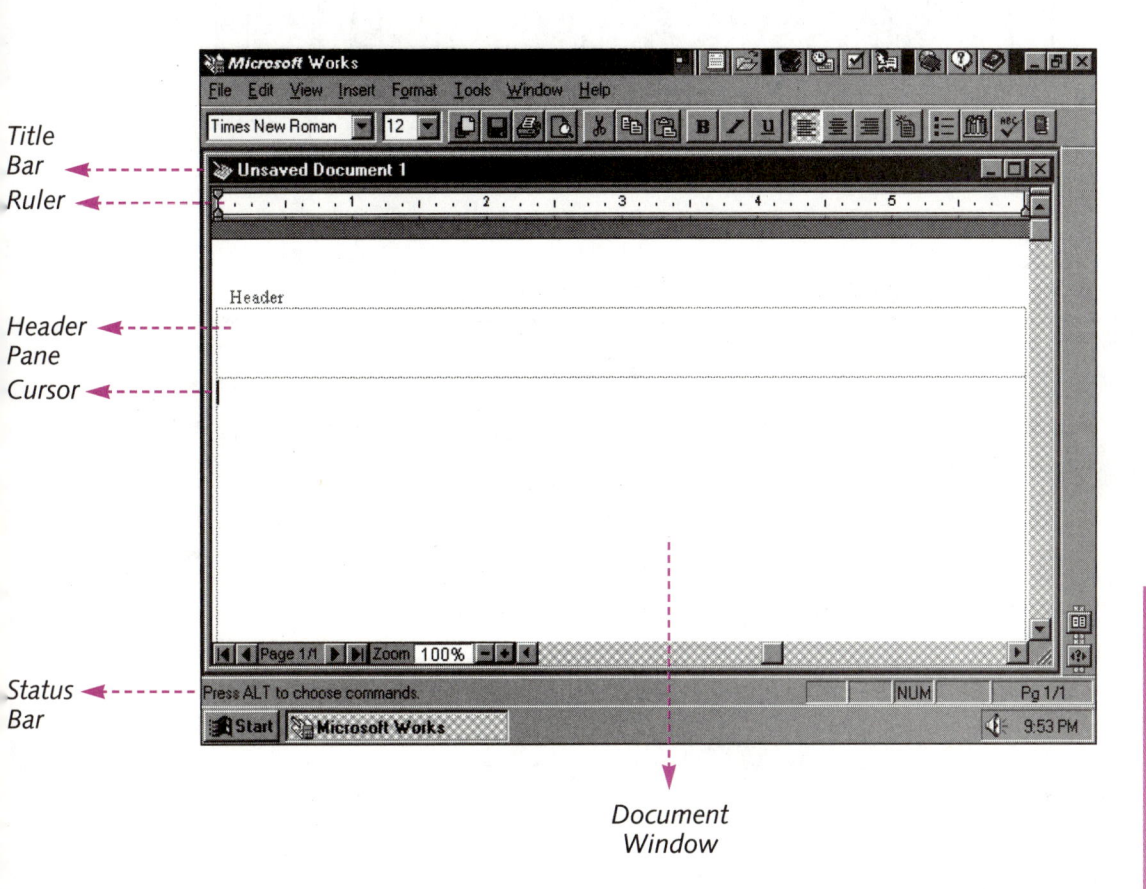

*Figure labels pointing to screenshot: Title Bar, Ruler, Header Pane, Cursor, Status Bar, Document Window*

**Figure 1–2**
The document window is where you will do your word processing work.

The title bar is located at the top of the window. It contains the name of the document in the window. The ruler, located below the title bar, displays indentions, tabs, and margins.

## ❖ ENTERING TEXT

The vertical blinking line in the document window is called the *cursor*. The cursor marks your place in the text and indicates where the next character you key will appear.

When you begin to enter text, you will notice that the cursor moves to the right in front of each letter you key. As you reach the right side of the window, the cursor automatically moves to the next line. This feature is called *word wrap*. If you want to end a line before it wraps, press Enter. You also press Enter to begin a new paragraph.

If you make a mistake while keying text, press the Backspace key to delete characters to the left of the cursor and then continue keying. If you hold down the Backspace key, it will continue to delete characters until you release the key. Figure 1–3 will help you locate the Backspace key.

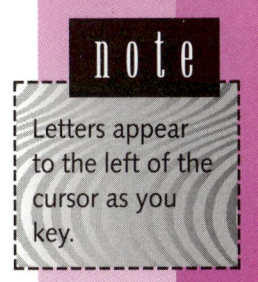

> **note**
> Letters appear to the left of the cursor as you key.

**lesson 1** *Creating and Saving a Document* **13**

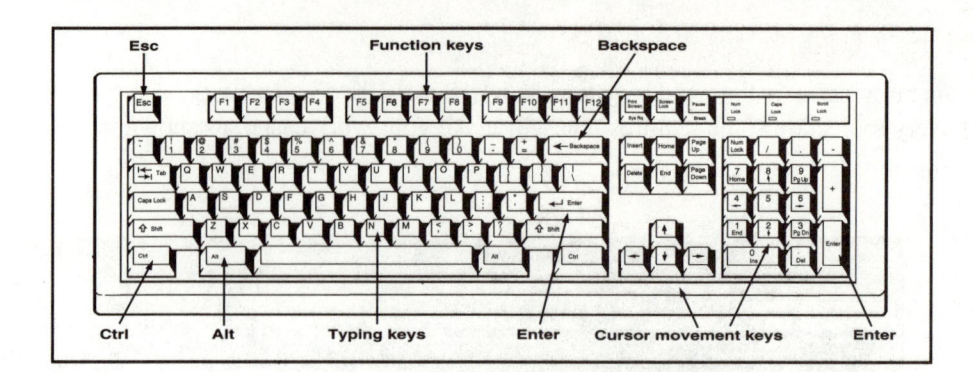

Figure 1–3
The Backspace key deletes characters to the left of the cursor.

## Exercise 1-3

**In this exercise, you will key a paragraph of text.**

1. Key the following text. As you key, watch what happens to the words as you reach the end of the line. Use the **Backspace** key to correct mistakes as you key.

---

In 1961, NASA launched the first chimpanzee into space. This chimp, named Ham, traveled a total distance of 422 miles at a top speed of 1,200 miles per hour. Ham helped pioneer safe space travel during the infancy of the United States Space Program.

---

2. Press **Enter** to move the cursor down one line.
3. Leave the document open for the next exercise.

### ❖ SAVING YOUR WORK

Saving is one of the most important features of any computer program. You can store files you have created on a floppy disk or on the computer's hard drive.

The Save and Save As commands are two ways to save a document. The first time you save a document, choose Save As from the File menu. Works will automatically present you with the Save As dialog box, shown in Figure 1–4. In this dialog box, you can type the name you wish to give your file, and choose a drive and directory where you want Works to save it. Works will then store the file in that location under the name you have supplied and return you to your document.

To save a document for the first time:

- Choose **Save As** from the **File** menu. The Save As dialog box appears.
- If saving to a floppy disk, place your disk in the floppy drive.
- Choose the appropriate drive and directory from the Save in list.
- Key the filename in the File name box.
- Click **Save.** Works saves the document on your disk.

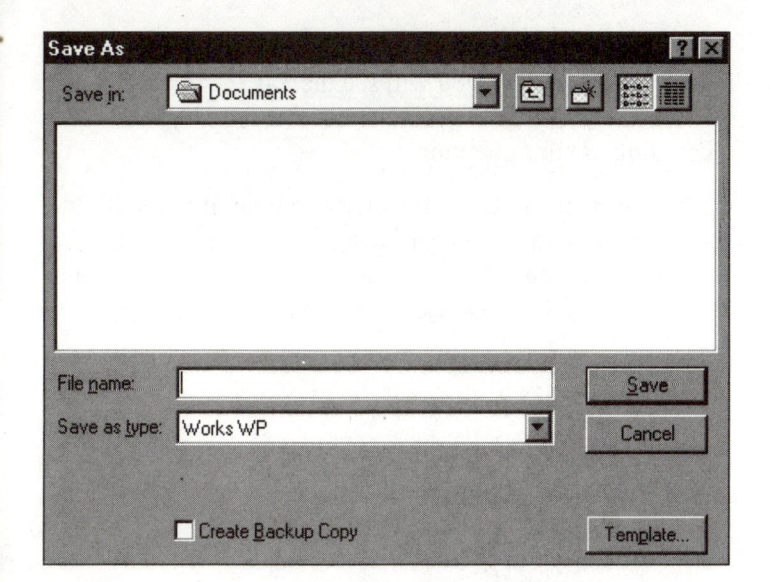

Figure 1–4
The Save As dialog box allows you to save a document with a specific name and in a specific directory or disk.

## Exercise 1-4

In this exercise, you will save a document you created in the previous exercise under a specific name.

1. Save the document you created in the previous activity as *Space First*.

The next time you want to save your document, choose Save from the File menu. Since your document has already been saved for the first time, you will not see a dialog box. Works will save the current document by overwriting the previous version of it.

**note**

Ask your instructor to specify a location for files you save from Works.

## Exercise 1-5

In this exercise, you will key an additional paragraph and save it in an existing file.

1. Press **Enter** to create a blank line.
2. Key this additional paragraph:

```
The Soviet Union was the first country to send a female into orbit.
Her name was Valentina Tereshkova. Sally Ride was the first American
woman to travel in space. Ride's job on the mission was to help
recover a stranded satellite.
```

3. Choose **Save** from the **File** menu. The file is saved under the name *Space First* and now includes the additional text you entered.
4. Close the document.

**lesson 1** *Creating and Saving a Document* 15

**note**

Using Save As to save an existing document with a new name does not rename the existing file. Instead, a new copy is saved with the new name, leaving the existing file with the original name.

If you wish to give your existing file a different name or save it to a new location, choose Save As from the File menu. Once again, you will see the Save As dialog box. Key the new name or choose a new destination for the file, click Save, and Works will store a new copy of the file according to your directions.

Sometimes you may be unable to finish an entire document at one time. If you have to quit a document before you are finished with it, you can save it following the instructions in the previous section. Then, when you are ready to work on the document again, open the document from the Works Task Launcher or by using the Open command from the File menu.

# activities

## ❖ TRUE/FALSE

*In the blank space before each sentence, place a **T** if the statement is true and an **F** if it is false.*

__T__ 1. The process of creating a new file is the same for all Works tools.

__F__ 2. Text cannot be entered in the active window.

__F__ 3. The cursor moves to the right in front of each letter you key.

__F__ 4. When entering text in the word processor, you must press Enter at the end of every line.

__T__ 5. You can choose Save As to give your existing file a different name or to save it to a new location.

## ❖ COMPLETION

*Answer the questions below in the space provided.*

1. What command is used to create a new document when Works is already running?

   file, new

2. What important information is supplied by the title bar?

   name of the document active

3. What is the vertical blinking line in the word processor window called?

   cursor

4. What happens if you hold down the Backspace key?

   erase

5. If a document has already been saved for the first time, what will choosing the Save command do?

   just save the correction

# review

## Review Exercise 1-1

**In this exercise you will create a new document and key a letter.**

Key the following letter in a new word processing document and save it as **Limo Letter**.

```
Lightfoot Luxury Limousines
111 Comfort Lane
San Antonio, TX 78227
October 25, 199-



Ms. Julie Reveiz
1971 Industrial Way
Miami, FL 33100

Dear Ms. Reveiz:

Thank you for your request for information regarding the use of our
limousine service during your convention this December. I am enclosing
our brochure.

If you have any questions after reviewing the brochure, please contact
me at (210) 555-1255.

Sincerely,



Bob Lightfoot

Enclosure: Brochure
```

# lesson 2

# Editing Text and Printing

## ❖ OBJECTIVES

Upon completion of this lesson, you will be able to:

1. Move the cursor.
2. Edit text.
3. Preview and print a document.

**Estimated Time:** 1/2 hour

## ❖ MOVING THE CURSOR

You can move the cursor using the mouse or the keyboard. To move the cursor with the mouse, place the pointer where you want the cursor to be and then click the mouse button. The cursor will appear. Often it is easier to move the cursor with the keyboard. Table 2–1 shows the keys you can press to move your cursor both short and long distances.

| Press | To Move the Cursor |
|---|---|
| → | Right one character |
| ← | Left one character |
| ↓ | To the next line |
| ↑ | To the previous line |
| End | To the end of the current line |
| Home | To the beginning of the current line |
| Page Down | To the next screen |
| Page Up | To the previous screen |
| Ctrl + Home | To the beginning of the document |
| Ctrl + End | To the end of the document |

Table 2–1

# Exercise 2-1

**In this exercise, you will use the mouse and keyboard methods to practice moving the cursor to locations in a document.**

1. Open *Exercise 2-1*.

2. Using the mouse, move the cursor to the blank line between the paragraphs.

3. Press **Ctrl** + **End** to move to the end of the document.

4. Using the mouse, move the cursor to the end of the first line of the second paragraph.

5. Press **Home** to move the cursor to the beginning of the line.

6. Use mouse and keyboard methods to practice moving the cursor to locations of your choice until you can quickly move the cursor anywhere in the document.

7. Leave the document open for the next exercise.

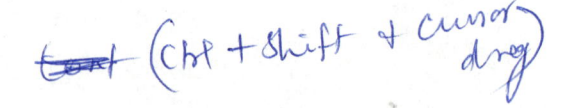

> **note**
> Clicking in the space just to the left of a line of text will highlight the whole line.

> **note**
> The Select All command in the Edit menu highlights the entire document.

## ❖ HIGHLIGHTING TEXT

Highlighting is the way you mark a block of text so you can work with the entire block at once. The block can be as small as one character or as large as an entire document. Highlighting speeds operations such as deleting a paragraph. Rather than pressing the Backspace or Delete key until the paragraph is deleted, you can highlight the paragraph and press Delete once. Highlighting text is also called *selecting* text.

To highlight text:

❖ Move the pointer to the position where you want the selection to begin.

❖ Press the mouse button.

❖ Drag to highlight the text.  *text (Ctrl + Shift + cursor drag)*

# Exercise 2-2

**In this exercise, you will practice highlighting text. *Exercise 2-1* should be on your screen.**

1. Practice highlighting text using the method outlined above.

2. Leave the document open for the next exercise.

## ❖ INSERTING TEXT

To insert text, move the cursor to the place you want the text and begin keying.

## Exercise 2-3

**In this exercise, you will practice inserting text. *Exercise 2–1* should be on your screen.**

1. Move the cursor to one space after the word *female* in the first line of the second paragraph. Key **astronaut**. Remember to leave one space before and one space after *astronaut*.

2. Highlight the word *orbit* in the first sentence of the second paragraph. Do not highlight the period. Press **Delete**. The word *orbit* disappears.

3. Key **space**.

4. Choose **Save As** from the **File** menu and save the document as *New Space*. Leave the document open for the next activity.

### ❖ MOVING TEXT

To move text from one location to another:

- Highlight the block you want to move.
- Choose **Cut** from the **Edit** menu.
  -or-
  Click the **Cut** icon on the toolbar (see Figure 2–1).
- Move the cursor to the new location.
- Choose **Paste** from the **Edit** menu.
  -or-
  Click the **Paste** icon on the toolbar (see Figure 2–1).

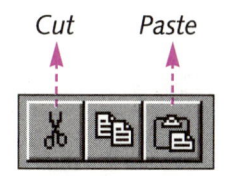

**Figure 2–1**
The Cut and Paste commands can be chosen by clicking buttons on the toolbar.

## Exercise 2-4

**In this exercise, you will cut text from a document and paste it to a different location within the document. *New Space* should be on your screen.**

1. Highlight the entire first paragraph.

2. Cut the paragraph.

3. Place the cursor at the end of the document and press **Enter** twice to create a blank line.

4. Paste the paragraph at the current cursor position.

5. Place the cursor at the top of the document. Press **Delete** to remove the blank line. Your screen should look like Figure 2–2.

6. Save the document and leave it open for the next exercise.

**lesson 2** *Editing Text and Printing*

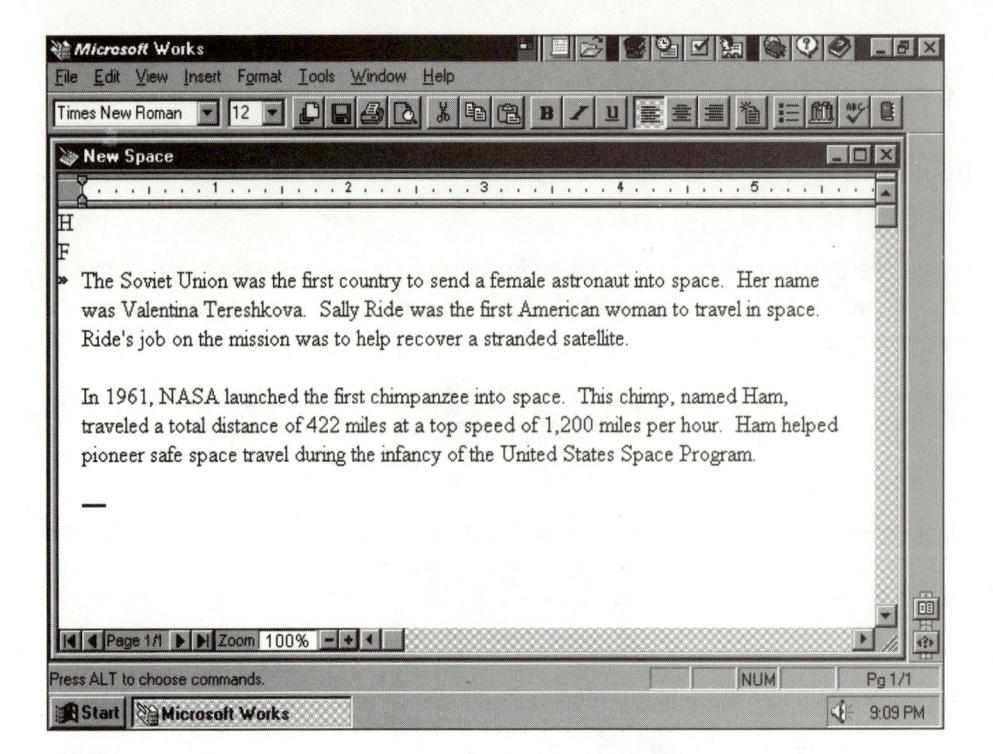

**Figure 2–2**
The Cut and Paste commands allow you to move highlighted text from one place to another in a document.

### ❖ COPYING TEXT

The Copy command is similar to the Cut command. When you choose the Copy command, however, a copy of your highlighted text is placed in the new location, leaving the original text unchanged.

To copy text:

- Highlight the block you want to move.
- Choose **Copy** from the **Edit** menu.
    -or-
    Click the **Copy** icon on the toolbar (see Figure 2–3).
- Move the cursor to the new location.
- Choose **Paste** from the **Edit** menu.
    -or-
    Click the **Paste** icon on the toolbar (see Figure 2–3).

**Figure 2–3**
The Copy and Paste commands are used to copy text.

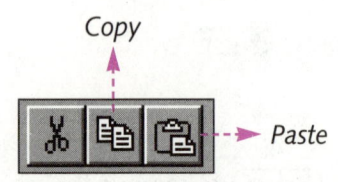

*Copy* → *Paste*

22 Microsoft Works 4.0 for Windows 95: QuickTorial™

# Exercise 2-5

In this exercise, you will copy text from a document and paste it in a different location within the document. *New Space* should be on your screen.

1. Copy the first paragraph and place it at the bottom of the document. A copy of the paragraph reappears. The original text remains at the top of the document.

2. Leave one blank line between the paragraphs.

3. Highlight the last paragraph of the document, including the blank line above it, as in Figure 2–4. Press the (Delete) key to delete the paragraph.

4. Save the document and leave it open for the next exercise.

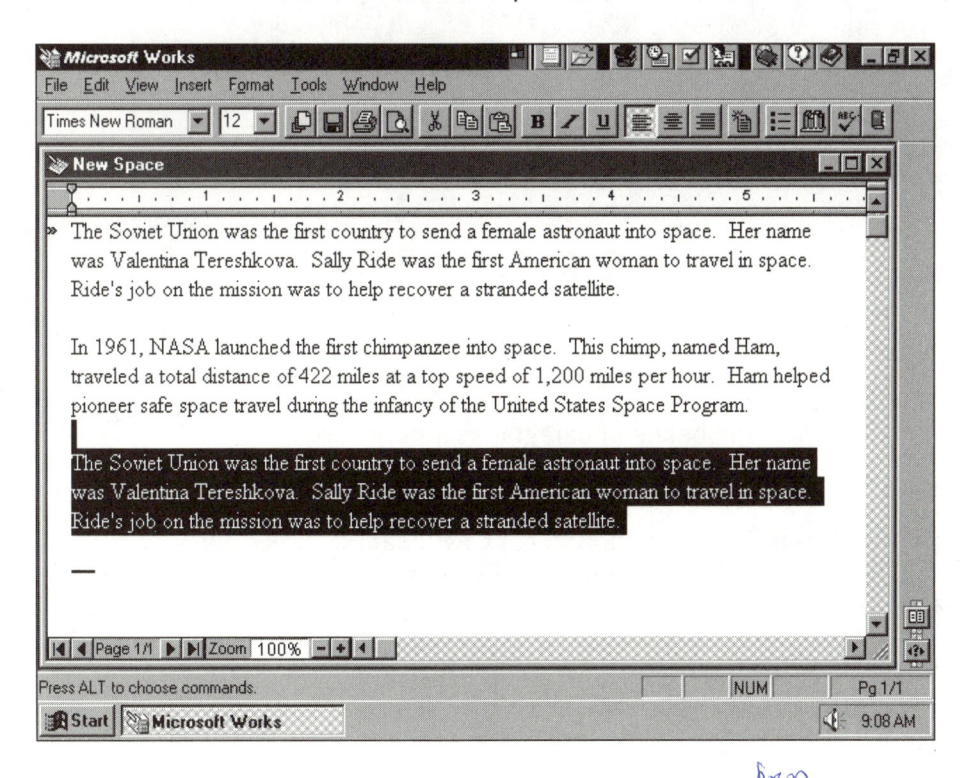

**Figure 2–4**
An entire block of text can be deleted at one time by highlighting the text and pressing Delete.

## ❖ DRAG AND DROP

You can copy and move text quickly using a method called drag-and-drop.

To use the drag-and-drop method:

- ❖ Highlight the text you want to copy or move and position the mouse pointer in the highlighted text. The pointer will change to an arrow with the word *DRAG* below it.

- ❖ Drag the text to the location where you want to move or copy the text. As you begin dragging, the word below the mouse pointer will change to *MOVE*.

- ❖ Release the mouse button to move the text, or press the (Ctrl) key and release the mouse button to copy the text.

**lesson 2** *Editing Text and Printing* 23

## Exercise 2-6

**In this exercise, you will practice using the drag-and-drop method to copy and move text within a document.** *New Space* **should be on your screen.**

1. Highlight the first paragraph of the document and the blank line that follows it.

2. Move the mouse pointer into the highlighted paragraph, as shown in Figure 2–5. Use the drag-and-drop method to move the paragraph to the bottom of the document.

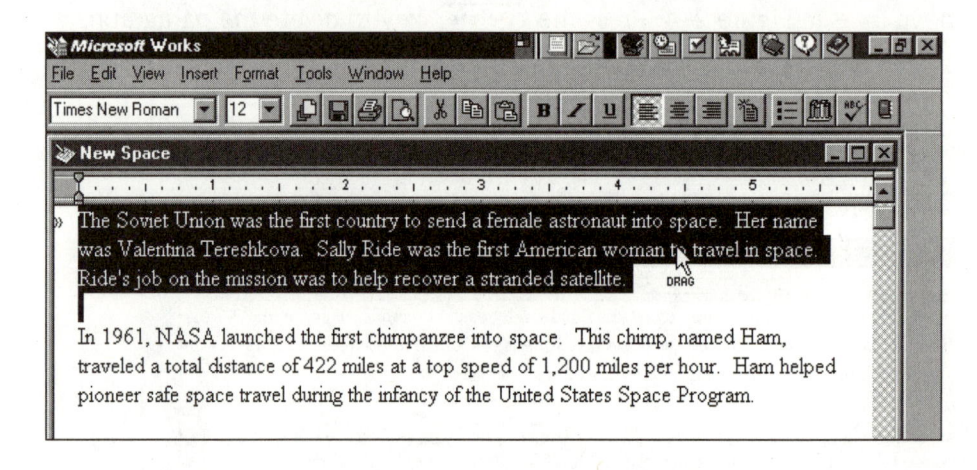

Figure 2–5
The drag-and-drop method can be used to move or copy text quickly.

3. Insert one blank line between paragraphs if necessary.

4. Highlight the word *astronaut* in the first sentence of the last paragraph.

5. Use the drag-and-drop method to copy *astronaut* between the words *woman* and *to* in the third sentence of the last paragraph. Adjust spacing as necessary.

6. Save the document and leave it open for the next exercise.

### ❖ PREVIEWING YOUR DOCUMENT

The Print Preview command enables you to look at a document as it will appear when printed. The Print Preview command is located in the File menu and is useful for viewing the layout of pages before you print your document.

To preview a document:

✛ Choose **Print Preview** from the **File** menu.
   -or-
   Click the **Print Preview** icon on the toolbar (see Figure 2–6).

Figure 2–6
The Print Preview button allows you to quickly preview a document.

----> Print Preview

24  Microsoft Works 4.0 for Windows 95: QuickTorial™

- Click **Zoom In** to increase the document size. Click **Zoom Out** to decrease the document size.
- Click **Cancel** to return to the document window.

## Exercise 2-7

In this exercise, you will practice previewing a document before printing. *New Space* should be on your screen.

1. Preview the document on your screen and then return to the document window.
2. Leave the document open for the next exercise.

### ❖ PRINTING YOUR DOCUMENT

The Print command enables you to print your document on paper.

To print a document:

- Choose **Print** from the **File** menu. The Print dialog box appears, as shown in Figure 2–7.
- Click **OK**.

> **note**
>
> The first time you choose the Print command, you may get a help message offering additional information on printing. Click OK to close the window. This first-time help message may also appear the first time you choose other commands.

**Figure 2–7**
The Print dialog box appears after you select the Print command.

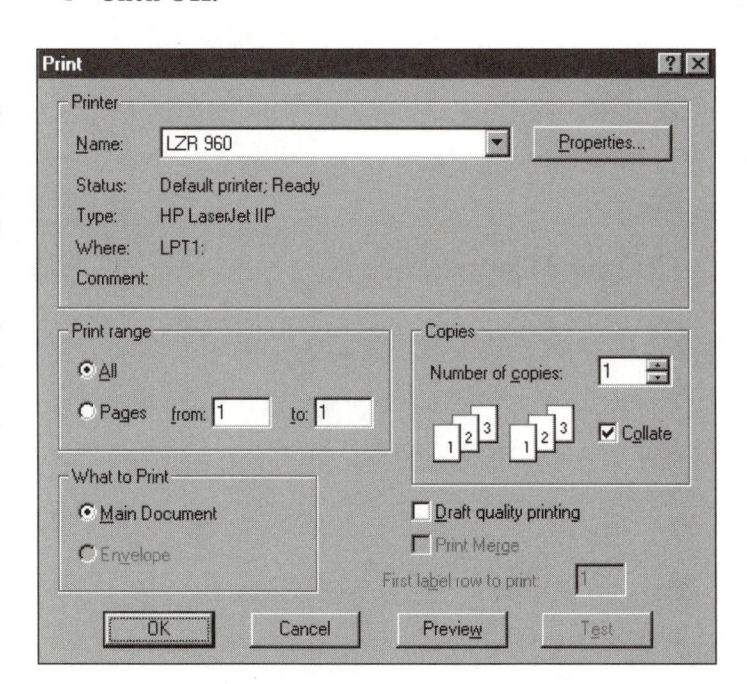

The Print button on the toolbar (to the left of the Print Preview button) can be used to print a document. The Print button, however, skips the Print dialog box and begins printing immediately.

**lesson 2** *Editing Text and Printing* 25

## Exercise 2-8

In this exercise, you will practice saving, printing, and closing a document. *New Space* should be on your screen.

1. Save, print, and close the document on your screen.

# activities

## ❖ TRUE/FALSE

*In the blank space before each sentence, place a **T** if the statement is true and an **F** if it is false.*

F  1. Pressing Ctrl + Home moves the cursor to the beginning of the current line.

T  2. Highlighting text is also called selecting text.

F  3. The Edit and Paste commands are used to move text from one location to another.

T  4. The Print Preview command is located in the File menu.

F  5. The Print dialog box appears after a document prints.

## ❖ COMPLETION

*Answer the questions below in the space provided.*

1. Using the keyboard, how do you move the cursor to the end of the document?

   Ctrl + end

2. Describe how highlighting can be used to make it easier to delete an entire sentence.

   Select the line + Del

3. What is the process for inserting a word in the middle of a paragraph?

   move the cursor + type (space)

4. Describe the drag-and-drop method for copying text.

   Select the entire text by dragging it and when you want the new lines return to

5. How does copying text differ from moving text?

lesson 2  activities  27

# review

## Review Exercise 2-1

**In the blank space, write the letter of the word that matches the correct definition.**

____ 1. The horizontal bar located at the top of a window that contains the name of the document in the window.

____ 2. The line that displays indention, tabs, and margins.

____ 3. The vertical blinking line that marks your place in the text and represents the point where the next keyed text will be inserted.

____ 4. The process of selecting a block of text.

____ 5. The window where you enter text and do your word processing work.

____ 6. A word processor feature that automatically moves text at the end of a line to the beginning of the next line.

a. highlighting
b. ruler
c. word wrap
d. cursor
e. document window
f. title bar

## Review Exercise 2-2

**In this exercise, you will practice editing text.**

1. Open *Review Exercise 2–2*.
2. In the first sentence of the document, insert an *f* in the word *efective*.
3. In the second sentence of the document, delete the word *can*.
4. In the third sentence, delete the comma and the word *meaningless* before the word *words*.
5. Insert the sentence *Use correct punctuation.* before the word *Correct* in item number 3. Remember to add two spaces after the period.
6. Use the Save As command to save the corrected document on your data disk as *Writing*.
7. Preview the document.
8. Print and close the document.

# Review Exercise 2-3

**In this exercise, you will practice editing text and moving copy within a document.**

1. Open *Review Exercise 2–3*.

2. Insert the words *Student Housing* before the word *orientation* in the last sentence of the first paragraph.

3. Insert an *m* in the word *roomate* in the first sentence of the second paragraph.

4. Replace the room number *607* in the third paragraph with *425*.

5. Replace the words *Junior and Senior students* in the third paragraph with *entering freshmen*.

6. Move the fourth paragraph, which begins with *Your roommate's name,* to the end of the second paragraph. Delete any extra lines that remain between paragraphs, and add spaces as necessary between sentences.

7. Save the revised document as *Housing*.

8. Preview the document.

9. Print and close document.

# lesson 3

# Margins, Indents, Spacing, and Alignment

## ❖ OBJECTIVES

Upon completion of this lesson, you will be able to:

1. Change margins.
2. Set indents.
3. Set spacing.
4. Align text.

**Estimated Time:** 1/2 hour

## ❖ MARGINS

Works provides default margins for a page. To change the top, bottom, right, or left margins:

- Choose **Page Setup** from the **File** menu. The Page Setup dialog box appears, as shown in Figure 3–1.
- Choose the **Margins** tab.
- Key margin settings in inches.
- Click **OK.**

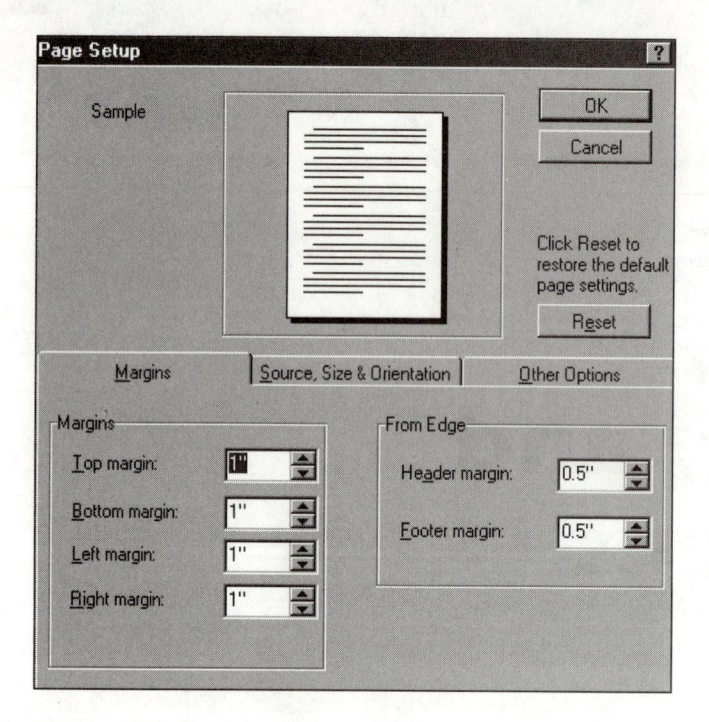

**Figure 3–1**
The Page Setup dialog box contains the document's default margins.

## Exercise 3-1

**In this exercise, you will change a document's margins.**

1. Open *Exercise 3–1*.

2. Change the margins of the document as follows:
    Top: **1.25**
    Bottom: **1.25**
    Left: **1.5**
    Right: **1.5**

3. Save the document as *Mountain*.

4. Leave the document open for the next exercise.

### ❖ INDENTING

You can indent text from either the left or the right margin, or from both margins. Indents can be used to make text more readable or to set off parts of the text from the rest of the text. Setting an indent affects the paragraph the cursor is currently in or all highlighted paragraphs.

#### FIRST-LINE INDENTS

The paragraphs shown in Figure 3–2 are examples of first-line indents.

```
    Indented paragraphs are used in documents of all types.
Reports, memos, newsletters, and magazine articles are just a few
documents that may contain indented paragraphs.

1. Lists of information and paragraphs that include numbers in the
   first line of text often are appropriate for hanging indents.
```

**Figure 3-2**
In the first example, the first line is indented. The second example is called a hanging indent.

To indent text:

- Highlight the text you want indented.
- Choose **Paragraph** from the **Format** menu. The Format Paragraph dialog box appears, as shown in Figure 3–3.

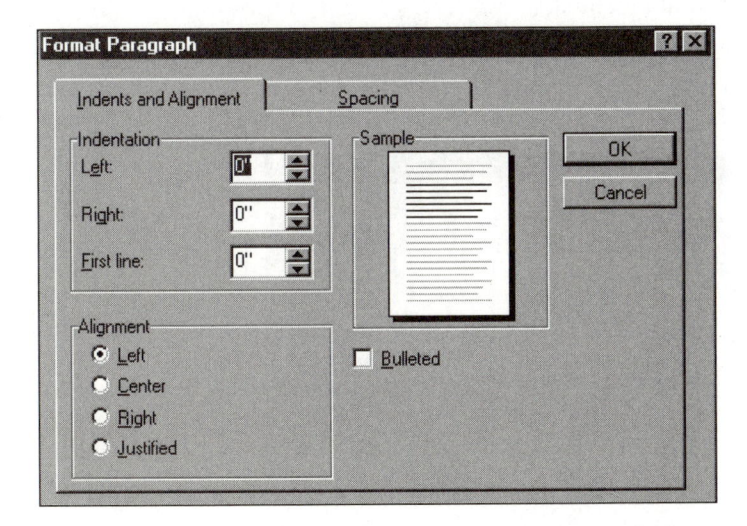

**Figure 3-3**
The Indents and Alignment tab in the Format Paragraph dialog box allows you to set indents.

- Key an indent in inches for the left side of the paragraph, the right side of the paragraph, and the first line of the paragraph.
- Click **OK**.

## Exercise 3-2

**In this exercise, you will practice indenting paragraphs.** *Mountain* **should be on your screen.**

1. Highlight the first paragraph of the document, which begins *A mountain can be defined* and ends with *Alaska to Central America.*

2. Set a hanging indent by entering **0.5** for the left indent and **-0.5** for the first line indent and clicking **OK.**

3. Highlight the entire document except the title and the table at the end of the document.

**lesson 3** *Margins, Indents, Spacing, and Alignment* 33

4. Set a first-line indent by entering **0** for the left indent and **0.25** for the first-line indent.

5. Save the document and leave it open for the next exercise.

### INDENTING FROM BOTH MARGINS

Indenting from both margins is useful for setting off paragraphs from the main body of the text. Often this is done when a paragraph is actually a quotation and needs to be set off from the surrounding paragraphs.

You can indent from both margins using the Format Paragraph dialog box with which you are already familiar. There is another method, however, called Easy Formats.

To indent text from both margins using Easy Formats:

❖ Highlight the text you want indented.

❖ Choose **Easy Formats** from the Format menu. The Easy Formats dialog box appears, as shown in Figure 3–4.

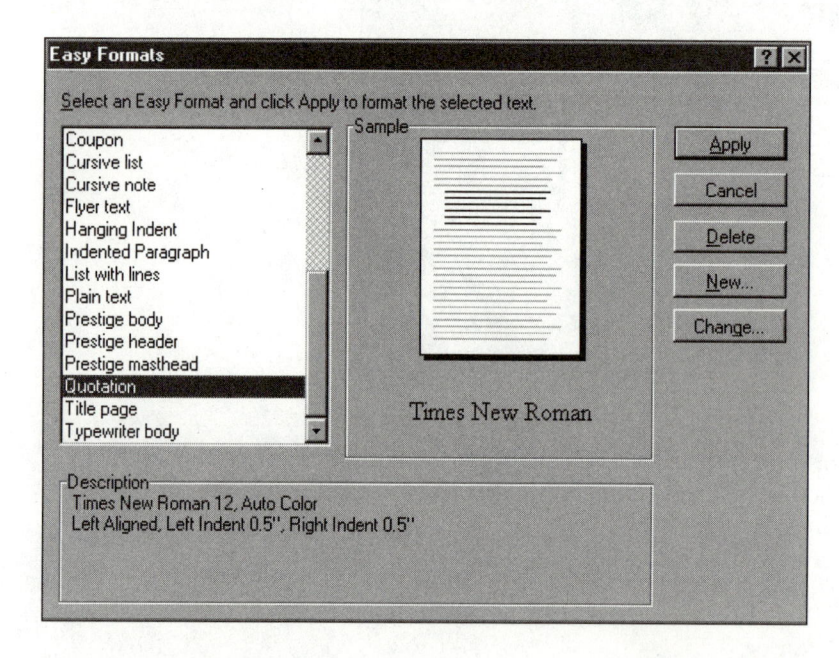

> **note**
>
> You can also set hanging and first-line indents using Easy Formats from the Format menu. The Hanging Indent format quickly sets a standard hanging indent, and the Indented Paragraph format gives you a first-line indent.

**Figure 3–4**
The Easy Formats dialog box allows you to quickly apply a variety of formats to highlighted text.

❖ Choose the **Quotation** format from the scrolling list of formats.

❖ Click **Apply.** The dialog box closes and the format is applied to the highlighted text.

## Exercise 3-3

In this exercise, you will indent a paragraph from both margins. *Mountain* should be on your screen.

1. Indent the fifth paragraph, which begins with *An orangy*, from both margins using the Quotation Easy Format.

2. Save the document and leave it open for the next exercise.

34 *Microsoft Works 4.0 for Windows 95: QuickTorial*™

## ❖ SPACING

Spacing refers to the distance between lines or paragraphs of text. Works allows you to single-space text, space text with 1.5 lines between the lines of text, double-space text, or use a custom setting. By default, Works single-spaces text.

You can key a line spacing in the Format Paragraph dialog box, or you can use shortcut keys to choose single-spacing, 1.5 spacing, or double-spacing. Table 3–1 shows the shortcut keys available for spacing text.

| Number of Spaces Between Lines | Shortcut |
|---|---|
| Single-spaced lines | Ctrl + 1 |
| One-and-a-half spaced lines | Ctrl + 5 |
| Double-spaced lines | Ctrl + 2 |

**note**

Setting line spacing affects the paragraph where the cursor is located or all highlighted paragraphs.

Table 3–1

When you want spacing other than one of the three standard options, you can specify exactly how much space to use:

- Choose **Paragraph** from the Format menu. The Format Paragraph dialog box appears.
- Choose the **Spacing** tab.
- In the Line Spacing box, key the number of lines you want to appear between the lines of the paragraph or paragraphs. You can also click the arrows at the end of the text box to increase or decrease spacing.
- Click **OK**.

When keying the number of lines you want, you can request fractions of numbers. For example, you might specify 1.66 to achieve just the right spacing.

## Exercise 3-4

In this exercise, you will adjust the spacing in a document. *Mountain* should be on your screen.

1. Double-space the entire document.
2. Single-space the paragraph that begins with *An orangy*.
3. Place the cursor immediately before the phrase *An orangy* and press **Enter** to create a blank line.
4. Save the document and leave it open for the next exercise.

## ❖ ALIGNMENT

Works allows you to align text in four ways: left-aligned, centered, right-aligned, and justified.

**lesson 3** *Margins, Indents, Spacing, and Alignment* 35

To align text:

- Highlight the text you want to align.
- Choose **Paragraph** from the **Format** menu. The Paragraph dialog box appears.
- Choose the **Indents and Alignment** tab.
- Choose the type of alignment desired from the Alignment box.
- Click **OK**.

You can also align text using the alignment options on the toolbar (see Figure 3–5) or by using the shortcuts in Table 3–2.

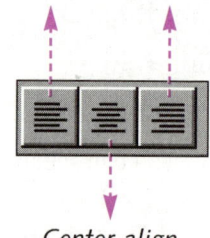

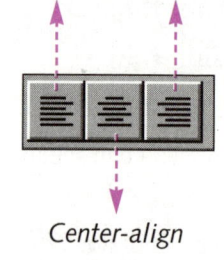

*Left-align   Right-align*

*Center-align*

**Figure 3–5**
Text can be aligned by clicking an alignment option on the toolbar.

| Alignment | Shortcut |
|---|---|
| Left-aligned | Ctrl + L |
| Centered | Ctrl + E |
| Right-aligned | Ctrl + Shift + R |
| Justified | Ctrl + J |

Table 3–2

## Exercise 3–5

In this exercise, you will align text within a document. *Mountain* should be on your screen.

1. Center the title of the document.
2. Right align the first paragraph.
3. Use Print Preview to see the right-aligned paragraph.
4. Return the paragraph to left alignment.
5. Print the document.
6. Save and close the document.

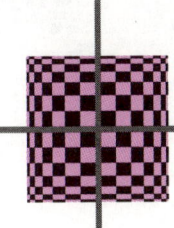

# activities

## ❖ TRUE/FALSE

*In the blank space before each sentence, place a **T** if the statement is true and an **F** if it is false.*

_____ 1. Works allows only the left and right margins to be changed.

_____ 2. Indents can be used to set off parts of the text from the rest.

_____ 3. Works provides shortcut keys for single, double, and triple spacing.

_____ 4. Setting line spacing always affects the entire document.

_____ 5. The alignment commands are located in the Format Paragraph dialog box.

## ❖ COMPLETION

*Answer the questions below in the space provided.*

1. What dialog box is used to change margins?

2. What part of the text is affected when an indent is set?

3. What are the shortcut keys for single spacing?

4. What are the four types of alignment available with Works?

5. List the keyboard shortcuts for two of the alignment options.

lesson 3 *activities* 37

# review

## Review Exercise 3-1

**In this exercise, you will format a document.**

1. Open *Review Exercise 3–1*.

2. Follow the instructions in the document, which direct you as to how to format the document.

3. Save the document as *Formats,* print, and close.

# lesson 4

# Fonts and Checking Spelling

❖ OBJECTIVES

Upon completion of this lesson, you will be able to:

1. Choose fonts.
2. Use the spelling checker.

**Estimated Time:** 1/2 hour

❖ FONTS

The term *font* refers to the shape of the characters belonging to a particular family of type. A font is also called a *typeface*.

What fonts are available to you will depend on what fonts are installed in Windows. The printer you are using may also affect the fonts available to you.

### CHANGING FONTS WITH THE TOOLBAR

You can choose fonts quickly from the toolbar. The name of the current font appears in the Font Name box on the left side of the toolbar, as shown in Figure 4–1. If no font is displayed, a default font will be used when the document is printed.

*Font Name Box*   *Font Size Box*

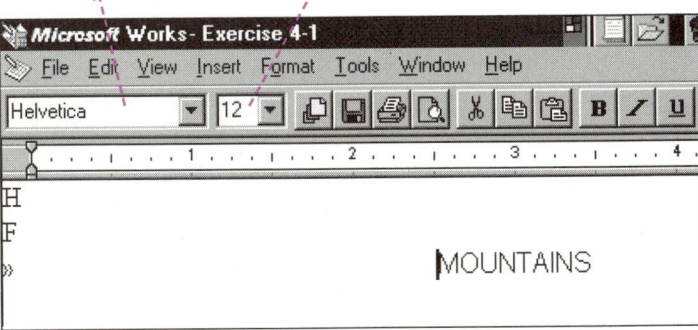

**Figure 4–1**
**The Font Name box on the toolbar displays the currently selected font.**

lesson 4 *Fonts and Checking Spelling* 39

**note**

If text is highlighted when you choose a font, the highlighted text will take on the new font. If no text is highlighted, the new font will be in effect as you key new text.

To change the font:

- Click the down arrow beside the Font Name box. A list of fonts will pull down, much like a pull-down menu.
- Click the desired font.

## Exercise 4–1

**In this exercise, you will change the font of the text in a document.**

1. Open *Exercise 4–1*.
2. Highlight the entire document.
3. Change the font of the entire document to **Times New Roman.** If this font is not available, choose a font that looks similar to the paragraph that begins this page.
4. Save the document as *Mountain 2,* and leave it open for the next exercise.

### STYLE

*Type style* refers to certain changes in the appearance of a font. Common styles are boldface, italic, and underline. These styles can be applied to change the appearance of any font.

When you begin keying a document in the word processor, you are using a normal style. This is the style you will most likely use for the body of your document. However, you will probably want to use other styles for particular features in your document. For example, you may want to make a specific word stand out by applying a boldface style to it. Titles of books and magazines should appear in italic style. More than one style can be applied to the same text. For example, you can boldface and italicize text.

To change the style of text:

- Highlight the text you want to change.
- Click the **boldface, italic,** or **underline** button on the toolbar.

In the toolbar are buttons for boldface, italic, and underline, as shown in Figure 4–2. Clicking on a style in the toolbar will apply that style to the text. Once the style is applied, it will be highlighted in the toolbar to show that it is chosen. Clicking the style in the toolbar again will remove the style from the text.

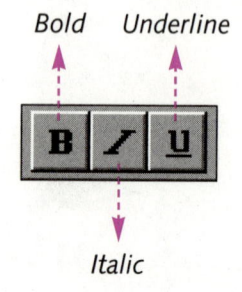

**note**

Like changing the font, changing the style affects the highlighted text or will affect text keyed after the style is chosen.

Figure 4–2
The toolbar can be used to change type style.

*Bold*   *Underline*

**B** *I* U

*Italic*

40  Microsoft Works 4.0 for Windows 95: QuickTorial™

You may find keyboard shortcuts to be the best way to boldface, italicize, or underline. Table 4–1 shows the shortcuts that can be used as an alternative to the toolbar.

| Style | Shortcut |
|---|---|
| Boldface | Ctrl + B |
| Italics | Ctrl + I |
| Underline | Ctrl + U |
| Normal | Ctrl + Space Bar |

Table 4–1

## Exercise 4-2

In this exercise, you will boldface and italicize elements within a document. *Mountain 2* should be on your screen.

1. Boldface the title of the document.
2. Italicize the word *mountain* in the first sentence of the first paragraph.
3. Save the document and leave it open for the next exercise.

### SIZE

You can change type size by using the Font Size box on the toolbar. The Font Size box operates just like the Font Name box.

## Exercise 4-3

In this exercise, you will change the type size of a headline within a document. *Mountain 2* should be on your screen.

1. Highlight the title of the document.
2. Change the size to 14 point.
3. Save the document, and leave it open for the next exercise.

### ❖ USING THE SPELLING CHECKER

Works contains a dictionary of more than 100,000 words to check the spelling of words in your document. You can check an entire document or parts of the document.

To use the spelling checker:

- Choose **Spelling** from the **Tools** menu.
  - or -
  Click the **Spelling Checker** button on the toolbar, as shown in Figure 4–3.

*Spelling Checker*

> **note**
>
> The spelling checker does not replace proof-reading. If you key *form* instead of *from*, the spelling checker will not detect the error.

Figure 4–3
The spelling checker can be accessed from the toolbar.

**lesson 4** Fonts and Checking Spelling  41

The Spelling dialog box, shown in Figure 4–4, allows you to check the spelling of words, ignore words, change misspelled words, or add words to your own custom dictionary. Table 4–2 explains the available options. The dictionary checks spelling only. It will *not* find grammatical errors.

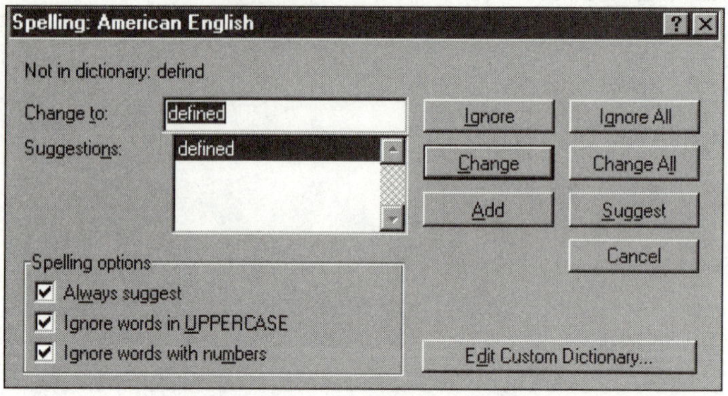

**Figure 4–4**
The Spelling dialog box contains several options for checking the spelling of a document.

| Option | Action |
| --- | --- |
| Ignore | Ignores only the highlighted word |
| Ignore All | Ignores all instances of the same word |
| Change | Changes only the highlighted word |
| Change All | Changes all instances of the same word |
| Add | Adds the highlighted word to the custom dictionary |
| Suggest | Displays a list of proposed spellings |

**Table 4–2**

## Exercise 4-4

**In this exercise, you will check your document for spelling errors.** *Mountain 2* **should be on your screen.**

1. Place the cursor at the beginning of the document and make sure that no text is highlighted.

2. Use the spelling checker to check the spelling of the document on your screen.

3. Print, save, and close the document.

**note**
If text is highlighted when the spelling checker is started, only the highlighted text will be checked.

# activities

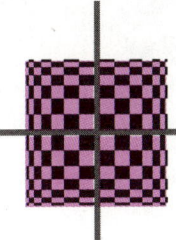

## ❖ TRUE/FALSE

In the blank space before each sentence, place a **T** if the statement is true and an **F** if it is false.

   T   1. A font is also called a typeface.

   ___ 2. The Font Name box and the Font Size box operate much like pull-down menus.

   T   3. You can make a word stand out from the rest of the text by applying a boldface style to it.

   F   4. The keyboard shortcut to make text normal is Ctrl + N.

   F   5. The spelling checker checks for spelling and grammatical errors.

## ❖ COMPLETION

Answer the questions below in the space provided.

1. What determines the fonts that are available on your computer?

2. If no text is highlighted when a font is chosen, what is affected by the new font choice?

3. What type style is used for titles of books and magazines?

4. Why can the spelling checker not replace proofreading?

5. What does the Suggest button in the Spelling dialog box do?

lesson 4  activities  43

# review

## Exercise 4-1

In this exercise, you will change the format features of a document and then check the document for spelling errors.

1. Open *Review Exercise 4-1*.

2. Center the title of the document. Choose a large font for the title and apply a bold style to it.

3. Choose a 12- or 14-point font for the body of the document.

4. Bold and italicize each occurrence of the word *Example:*.

5. Add the following hyphen rule to the bottom of the document.

    ```
    7. to show consecutive numbers or the passage of time.
    ```

    **Example:** The pages are numbered 1-500.

6. Spell check the document.

7. Save the document as *Hyphen Rules*, print, and close.

# lesson 5

# Tabs, Page Breaks, and Search and Replace

## ❖ OBJECTIVES

Upon completion of this lesson, you will be able to:

1. Set tabs.
2. Insert page breaks.
3. Quickly search and replace text.

**Estimated Time:** 1/2 hour

## ❖ TABS

Tabs mark the place the cursor will stop when the Tab key is pressed. Tabs are useful for creating tables or aligning numbered items. Default tabs are set every half inch. You can, however, set tabs yourself. Text can be aligned with decimal, left-aligned, right-aligned, or centered tabs, as shown in Figure 5–1. Notice that different tab symbols appear over the different types of tab settings.

| Symbol | Element | Atomic Number | Atomic Weight |
|---|---|---|---|
| Au | Gold | 79 | 196.967 |
| H | Hydrogen | 1 | 1.00797 |
| Fe | Iron | 26 | 55.847 |
| Pb | Lead | 82 | 207.19 |
| Ni | Nickel | 28 | 58.71 |
| Ag | Silver | 47 | 107.868 |
| Zn | Zinc | 30 | 65.37 |

Left-Aligned Tab   Center-Aligned Tab   Right-Aligned Tab   Decimal-Aligned Tab

**Figure 5–1**
Use tabs to align columns in a table or list.

lesson 5  *Tabs, Page Breaks, and Search and Replace*  45

# Exercise 5-1

**In this exercise, you will set different tab stops.**

1. Open *Exercise 5–1*.

2. Place the cursor after the period following *27,923 ft.* in the last line of the table. Press **Enter**. Notice the tab markers on the ruler. These markers indicate that the tabs in the table have already been set. You will now key the last entry in the table.

3. Press **Tab**. The cursor moves to the decimal tab at 1 inch. Key **5**. Remember to key a period after the 5.

4. Press **Tab**. The cursor moves to the left-aligned tab at 1.37 inches. Key **Makalu 1**.

5. Press **Tab**. The cursor moves to the left-aligned tab at 2.75 inches. Key **Nepal/China**.

6. Press **Tab**. The cursor moves to the right-aligned tab at 5 inches. Key **27,824 ft.** Remember to key a period after *ft*.

7. In the last line of copy preceding the table, change the four to five so the sentence reads, "The following table lists the five highest mountains in the world."

8. Save the document as *Mountain 3* and leave it open for the next exercise.

## SETTING TABS

To set your own tabs:

✦ Place the cursor in the paragraph that needs the tabs.
  - or -
  Highlight the paragraphs that the tabs will affect.

✦ Choose **Tabs** from the **Format** menu. The Format Tabs dialog box appears, as shown in Figure 5–2.

> **note**
> A tab leader is a line of characters that precedes a tab. Tab leaders are used to guide the reader's eye from one column to the next. You may have seen leaders in a table of contents.

**Figure 5–2**
The Tabs dialog box allows you to insert and customize tabs.

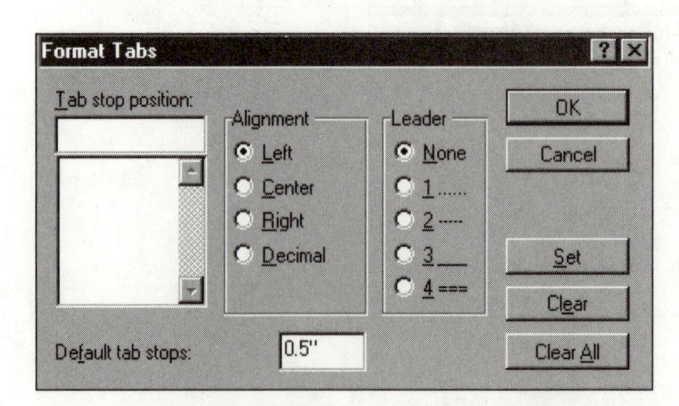

✦ Key the first tab position (in inches) in the Tab stop position box.

✦ Choose an alignment for the tab.

46  *Microsoft Works 4.0 for Windows 95: QuickTorial*™

- If desired, choose a tab leader.
- Click **Set**.
- If necessary, insert other tab positions.
- Click **OK** when all tabs are inserted.

## Exercise 5-2

**In this exercise, you will set tabs to align columns.** *Mountain 3* **should be on your screen.**

1. Place the cursor after the period following the sixth paragraph, the paragraph ending with the word *world*. Press **Enter**.
2. Insert a centered tab at 1.8 inches.
3. Insert a second centered tab at 3.2 inches.
4. Insert a third centered tab at 4.65 inches.
5. Key the column headings using the tabs just set.
   a. Press **Tab**. Key **Mountain**.
   b. Press **Tab**. Key **Location**.
   c. Press **Tab**. Key **Height**.
6. Underline each heading individually. Your screen should appear similar to Figure 5–3.
7. Save the document and leave it open for the next exercise.

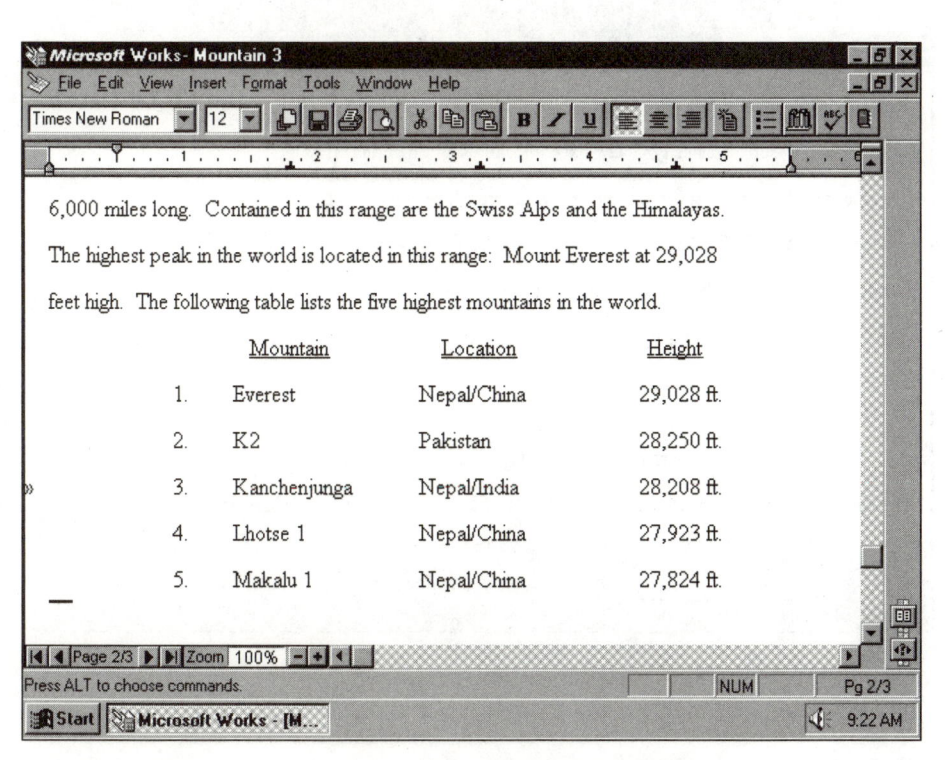

**note**

The ruler shows where tabs are set in a document. The tab markers can be dragged to new settings on the ruler.

**Figure 5–3**
Tabs make it easy to center headings in a table.

**lesson 5** *Tabs, Page Breaks, and Search and Replace* 47

REMOVING TABS

Tabs can be removed using the Format Tabs dialog box. Highlight the tab position you want to remove and click the Clear button in the dialog box. If you want to remove all the tabs at the same time, click Clear All.

## ❖ PAGE BREAKS

Works automatically inserts page breaks where they are necessary. You can, however, insert a page break manually. An example of when you would want to insert a page break manually is when an automatic page break separates a heading from the text that follows it.

To insert a page break manually:

- Move the cursor to the beginning of the line where the new page is to begin.
- Choose **Page Break** from the **Insert** menu.
  - or -
  Press **Ctrl** + **Enter**.

An automatic page break is indicated by a small >> symbol at the left side of the screen. A page break that is inserted manually is indicated by a dotted line across the screen in addition to the >> symbol. Figure 5–4 illustrates a manual and an automatic page break.

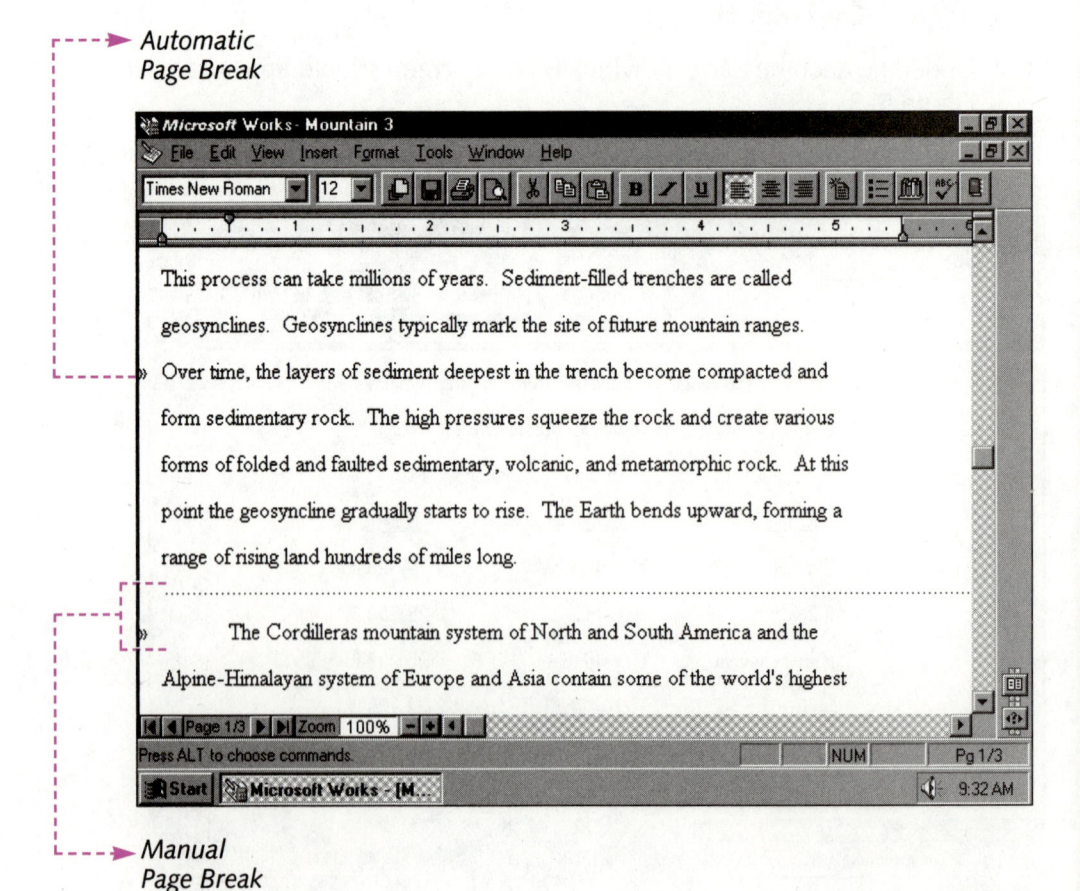

*Figure 5–4 The two types of page breaks differ in appearance.*

48  *Microsoft Works 4.0 for Windows 95: QuickTorial*™

## Exercise 5-3

**In this exercise, you will insert a page break.** *Mountain 3* **should be on your screen.**

1. Insert a page break in the table before the column heading *Mountain* to cause the table to appear at the top of a new page.
2. Save the document and leave it open for the next exercise.

## ❖ FIND

Using the Find command, you can quickly search a document for every occurrence of a specific word or phrase. Find moves the cursor from its present position to the next occurrence of the word or phrase for which you are searching.

To find a word or phrase:

- Choose **Find** from the **Edit** menu. The Find dialog box appears, as shown in Figure 5-5.

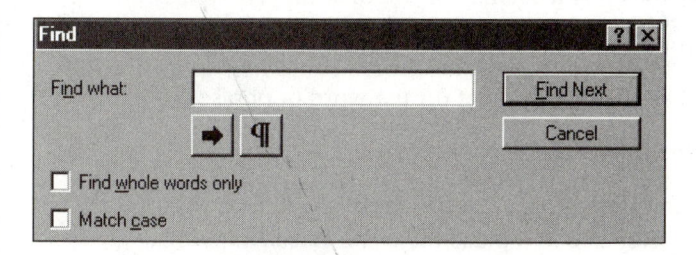

**Figure 5-5**
The Find dialog box is used to find a specific word or phrase in a document.

- In the Find what box, key the word or phrase you want to find.
- Click **Find Next.**
- Works will highlight the next occurrence.
- Click **Find Next** to continue the search; click **Cancel** to stop Find.

The Find command can find whole or partial words. For example, Works can find the word *all* or any word with *all* in it, such as *fall*, *horizontally*, or *alloy*. Find can look for words that match a specific capitalization. For example, if you wanted to search for the word *page* in lowercase letters, you would click Match case in the Find dialog box. Works would find *page*, but not *Page* or *PAGE*.

## Exercise 5-4

**In this exercise, you will use the Find command.** *Mountain 3* **should be on your screen.**

1. Place the cursor at the beginning of the document.
2. Search the document for the word *peak*. It appears three times.
3. Leave the document open for the next exercise.

**lesson 5** *Tabs, Page Breaks, and Search and Replace* 49

### ❖ REPLACE

The Replace command is an extended version of the Find command. Replace has all the features of Find. In addition, however, the Replace dialog box, shown in Figure 5–6, allows you to replace a word or phrase with another word or phrase that you specify. The replacements can be done individually, or all occurrences can be replaced at once.

**Figure 5–6
The Replace dialog box contains different options to find and replace words.**

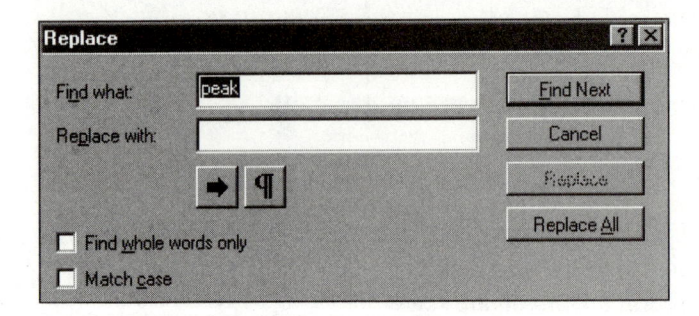

To use the Replace command:

- Place the cursor at the beginning of the document.
- Choose **Replace** from the **Edit** menu.
- Key the word or phrase you wish to replace in the Find what box.
- In the Replace with box, key the replacement for the word or phrase.
- Click **Find Next** to find the first occurrence of the word.
- Click **Replace** to replace the first occurrence and move to the next occurrence. You may continue clicking Replace to replace the occurrences individually.
  - or -
  Choose **Replace All** to replace all occurrences with no prompts.

## Exercise 5-5

In this exercise, you will use the Replace command. *Mountain 3* should be on your screen.

1. Place the cursor at the top of the document.
2. Replace all occurrences of the word *squeeze* with the word *compress*. One occurrence will be replaced, as indicated in the bottom left of your screen.
3. Save, print, and close the document.

# activities

## ❖ TRUE/FALSE

In the blank space before each sentence, place a **T** if the statement is true and an **F** if it is false.

_____ 1. Tabs mark the place the cursor will stop when the Enter key is pressed.

_____ 2. A tab leader is a line of characters that precedes a tab.

_____ 3. A page break can be inserted by pressing Shift + Enter.

_____ 4. The Find command can locate partial words.

_____ 5. The Find command is an extended version of the Replace command.

## ❖ COMPLETION

Answer the questions below in the space provided.

1. What are the default tab settings in Works?

   _____
   _____

2. What are the four available tab alignments?

   _____
   _____
   _____

3. What kind of table often uses tab leaders?

   _____
   _____

4. Give an example of a time when you would need to insert a page break manually.

   _____
   _____

5. What does the Match case option in the Find dialog box do?

   _____
   _____

# review

## Review Exercise 5-1

**In the blank space, write the letter of the word that matches the correct definition.**

____ 1. Marks the place that the cursor will stop when the Tab key is pressed.

____ 2. Refers to changes in the appearance of a font, such as bold or italics.

____ 3. The amount of space between the edge of a page and the text in a document.

____ 4. Determines how text is placed horizontally in relation to the margins.

____ 5. A space set between text and a document's margins.

____ 6. The distance between lines of text or paragraphs.

____ 7. The place where one page ends and another begins.

____ 8. Refers to the shape of characters belonging to a particular family of type.

a. margin
b. indent
c. spacing
d. font
e. type style
f. tab
g. alignment
h. page break

## Review Exercise 5-2

**In this exercise, you will create a new document and make formatting changes.**

1. Create a new document.
2. Key **TABLE OF CONTENTS** at the top of the document. Center the title. Make the title bold.
3. Press (Enter) twice. Change alignment back to Left.
4. Set a right-aligned tab with dots (...) as a leader at 5.75 inches.

5. Enter the following into the table:

```
What Were Dinosaurs?..................1
Where Did the Dinosaurs Live?.........4
The Triassic Period...................5
The Jurassic Period...................6
The Cretaceous Period.................8
The Extinction of the Dinosaurs.......9
```

6. Save the document as *Contents*. Print and close the document.

# lesson 6

# Advanced Copying, Headers, and Footers

## ❖ OBJECTIVES

Upon completion of this lesson, you will be able to:

1. Copy text between documents.
2. Copy character style and paragraph format.
3. Insert special characters, headers, and footers.

**Estimated Time:** 1/2 hour

## ❖ COPYING TEXT BETWEEN DOCUMENTS

The Copy command can be used to copy text from one document to another. Copying text between documents is similar to copying text within a document.

- Open the document you are copying from and the document you are copying to.
- Make the document you are copying from active, and highlight the text you want to copy.
- Click the **Copy** button on the toolbar.
- Switch to the document you are copying to.
- Position the cursor where you want to insert the text and click the **Paste** button on the toolbar.

> **note**
> To move text from one document to another, use the Cut command.

## ❖ COPYING FORMAT AND STYLE

Often you will spend time formatting a paragraph with indents or tabs and then find that you need the same format in another part of the document. The Paste Special command allows you to copy the format of a block of text, rather than the text itself. The command can be used to quickly apply a complicated format to text.

To copy character style or paragraph format:

- Highlight the text with the format you want to copy.
- Click the **Copy** button on the toolbar.
- Highlight the text to which you want to apply the copied format.

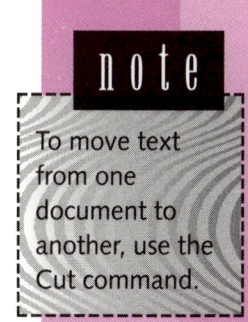

**lesson 6** *Advanced Copying, Headers, and Footers* 55

✤ Choose **Paste Special** from the **Edit** menu. The Paste Special dialog box appears, as shown in Figure 6–1.

✤ Choose character style or paragraph format.

Figure 6–1
The Paste Special dialog box allows you to choose whether to copy character style or paragraph format.

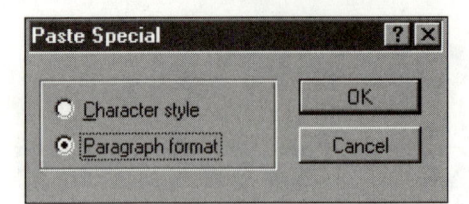

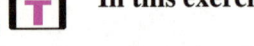

## Exercise 6–1

In this exercise, you will copy the format and style of text.

1. Open *Exercise 6–1*.

2. Boldface the first heading, *Respect for the Flag*.

3. Copy the bold style (character style) from the first heading to the second heading, *Time and Occasions for Display*.

4. Highlight the paragraphs under the *Respect for the Flag* heading, except for the first paragraph.

5. Create a custom hanging indent by setting a left indent of 0.25 and a first line indent of -0.25.

6. Copy the paragraph format of the paragraphs with the hanging indents to the paragraphs under the *Time and Occasions for Display* heading.

7. Save the document as *Flag Etiquette* and leave it open for the next exercise.

### ❖ SPECIAL CHARACTERS

Works has a number of special characters that can help you format your document. You insert these characters using the Special Character command. For example, you can insert characters that control hyphenation and that automatically print the time or the date. Special characters are particularly useful in headers and footers, as you will see in the next section.

Special characters are inserted from the Insert menu. Some special characters can be inserted directly from the Insert menu. You can insert the page number, document name, or date and time in a document. These items will be updated automatically each time you print the document.

Other special characters must be inserted using the Special Character command:

✤ Place the cursor where you want the character to appear.

✤ Choose **Special Character** from the **Insert** menu. The Insert Special Character dialog box will appear, as shown in Figure 6–2.

56  *Microsoft Works 4.0 for Windows 95: QuickTorial*™

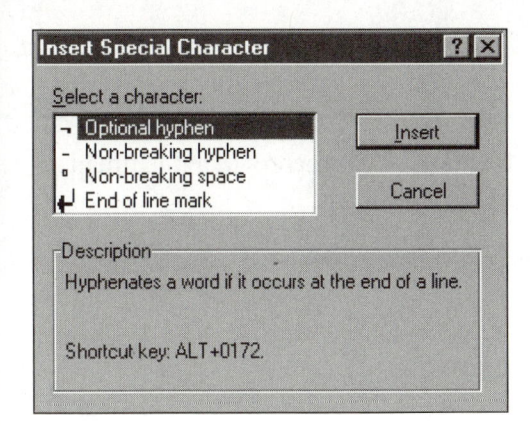

Figure 6–2
The Insert Special Character dialog box contains special character choices you can add to a document.

- Choose the special character you want from the list.
- Click **Insert.**

### ❖ VIEW ALL CHARACTERS

The All Characters command is used to view hidden formatting characters, such as carriage returns or end-of-line marks. Being able to see these hidden characters can help you in editing your text.

To view hidden characters:

- Choose **All Characters** from the **View** menu. The hidden formatting characters appear, as shown in Figure 6–3.

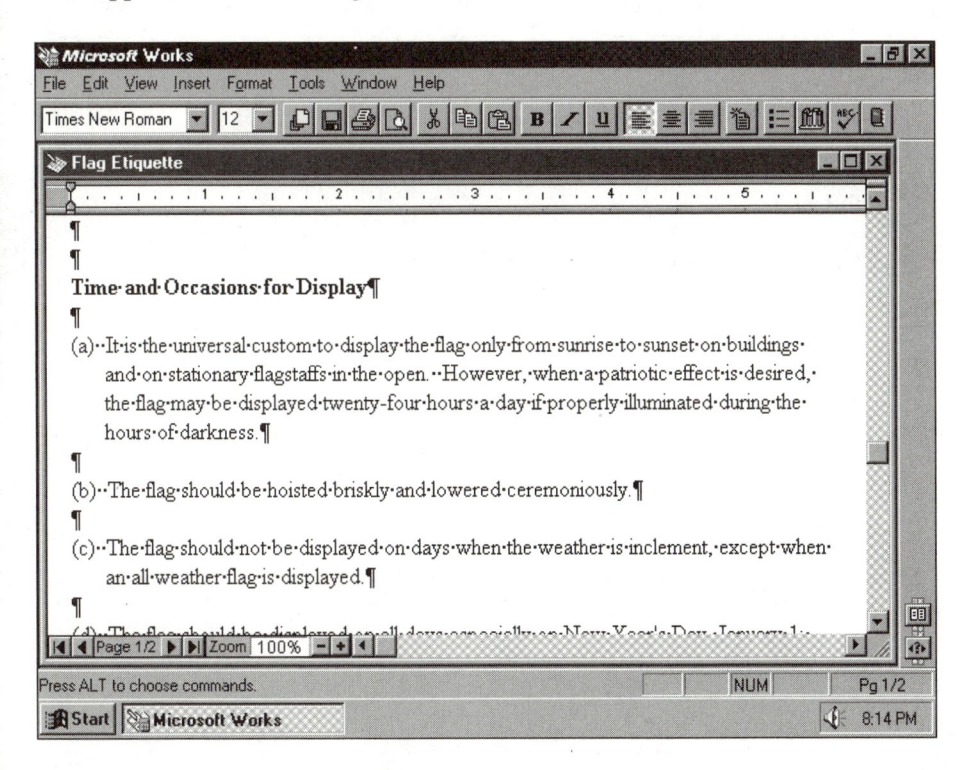

Figure 6–3
Choosing the All Characters command from the View menu makes hidden formatting characters appear.

To hide the characters:

- Choose **All Characters** from the **View** menu.

**lesson 6** *Advanced Copying, Headers, and Footers* 57

## Exercise 6–2

**In this exercise, you will view hidden formatting characters in a document. *Flag Etiquette* should be on your screen.**

1. Show the hidden formatting characters in the document on your screen.
2. Hide the formatting characters.
3. Leave the document open for the next exercise.

> **note**
>
> The H and F lines appear only when the document is in Normal view. Normal view can be chosen from the View menu.

### ❖ HEADERS AND FOOTERS

A header is a small amount of text that appears at the top of each page of a document. A footer is a small amount of text that appears at the bottom of each page of a document. Headers and footers are often used to provide the title of a document, the date the document was created or printed, or the page number.

In Works, there is an area at the top of a document labeled H and F, as shown in Figure 6–4. What you key next to the H line will appear as a header at the top of each page. What you key next to the F line will appear as a footer at the bottom of each page.

*Header Line*
*Footer Line*

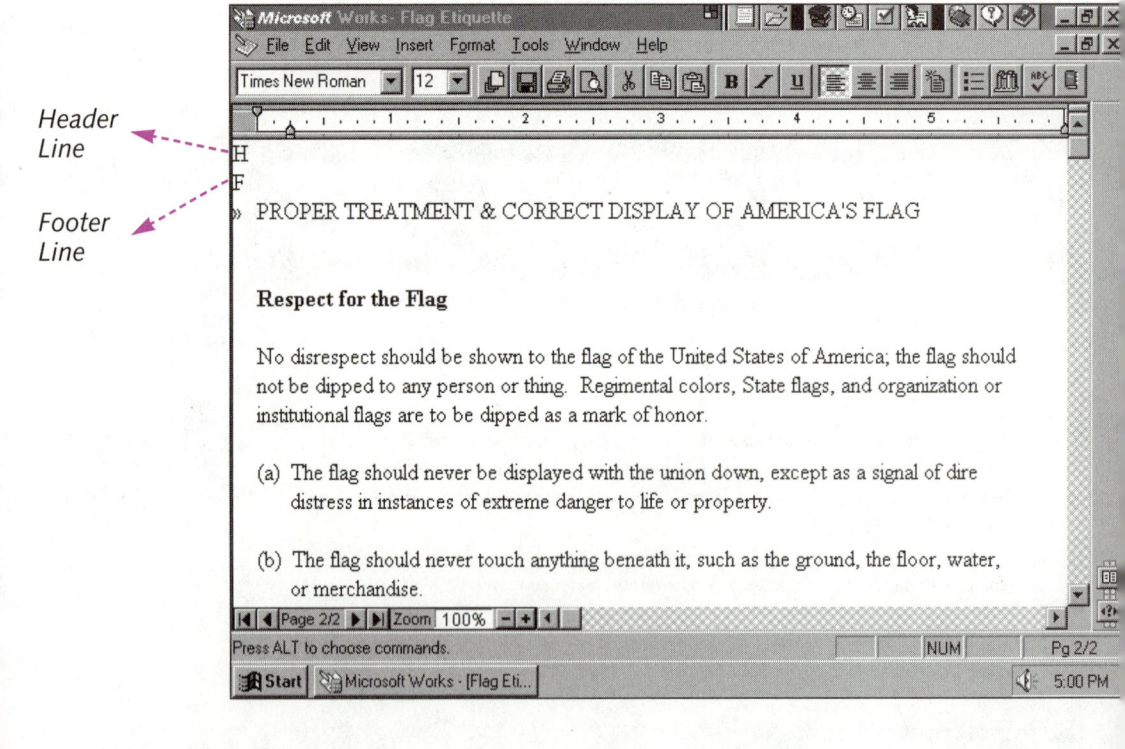

**Figure 6–4**
Headers and footers are keyed into special areas on the document.

To add headers and footers:

❖ Make sure the document is in Normal view and scroll to the very top of the document.

❖ Key your header on the line marked H, and key your footer on the line marked F.

58 Microsoft Works 4.0 for Windows 95: QuickTorial™

# Exercise 6-3

**In this exercise, you will create a header and footer.** *Flag Etiquette* **should be on your screen.**

1. Create a header with your name at the left margin. Press Tab two times and create the page number at the right margin. Use the Page Number command in the Insert menu to insert the page number.

2. Create a footer which reads **U.S. Code TITLE 36**. Center the text.

3. Change the font of the header and footer to a 9- or 10-point font.

4. Boldface the title, *PROPER TREATMENT & CORRECT DISPLAY OF AMERICA'S FLAG*.

5. Save, print, and close the document.

# activities

## ❖ TRUE/FALSE

*In the blank space before each sentence, place a **T** if the statement is true and an **F** if it is false.*

_____ 1. The Copy command can be used to copy text from one document to another.

_____ 2. Special characters can perform such tasks as print the current date or page number.

_____ 3. The Show command can be used to show hidden formatting characters.

_____ 4. A footer is a small amount of text which appears at the top of each page of a document.

_____ 5. The page number is often included in a header or footer.

## ❖ COMPLETION

*Answer the questions below in the space provided.*

1. What command is used to move text between documents?
   _____
   _____

2. What choice does the Paste Special dialog box present?
   _____
   _____

3. Which Paste Special option copies the indents of a paragraph?
   _____
   _____

4. Beside what indicator do you key the text for a header?
   _____
   _____

5. In what view do the header and footer lines appear at the top of the document?
   _____
   _____

# review

## Review Exercise 6-1

**In this exercise, you will format a document.**

1. Open *Review Exercise 6–1*.

2. Change the top and bottom margins to .75 inches.

3. Center and boldface the title of the document. If possible, change the font size of the title to 18 point or some other size larger than 12 point.

4. Place the cursor after the words *Briarcliff High School* below the title. Set a centered tab at 3 inches and a right-aligned tab near the right margin (approximately 5.8 inches).

5. On the same line as the words *Briarcliff High School*, key **Issue 22** at the 3-inch tab. Key **March 20, 19—** at the right-aligned tab.

6. Boldface each paragraph heading.

7. Left-align the first paragraph.

8. Save the document as *Update*. Print and close the document.

## Review Exercise 6-2

**In this exercise, you will create a new document with hanging indents.**

Create a new document and key the resume in Figure 6–5. Use hanging indents to format the Work Experience section of the resume. Save the document as *Resume*. Print and close the document.

### Justin Reed
**111 Creekview Drive**
**Spartanburg, SC 29302-1110**
**(803) 555-3456**

**Education**

*1987–1992*   Southwest University
Magna Cum Laude, 3.72 GPA
Bachelor of Arts Degree in English

*1984–1987*   Franklin High School
Honors Graduate, 3.9 GPA

**Work Experience**

*1988–present*   **Toys Toys Toys.** Employed as store assistant manager which entailed writing weekly employee schedules, ordering merchandise, and maintaining harmonious relations between upper management and employees.

*1981–1988*   **Milner's Wholesale Warehouse.** Employed as cashier and stocker. Served on the hiring committee which interviewed and hired new employees. Organized the children's telethon which was sponsored by Milner's Wholesale Warehouse.

*1984–1985*   **Burger Barn.** Employed as cook and customer assistant.

**Activities**

*1986–1987*   Senior Class President of Franklin High School

*1991–1992*   Secretary of the English Honor Society

*1990–1994*   Senior Citizens Home volunteer

**References**   Available Upon Request

Figure 6–5

## Review Exercise 6-3

In this exercise, you will create a memo.

Create a new document and key the memo in Figure 6–6. Save the document as *Memo*. Print and close the document.

---

### MEMORANDUM

TO: All Associates
FROM: Adam J. Hall
DATE: April 4, 19—
SUBJECT: Spring Picnic

It's that time of year again. The spring picnic is just two short weeks away. This year the picnic will be on April 18 at the Municipal Park northeast complex and will start promptly at 11:30 a.m.

There will be baseball, volleyball, and an awards ceremony. Come join the fun!

---

Figure 6–6

# lesson 7

# Moving the Highlight, Entering Data, and Saving

## ❖ OBJECTIVES

Upon completion of this lesson, you will be able to:

1. Identify the parts of the spreadsheet.
2. Move the highlight in the spreadsheet.
3. Enter data in the spreadsheet.
4. Save a spreadsheet.

**Estimated Time:** 1/2 hour

## ❖ CREATING AND OPENING SPREADSHEETS

To create a new spreadsheet or open an existing one, use the same process you used in the word processor. When you click on the Spreadsheet button in the Works Task Launcher, Works automatically opens a new spreadsheet titled *Unsaved Spreadsheet 1*.

## Exercise 7–1

**In this exercise, you will open an existing spreadsheet file.**

1. Open *Exercise 7–1*.
2. Leave the document open for the next exercise.

## ❖ PARTS OF A SPREADSHEET

Spreadsheets have some of the basic features that you learned in the word processor: the title bar, the menu bar, and the toolbar. However, other parts of the spreadsheet, such as the formula bar and the grid of cells created by columns and rows, do not appear in the word processor. Figure 7–1 shows the parts of the spreadsheet.

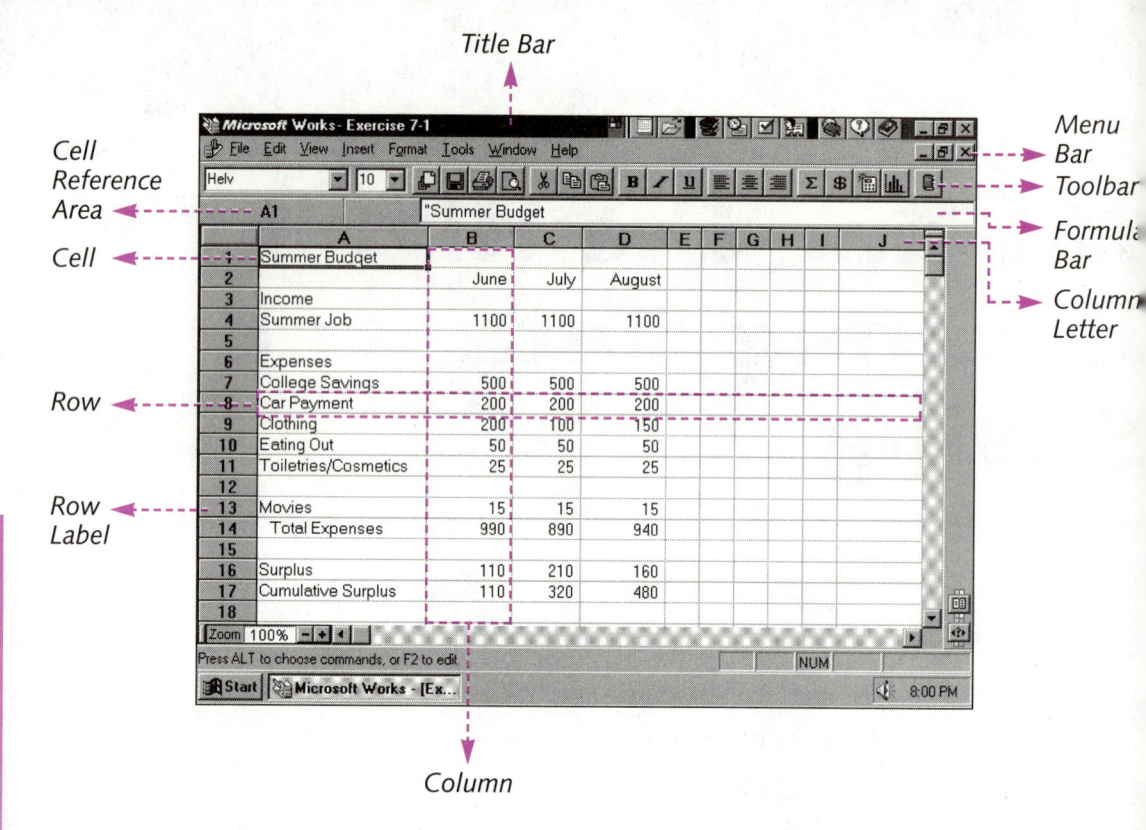

**Figure 7-1**
**A spreadsheet with labeled parts.**

Labels on figure: Cell Reference Area, Cell, Row, Row Label, Title Bar, Menu Bar, Toolbar, Formula Bar, Column Letter, Column

*Columns* appear vertically and are identified by letters at the top of the spreadsheet screen. *Rows* appear horizontally and are identified by numbers on the left side of the spreadsheet screen. A *cell* is the intersection of a row and column and is identified by a *cell reference*, the column letter, and row number (for example, A1, B2, C4).

The *formula bar* appears directly below the toolbar in the spreadsheet. On the far left side of the formula bar is the cell reference area that identifies the *active cell*. The active cell is the cell ready for data entry. On the grid of cells, the active cell is surrounded by a dark border. Your screen currently shows a border around the active cell on the spreadsheet, and the reference of the cell, A1, appears in the cell reference area of the formula bar.

In the word processor, the point at which a character is keyed is indicated by the cursor. In the spreadsheet, the entry point is called a *highlight*. You may change the active cell by moving the highlight from one cell to another.

❖ MOVING THE HIGHLIGHT IN A SPREADSHEET

You can move the highlight to different parts of the spreadsheet using the mouse, the direction keys, or the Go To command in the Edit menu.

USING THE MOUSE TO MOVE THE HIGHLIGHT

You can quickly move the highlight to any cell by clicking on that cell or you can use the scroll bars to move to cells that are not displayed on the screen.

## USING KEYS TO MOVE THE HIGHLIGHT

You can move the highlight using the keys listed in Table 7–1. You will see that many of these keys and key combinations are familiar to you from the word processor.

| To Move | Press |
|---|---|
| Left one column | ← |
| Right one column | → |
| Up one row | ↑ |
| Down one row | ↓ |
| To the first cell of a row | Home |
| To the last cell of a row containing data | End |
| To cell A1 | Ctrl + Home |
| To the last row or column containing data | Ctrl + End |
| Up one window | Page Up |
| Down one window | Page Down |
| Left one window | Ctrl + Page Up |
| Right one window | Ctrl + Page Down |

**note**: When the arrow keys, Page Up, or Page Down keys are held down, the movement will repeat, allowing you to move quickly.

Table 7–1

## USING THE GO TO COMMAND

You may want to move the highlight to a cell that does not appear on the screen using the Go To command.

To use the Go To command:

- Choose **Go To** from the **Edit** menu.

    -or-

    Press **F5**.

- Key the cell reference of the cell in which you want the highlight to appear.

- Click **OK**.

## Exercise 7-2

In this exercise, you will move the highlight in a spreadsheet. Exercise 7–1 should be on your screen.

1. Practice using the keys in Table 7–1 to move the highlight.

**lesson 7** *Moving the Highlight, Entering Data, and Saving*

2. Move to cell B4 using the Go To command.

3. Leave the spreadsheet open for the next exercise.

❖ ENTERING DATA INTO A CELL

Spreadsheet cells may contain data in the form of text, numbers, or formulas. Text consists of alphabetic characters and is usually in the form of headings, labels, or explanatory notes. In the formula bar, textual data is preceded by a quotation mark that indicates the data in the cell will not be used in calculations performed by the spreadsheet. Numbers can be in the form of values, dates, or times. Formulas are equations that calculate a value stored in a cell. (Formulas will be discussed in Lesson 10.) Whether the data consists of text, numbers, or formulas, it is entered by keying the information and then either pressing the Enter key or clicking the Enter button (the check mark (✔) located to the right of the cell reference area in the formula bar).

## Exercise 7-3

In this exercise, you will enter text and numbers into cells of a spreadsheet. Exercise 7-1 should be on your screen.

1. Move the highlight to A12 and key **Compact Discs**. As you key, the letters will appear both in the cell and in the formula bar.

2. Press **Enter**. Notice that the words in the formula bar are preceded by a quotation mark to indicate that they are textual data that will not be used in calculations.

3. Move to B12 and key **25**. Before entering the data by pressing the Enter key, notice the total expenses for June are 990.

4. Press **Enter**. The amount of total expenses for June has changed from 990 to 1015.

5. Enter **25** into C12 and D12, and notice how the spreadsheet recalculates the amounts each time you make a change.

6. Leave the spreadsheet open for the next exercise.

> **note**
> You can appreciate the value of the spreadsheet in making quick calculations when data changes.

❖ ADJUSTING COLUMN WIDTH

Sometimes the data you key will not fit in the column. When the data is wider than the column, Works will respond in one of three ways. If the data is a value, date, or time, Works will display a series of number signs (######) in the cell, as shown in Figure 7-2. If the data is text, the data will either flow into the next cell or Works will only display what fits in the cell.

**Figure 7-2**
A series of number signs indicates that a value, date, or time is too wide to fit in the cell.

To adjust a column's width:

- Highlight the column to adjust.

- Choose **Column Width** from the **Format** menu. The Column Width dialog box, shown in Figure 7–3, will appear.

**Figure 7-3**
The Best Fit button in the Column Width dialog box automatically selects the optimal width for your data.

- Key the column width you desire and click **OK**.
  -or-
  Click the **Best Fit** button to adjust the column to a width that accommodates the data.

  OR

- Place the mouse pointer on the boundary line to the right of the column letter. (The pointer changes into two arrows with the word *ADJUST* under it.)

- Drag to the right or left until the column is the desired size.

**note**

You can quickly apply the Best Fit option to a column by double-clicking the column letter.

## Exercise 7-4

In this exercise, you will change the width of a column on a spreadsheet. Exercise 7–1 should be on your screen.

1. Key **September** into E2, and press **Enter**. Because the word is recognized as a date and is too large for the column, a series of number signs (#) will appear in the cell.

2. Use the **Best Fit** option from the Column Width dialog box to widen the column.

3. Leave the spreadsheet open for the next exercise.

lesson 7  *Moving the Highlight, Entering Data, and Saving*  69

## ❖ CHANGING DATA IN A CELL

As you work with the spreadsheet, you may make a mistake or want to change data. If so, you may edit, replace, or clear existing data in cells of the spreadsheet.

### EDITING DATA

Editing is performed when only minor changes to cell data are necessary. Data in a cell may be edited in the formula bar by using the Edit key, which is F2 on your keyboard.

To edit data in a cell:

- Double-click the cell you want to edit. A cursor will appear in the cell.
    -or-
    Click the cell you want to edit and press (F2). A cursor will appear in the cell.
- Make the changes and press (Enter).

### REPLACING DATA

To replace cell contents:

- Highlight the cell.
- Key the new data.
- Press (Enter).

### CLEARING DATA

Clearing a cell will empty the cell of all its contents.

To clear cell contents:

- Highlight the cell.
- Press the (Delete) key.
    -or-
    Choose **Clear** from the **Edit** menu.

## Exercise 7-5

**In this exercise, you will edit, replace, and clear data from spreadsheet cells. Exercise 7–1 should be on your screen.**

1. Cell A16 contains the word *Surplus*. Edit the cell so it contains the words *Cash Surplus*.

2. Cell A3 now contains the word *Income*. Replace this word with the word *Revenue*.

3. Clear the word *September* from cell E2. Your screen should appear similar to Figure 7–4.

4. Leave the spreadsheet open for the next exercise.

[Screenshot of Microsoft Works - Exercise 7-1 spreadsheet showing Summer Budget data]

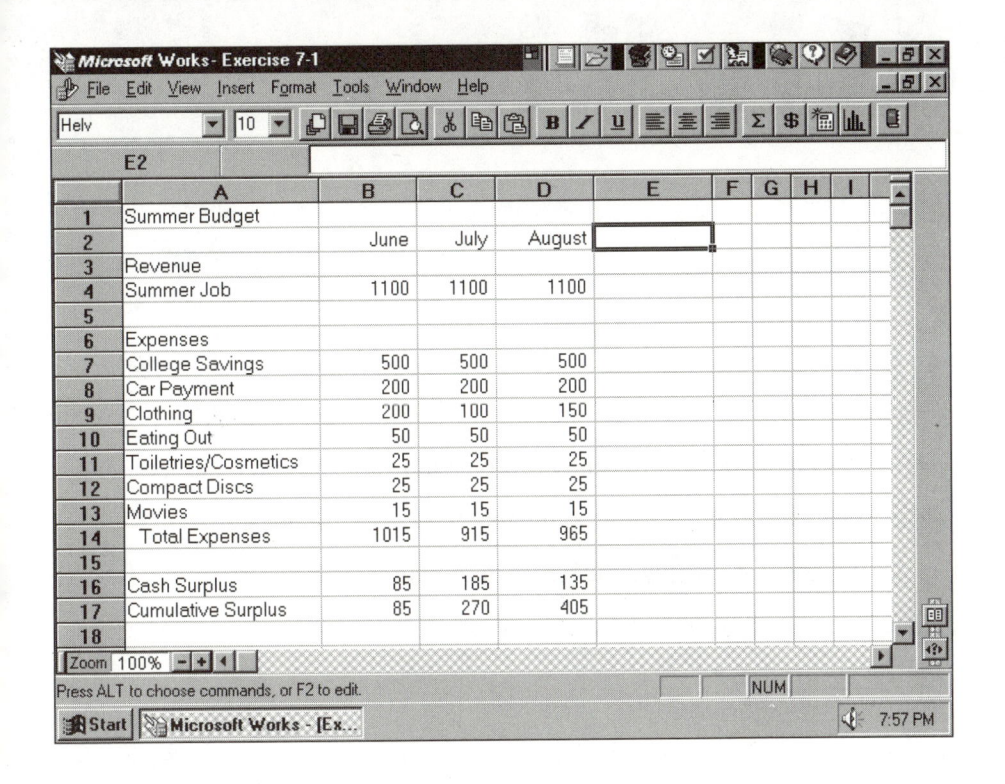

Figure 7–4
Changes may be made to a cell in a spreadsheet by editing, replacing, or clearing existing data.

## ❖ SAVING A SPREADSHEET

You may save and close the spreadsheet file by choosing the Save and Close commands from the File menu, just as you did in the word processor tool. Because you are currently working on a file that has already been named, you must choose Save As to save it to a new name and location.

### Exercise 7-6

**In this exercise, you will save a spreadsheet.**

1. Use the Save As command to save the spreadsheet as *Budget*.
2. Close the file.

**note**

If you are saving your data to a hard disk or network drive, locate the appropriate directory in the Save As dialog box rather than inserting a floppy disk.

# activities

❖ TRUE/FALSE

In the blank space before each sentence, place a **T** if the statement is true and an **F** if it is false.

_T_ 1. Opening a spreadsheet is similar to opening a word processor file.

_F_ 2. Columns are identified by numbers on the left side of the spreadsheet screen.

_F_ 3. Rows are identified by letters at the top of the spreadsheet screen.

_T_ 4. Pressing Ctrl + Home moves the highlight to cell A1.

_T_ 5. The Delete key can be used to clear a cell.

❖ COMPLETION

Answer the questions below in the space provided.

1. What is the intersection of a row and a column?

   _Cell_

2. What key moves the highlight to the first cell in a row?

   _Home_

3. What does the Best Fit button in the Column Width dialog box do?

   _column width proper_

4. What key is pressed to edit the contents of the active cell?

   _F2_

5. What command saves a file with a new name?

   _Save as_

# review

## Review Exercise 7-1

In the blank space, write the letter of the keystroke that matches the highlight movement.

_f_ 1. Left one column
_g_ 2. Right one column
_i_ 3. Up one row
_k_ 4. Down one row
_d_ 5. To the first cell of a row
_c_ 6. To the last cell of a row containing data
_a_ 7. To cell A1
_h_ 8. To the last row or column containing data
_Pg Up_ 9. Up one window
_Pg dn_ 10. Down one window
_Ctrl Pg up_ 11. Left one window
_Ctrl Pg dn_ 12. Right one window

a. Ctrl + Home
b. Page Up
c. End
d. Home
e. Ctrl + Page Up
f. ←
g. →
h. Ctrl + End
i. ↑
j. Ctrl + Page Down
k. ↓
l. Page Down

## Review Exercise 7-2

In this exercise, you will enter and edit data in a spreadsheet.

As a volunteer for a local environmental awareness group, you have agreed to collect and survey the type of trash discarded on a one-mile stretch of highway in your community. To help with your survey calculations, you have prepared the spreadsheet *Review Exercise 7–2* to account for trash items you have collected. Complete the spreadsheet by performing the following steps:

1. Open the file *Review Exercise 7–2*.

2. Enter the following numbers of trash items collected for Week 4. The totals for each category should change as you enter the data.

    Beer Cans         15
    Soda Cans          5
    Fast Food Items   20

| | |
|---|---|
| Newspaper Pages | 3 |
| Other Paper Items | 10 |
| Cigarette Butts | 17 |

3. In addition to the items above, you picked up a tennis shoe. Enter a new category in A11 called **Clothing**. Then enter the number **1** in E11.

4. You made a mistake when entering data for Week 3. Edit the cell for cigarette butts to show 18 rather than 16.

5. Save the file as *Litter*, print, and close it.

## Review Exercise 7-3

**In this exercise, you will create a new spreadsheet.**

1. Create a new spreadsheet document.

2. Enter the data below into the spreadsheet.

   **City Populations (in thousands)**

   | | 1970 | 1980 | 1990 |
   |---|---|---|---|
   | Boston | 641 | 563 | 574 |
   | Dallas | 644 | 905 | 1007 |
   | Phoenix | 584 | 790 | 983 |
   | St. Louis | 622 | 453 | 397 |

   Data source: U.S. Bureau of the Census, *Statistical Abstract of the United States*, 1990.

3. Save the file as *City Populations*, print, and close it.

# lesson 8

# Cell Appearance and Inserting and Deleting Rows and Columns

## ❖ OBJECTIVES

Upon completion of this lesson, you will be able to:

1. Select a group of cells.
2. Change cell appearance.
3. Insert and delete rows and columns.

**Estimated Time:** 1/2 hour

## ❖ SELECTING A GROUP OF CELLS

Often you will perform operations on several cells at once. A selected group of cells is referred to as a *range*. In a range, all cells touch each other and form a rectangle. The range is identified by the cell in the upper left corner and the cell in the lower right corner, separated by a colon (for example, B7:D11). The reference for a selected range will appear in the cell reference area at the far left of the formula bar.

To select a group of cells:

- Place the highlight in the first cell of the range and drag to the last cell. As you drag the highlight, the range of selected cells will become shaded (except for the first cell).

## ❖ CHANGING CELL APPEARANCE

You can change the appearance of cell contents to make them easier to read. In this section, you will learn to alter the appearance of cell contents by changing the font, font size, style, alignment, format, and borders. Figure 8–1 shows examples of the changes you can make to a cell's contents.

**Figure 8–1**
The appearance of cell contents may be changed by changing style, alignment, and format, or by adding borders.

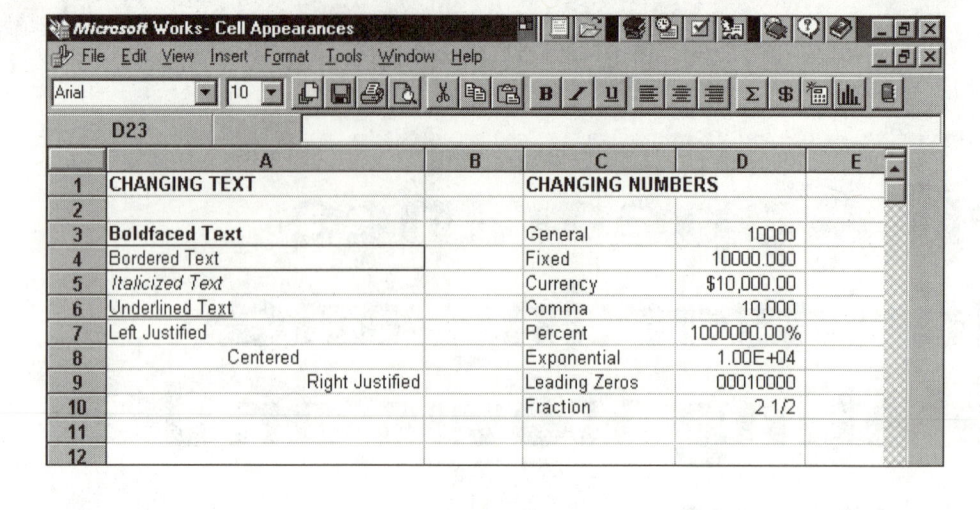

> **note**
> The number and types of fonts available in the spreadsheet will vary depending on the fonts installed in your system.

> **note**
> You can also use the same keyboard shortcuts to apply styles as you did in the word processor.
>
> Ctrl + B
> Bold
>
> Ctrl + I
> Italics
>
> Ctrl + U
> Underline

## FONTS AND FONT SIZES

The font and font size may significantly affect the readability of the spreadsheet if you decide to print it. You can choose different fonts or font sizes for different parts of the spreadsheet.

To change the font and font size of part of the spreadsheet:

- Highlight the cell or cells you want the change to affect.
- Choose a font from the **Font Name** box.
- Choose a size from the **Font Size** box.

## STYLE

Boldfacing, italicizing, or underlining can add emphasis to the contents of a cell.

To apply a style:

- Highlight the cell or cells you want to change.
- Click the desired style button in the toolbar.
  -or-
- Highlight the cell or cells you want to change.
- Choose **Font** and **Style** from the **Format** menu. The Format Cells dialog box will appear with the Font section visible.
- Choose the desired style(s) in the Style box.
- Click **OK**.

## CELL ALIGNMENT

You may align the contents of a cell or cells in three ways: against the left margin of the cell, in the center of the cell, or against the right margin of the cell. Works will automatically align all text entries (those preceded by a quotation mark when viewed in the formula bar) at the left side of the cell. All numbers are automatically aligned on the right side of the cell.

To change the alignment of the cell:

- Highlight the cell or cells you want to change.
- Click on the desired alignment button in the toolbar.
  -or-
- Highlight the cell or cells you want to change.
- Choose **Alignment** from the **Format** menu. The Format Cells dialog box will appear with the Alignment section visible.
- Choose the desired horizontal and vertical alignments.
- Click **OK**.

## FORMATS

Several cell formats are available. The default format, called general format, accommodates both text and numerical data. However, you can use several other formats (see Table 8–1).

> **note**
>
> The keyboard shortcuts for alignment you learned in the word processor can be used to align the contents of a spreadsheet cell.
>
> **Ctrl** + L
> Left alignment
>
> **Ctrl** + E
> Center alignment
>
> **Ctrl** + **Shift** + R
> Right alignment

| Format | Display |
| --- | --- |
| General | The default format; displays both text and numerical data as keyed |
| Fixed | Displays numerical data with a fixed amount of places to the right of the decimal point |
| Currency | Displays numerical data preceded by a dollar sign |
| Comma | Displays numerical data with commas every third decimal place |
| Percent | Displays numerical data followed by a percent sign |
| Exponential | Displays numerical data in scientific notation |
| Leading Zeros | Displays numerical data with a specified number of decimal places to the left of the decimal point |
| Fraction | Displays numerical data as a fractional value |
| True/False | Displays the word *True* for all non-zero number values and *False* for zero |
| Date | Displays text and numerical data as dates |
| Time | Displays text and numerical data as time |
| Text | Displays cell contents as text even if the data contains numbers or special characters that would normally be considered numeric |

Table 8–1

**lesson 8** *Cell Appearance and Inserting and Deleting Rows and Columns* 77

To change the format of a cell:

- Highlight the cell or cells you want to change.
- Choose **Number** from the **Format** menu. The Format Cells dialog box will appear with the Number section visible.
- Choose the desired format in the Format box.
- Click **OK**.

## BORDERS

Emphasis may be added to a cell by placing a border around its edges. You may place the border around the entire cell or only on certain sides of the cell.

To place a border around a cell:

- Highlight the cell or cells you want to change.
- Choose **Border** from the **Format** menu. The Border dialog box will appear.
- Click the **Outline** box in the Border box. A line should appear in the box.
- Click **OK**.

## Exercise 8-1

In this exercise, you will change the appearance of the cells in a spreadsheet.

1. Open *Exercise 8–1*.
2. Boldface cell A1.
3. Place a border around the spreadsheet title, *Summer Budget*, in A1.
4. Boldface the range A16:A17.
5. Underline the names of the months (range B2:D2) to show they are column headings.
6. Center the names of the months.
7. Center cells A3 and A6.
8. Format ranges B4:D4, B7:D7, and B16:D17 in Currency format.
9. If necessary, widen any cells that are too narrow to accommodate the data.
10. Format range B8:D14 in Comma format. Your screen should appear similar to Figure 8–2.

# activities

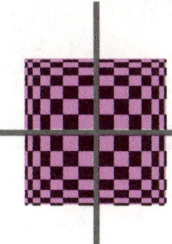

## ❖ TRUE/FALSE

In the blank space before each sentence, place a **T** if the statement is true and an **F** if it is false.

_T_ 1. A selected group of cells is referred to as a range.
_T_ 2. Works permits more than one font in a single spreadsheet.
_T_ 3. Numbers are right aligned unless a different alignment is specified.
_F_ 4. The Leading Zeros format displays numerical data in scientific notation.
_F_ 5. The Insert Row command can be used to bring back a deleted row immediately after deleting a row.

## ❖ COMPLETION

Answer the questions below in the space provided.

1. What is the process for selecting a group of cells?

    _Range_

2. What styles are available for emphasizing cell contents?

    _Bold  Italicizing  underling_

3. What alignment is used automatically to align text?

    _Left_

4. What format is used to display dollar amounts?

    _Currency_

5. What happens to the data in a deleted row or column?

    _gone_

lesson 8 activities 81

# review

## Review Exercise 8-1

In this exercise, you will widen columns and change the appearance of the cells in a spreadsheet.

1. Open the file *Review Exercise 8–1*.
2. Widen columns B through E to 10 characters each.
3. Widen column A to 18 characters.
4. Widen column F to 16 characters.
5. Change the appearance of the following cells and cell ranges to the style indicated:

   | Cell(s) | Change to |
   |---------|-----------|
   | A1 | Boldface |
   | A3:E3 | Underline |
   | A3:F3 | Center |
   | F3 | Italics |
   | A13 | Italics |
   | A13:F13 | Boldface |
   | F3:F11 | Boldface |

4. Save the file as *Litter 2*, print, and close it.

# lesson 9

# Copying and Moving Data and Printing

## ❖ OBJECTIVES

Upon completion of this lesson, you will be able to:

1. Copy data in a spreadsheet.
2. Move data in a spreadsheet.
3. Print a spreadsheet.

**Estimated Time:** 1/2 hour

## ❖ COPYING DATA

When creating or enlarging a spreadsheet, you may want to use the same text or numbers in another portion of the spreadsheet. Rather than key the same data over again, you can copy the data. There are several ways to copy data in a spreadsheet.

### COPY AND PASTE

The Copy command duplicates the contents of a cell or cells on the Clipboard so that you can enter the data in another part of the spreadsheet. The Copy command, however, will not affect the data in the original cell(s). Although there are commands to Copy and Paste on the Edit menu, the easiest way to access the Copy and Paste commands is using the toolbar (see Figure 9–1).

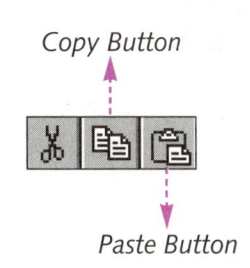

*Copy Button*

*Paste Button*

> **note**
> Data copied into a cell will replace data already in that cell. Check your destination cells for existing data before copying.

**Figure 9–1**
The Copy and Paste buttons on the toolbar provide a shortcut for the Copy and Paste commands.

To use the copy command:

- Highlight the cell or range to be copied.
- Click the **Copy** button in the toolbar.
- Place the highlight in the upper left corner of the range into which the data will be copied.
- Click the **Paste** button in the toolbar, and the copied data will fill the new range of cells. If you would like to make copies in yet another area of the spreadsheet, move the highlight to that area and click the Paste button on the toolbar.

## Exercise 9-1

**In this exercise, you will practice copying and pasting.**

1. Open *Exercise 9-1*. The spreadsheet contains columns for grades and percentages of homework and examinations.

2. Expand the spreadsheet to calculate grades for a history class by copying the range A4:D9 to A11:D16.

3. Key **History 101** in A10.

4. Expand the spreadsheet to calculate grades for a biology class by highlighting cell A18 and clicking the **Paste** button in the toolbar. The range of cells should be copied from A4:D9 to A18:D23.

5. Key **Biology 101** in A17.

6. Boldface the contents of cells A10 and A17.

7. Save the spreadsheet as *Grades* and leave it open for the next exercise. Your screen should look similar to Figure 9-2.

Figure 9-2
Copying speeds up the process of creating a spreadsheet.

### FILL DOWN AND FILL RIGHT

The Fill Down and Fill Right commands copy data into cell(s) adjacent to the original (see Figure 9-3).

The Fill Down command will copy data into the cell(s) directly below the original cell.

- Highlight the cell to be copied and the cells below it where you want the data copied.
- Choose **Fill Down** from the **Edit** menu.

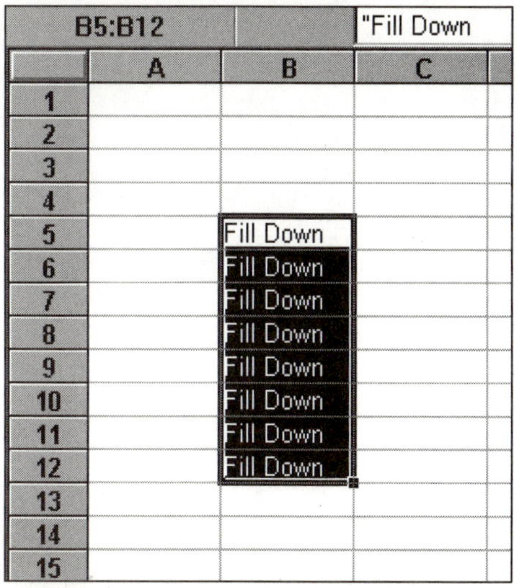

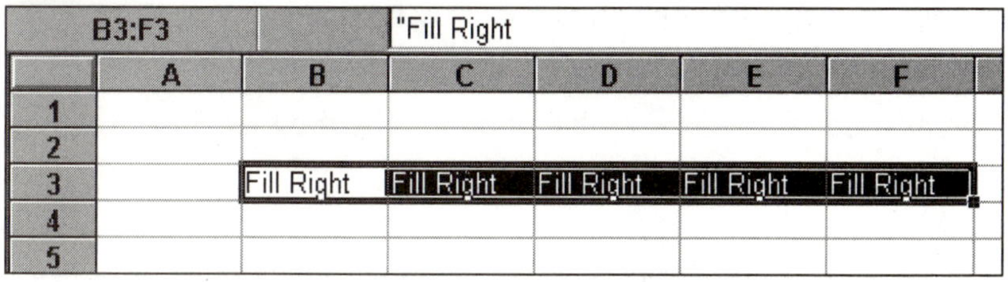

**Figure 9-3**
Fill Down copies data to adjacent cells below the original cell, while Fill Right copies to adjacent cells to the right of the original cell.

The Fill Right command will copy data into the cell(s) to the right of the original cell.

* Highlight the cell to be copied and the cells to the right of it where you want the data copied.
* Choose **Fill Right** from the **Edit** menu.

> **note**
>
> Filling can be used only when the destination cells are adjacent to the original cell.

## Exercise 9-2

In this exercise, you will use the Fill Down command to copy data in a spreadsheet. *Grades* should be on your screen.

The table shows the data for grades earned in classes.

| Subject | Grade | Percent |
|---|---|---|
| **English 101** | | |
| Homework | 87 | 10.00% |
| Exam 1 | 82 | 20.00% |
| Exam 2 | 75 | 20.00% |
| Exam 3 | 78 | 20.00% |
| Final Exam | 81 | 30.00% |
| **History 101** | | |
| Homework | 76 | 5.00% |
| Exam 1 | 74 | 20.00% |
| Exam 2 | 80 | 20.00% |
| Exam 3 | 77 | 20.00% |
| Final Exam | 79 | 35.00% |

**lesson 9** *Copying and Moving Data and Printing*

**Biology 101**

| Homework | 89 | 30.00% |
|---|---|---|
| Exam 1 | 92 | 15.00% |
| Exam 2 | 87 | 15.00% |
| Exam 3 | 95 | 15.00% |
| Final Exam | 93 | 25.00% |

**Follow the steps below to enter the data in the spreadsheet.**

1. Enter **0.2** in C5. (0.2 is the decimal equivalent of 20%.)
2. Use the Fill Down command to copy data from C5 to C6:C7.
3. Enter **0.2** in C12 and **0.15** in C19.
4. Use the Fill Down command to copy data from C12 to C13:C14 and C19 to C20:C21.
5. Enter the remaining data into the spreadsheet by inserting the percentages shown for homework and final exams, and enter the grades for all items.
6. Save your spreadsheet and leave the file open for the next exercise.

> **note**
> After completing the spreadsheet, you may notice that the semester grades have been calculated based on the data entered.

## ❖ MOVING DATA

Like the Copy command, the Cut command places selected data on the Clipboard so that it may be pasted into another part of the spreadsheet. The Cut command, however, will remove the data from the original cell(s) in the spreadsheet. Because cut data is stored on the Clipboard, you may restore the data at any time by simply choosing the Paste command.

To move data:

- Highlight the cells to be moved.
- Click the **Cut** button on the toolbar (see Figure 9–4). The data in the range will disappear from the spreadsheet.
- Highlight the part of the spreadsheet where the data is to be moved.
- Click the **Paste** button on the toolbar. The data will appear in the new position.

*Figure 9–4 The Cut command removes the data from a cell and places it on the Clipboard.*

Cut Button
Paste Button

### Exercise 9-3

In this exercise, you will use the Cut and Paste commands to move data in a spreadsheet. *Grades* should be on your screen.

1. Use the Cut and Paste commands to move the data for Biology 101 (A17:D23) down two rows. The data should appear in the range A19:D25.

2. Move the data for History 101 (A10:D16) down one row. The data should appear in the range A11:D17. Your screen should look similar to Figure 9–5.

3. Save the spreadsheet and leave it open for the next exercise.

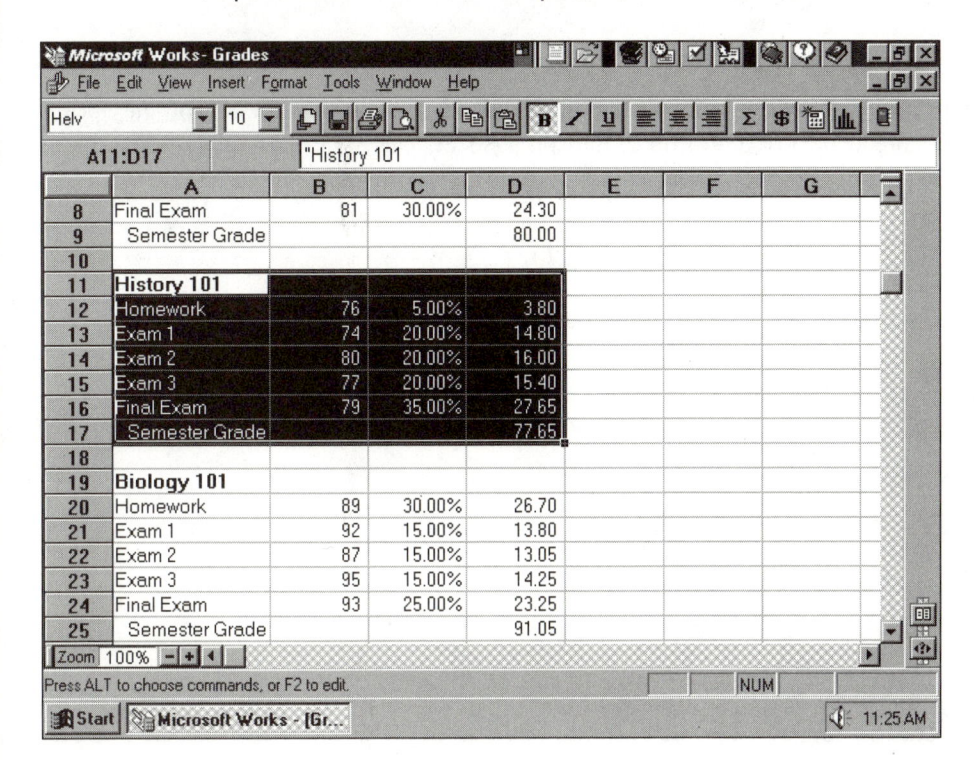

**Figure 9–5**
The Cut command removes data from its original position, and the Paste command places it in another part of the spreadsheet.

### ❖ FREEZING TITLES

Freezing will keep the row or column titles on the screen no matter where you scroll in the spreadsheet. To freeze titles:

* Position the highlight to the right of the columns you want to freeze and below the rows you want to freeze.

* Choose **Freeze Titles** from the **Format** menu.

To unfreeze the rows and columns:

* Choose **Freeze Titles** again.

## Exercise 9-4

In this exercise, you will freeze the column headings in a spreadsheet. **Grades** should be on your screen.

1. Highlight A3.

2. Choose **Freeze Titles** from the **Format** menu. The column headings on Rows 1 and 2 are now frozen.

**lesson 9** *Copying and Moving Data and Printing* **87**

3. Scroll to the lower part of the spreadsheet. You will notice that the column headings remain at the top of the screen no matter where you move.

4. Leave the spreadsheet open for the next exercise.

❖ PRINTING A SPREADSHEET

Printing a spreadsheet is similar to printing a word processor document. You may print the entire spreadsheet or a portion of the spreadsheet. The Set Print Area command tells Works the part of the spreadsheet you want to print. To designate the area you want to print:

- Highlight the range you want to print.
- Choose **Set Print Area** from the **Format** menu.
- Click **OK**.

Once the print area is set, print the spreadsheet.

- Choose **Print** from the **File** menu.
- Select the options you want from the Print dialog box.
- Click **OK**.

## Exercise 9-5

In this exercise, you will print a spreadsheet. *Grades* should be on your screen.

1. Unfreeze the titles.
2. Set the print area to A1:D25.
3. Change the left margin to 2 inches using the Page Setup command.
4. Print the spreadsheet.
5. Save and close the file.

# activities

## TRUE/FALSE

In the blank space before each sentence, place a **T** if the statement is true and an **F** if it is false.

__F__ 1. Data copied into a cell will move data already in that cell down to make room for the data being copied.

__T__ 2. The Fill Down command will copy data into the cells directly below the original cell.

__T__ 3. The Cut command removes the data from the original cell(s) in the spreadsheet.

__F__ 4. You can unfreeze frozen titles using the Unfreeze Titles command.

__T__ 5. The Set Print Area command tells Works the part of the spreadsheet to print.

## COMPLETION

Answer the questions below in the space provided.

1. What is the result of choosing the Copy command?

   *Copy the contents*

2. What command copies data into the cells directly to the right of the original cell?

   *fill right*

3. What is the process for moving spreadsheet data?

   *Cut + paste*

4. Before freezing titles, where should the highlight be placed?

   *titles*

5. When can filling be used?

   *Same contents*

lesson 9 activities 89

# review

## Review Exercise 9-1

In the blank space, write the letter of the spreadsheet command that will solve the spreadsheet problem.

**Spreadsheet Problems**

____ 1. You are tired of keying repetitive data.

____ 2. A portion of the spreadsheet would be more useful in another area of the spreadsheet.

____ 3. You forgot to key a row of data in the middle of the spreadsheet.

____ 4. You no longer need a certain column in the spreadsheet.

____ 5. Column headings cannot be viewed on the screen when you are working in the lower part of the spreadsheet.

____ 6. Your boss would rather not view your spreadsheet on the screen and has requested a copy on paper.

____ 7. You would like to print only a portion of the spreadsheet.

**Spreadsheet Commands**

6 a. Print command
1 b. Fill Right, Fill Down, or Copy command
3 c. Insert Row command
2 d. Cut and Paste command
7 e. Set Print Area command
4 f. Delete Column command
5 g. Freeze Titles command

# Review Exercise 9-2

In this exercise, you will create and print a spreadsheet.

The file *Review Exercise 9-2* is a spreadsheet for the Bates family, who are preparing to purchase furniture for a new home. The spreadsheet is not currently organized by rooms in the house. In addition, the family wants to purchase more than one piece of certain items.

1. Open *Review Exercise 9-2*. Organize the spreadsheet following the format given in the table. The new spreadsheet should have furniture items organized by rooms, with proper headings and cell formats. Remember to use the Fill Down command to copy repetitive items and the Insert Row command to provide headings. Use the Cut and Paste commands to move some of the data.

   **Furniture Purchase Worksheet**

   | Item | Purchase Price |
   |---|---|
   | **Utility Room** | |
   | Washer | $340.00 |
   | Dryer | $299.00 |
   | | |
   | **Living Room** | |
   | Couch | $500.00 |
   | Arm Chair | $260.00 |
   | End Table | $250.00 |
   | End Table | $250.00 |
   | | |
   | **Bedroom** | |
   | Bed | $550.00 |
   | Dresser | $400.00 |
   | Drawers | $250.00 |
   | | |
   | **Dining Room** | |
   | Table | $400.00 |
   | Dining Chair | $120.00 |
   | Dining Chair | $120.00 |
   | Dining Chair | $120.00 |
   | Dining Chair | $120.00 |

2. Print the spreadsheet.

3. Save the spreadsheet as *Furniture* and close the file.

## Review Exercise 9-3

In this exercise, you will change the appearance of the cells in a spreadsheet, widen columns, insert rows, and print the spreadsheet.

The file *Review Exercise 9–3* is similar to the spreadsheet you created in Review Exercise 7-3 showing city populations.

1. Open *Review Exercise 9–3*.
2. Boldface the contents of cell A1.
3. Boldface, underline, and center the titles in the range B3:D3.
4. Insert the following cities in alphabetical order using the Insert Row command.

   | City | 1970 | 1980 | 1990 |
   |---|---|---|---|
   | Atlanta | 495 | 425 | 394 |
   | Grand Rapids | 198 | 182 | 189 |
   | Los Angeles | 2812 | 2967 | 3486 |
   | New York | 7896 | 7072 | 7323 |

5. Adjust the width of column A using the Best Fit option.
6. Save the spreadsheet as *Cities*, print the spreadsheet, and close.

# lesson 10

# Using Formulas

❖ OBJECTIVES

Upon completion of this lesson, you will be able to:

1. Define a spreadsheet formula.
2. Create spreadsheet formulas.
3. Enter and edit formulas.
4. Use formula helpers.

**Estimated Time:** 1/2 hour

❖ WHAT ARE FORMULAS?

A *formula* is an equation that calculates a new value from existing values. Works recognizes the contents of a cell as a formula when an equals sign (=) is the first character in the cell. For example, if the formula =8+6 were entered into Cell B3, the value of 14 would be displayed in the spreadsheet. The formula bar displays the characters =8+6, as shown in Figure 10–1.

*A formula is preceded by an equals sign and is displayed in the formula bar.*

*The result of a formula is displayed in the cell.*

Figure 10–1
Works recognizes an entry as a formula when an equals sign is the first character in the cell.

### STRUCTURE OF A FORMULA

A spreadsheet formula is composed of two types of characters: operands and operators. An *operand* is a number or cell reference used in formulas. An *operator* tells Works what to do with the operands. For example, in the formula =B3+5, B3

lesson 10 *Using Formulas* 93

and 5 are operands. The plus sign (+) is an operator that tells Works to add the value contained in cell B3 to the number 5. The operators used in formulas are shown in Table 10–1.

Table 10–1

| Operator | Operation | Example | Meaning |
|---|---|---|---|
| + | Addition | B5+C5 | Adds the values in B5 and C5 |
| - | Subtraction | C8-232 | Subtracts 232 from the value in C8 |
| * | Multiplication | D4*D5 | Multiplies the value in D4 by the value in D5 |
| / | Division | E6/4 | Divides the value in E6 by 4 |
| ^ | Exponentiation | B3^3 | Raises the value in B3 to the third power |

### ORDER OF EVALUATION

Formulas containing more than one operator are called *complex formulas*. For example, the formula =C3*C4+5 will perform both multiplication and addition to calculate the value in the cell. The sequence used to calculate the value of a formula amount is called the *order of evaluation*. Formulas are evaluated in the following order:

1. Contents within parentheses are evaluated first. You may use as many sets of parentheses as you desire. Works will evaluate the innermost set of parentheses first.

2. Mathematical operators are evaluated in the following order: exponentiation, negative signs, multiplication and division, addition and subtraction.

3. Equations are evaluated from left to right if two or more operators have the same order of evaluation. For example, in the formula =20/5/2, twenty would be divided by five, then the quotient (four) would be divided by two.

❖ ENTERING AND EDITING FORMULAS

To enter a formula:

- Highlight the cell in which you want to enter the formula.
- Key the formula and press **Enter**.

If you enter a formula incorrectly, an error dialog box will appear. Works may suggest a correct formula as an alternative, or may highlight the incorrect portion of the formula. If the entry is badly flawed, Works may make no suggestion or not highlight any portion of the formula. Regardless of what Works may suggest, you may edit the formula and enter it again.

To edit formulas already entered in the spreadsheet:

- Highlight the cell.
- Press **F2**, the Edit key.
- Edit the data and press **Enter**.

> **note**
> You can edit a formula using the mouse by clicking the cell and then clicking in the formula bar.

94 Microsoft Works 4.0 for Windows 95: QuickTorial™

## Exercise 10-1

In this exercise, you will create formulas that perform calculations.

1. Open *Exercise 10-1*.

2. Enter the following formulas in the cells. Remember to key an equals sign before you key each formula. After you enter a formula, the formula result value will appear in the cell.

   | Cell | Formula    | Resulting Value |
   |------|------------|-----------------|
   | C3   | =A3+B3     | 380             |
   | C4   | =A4-B4     | -246            |
   | C5   | =A5*B5     | 18850           |
   | C6   | =A6/B6     | 2               |
   | D3   | =(A3+B3)*20| 7600            |
   | E3   | =A3+B3*20  | 4921            |

3. Enter your name in A1.

4. Print the range A1:E6.

5. Save the spreadsheet as *Calculate* and close the file.

> **note**
>
> You can see from the last two formulas in this exercise the importance of the parentheses in the sequence of calculation.

## USING THE HIGHLIGHT TO CREATE FORMULAS

Until now, you constructed formulas by keying the entire formula in the cell of the spreadsheet. You may enter a formula quickly by using the highlight to enter cell references in a formula rather than keying the reference.

For example, to enter the formula =*A3+B3* in a cell, you would:

- Highlight the cell that will contain the formula.
- Press =.
- Highlight A3.
- Press +.
- Highlight B3.
- Press **Enter**.

## Exercise 10-2

In this exercise, you will use the highlight to create formulas.

The file *Exercise 10-2* is a spreadsheet that records the portions of meat and cheese sold in a sandwich shop during a month. In this exercise, you will create formulas to calculate the total ounces of meat and cheese sold during the month.

Portions are allocated as follows:

|  | Large | Small |
|---|---|---|
| **Meat** | 6 ounces | 3 ounces |
| **Cheese** | 4 ounces | 2.5 ounces |

1. Open the spreadsheet file *Exercise 10–2*.

2. Use the highlight to create the following formulas:

   | Cell | Formula | Resulting Value |
   |---|---|---|
   | D4 | =(6*B4)+(3*C4) | 1440 |
   | D8 | =(4*B8)+(2.5*C8) | 1818.5 |

3. Use the **Fill Down** command to copy the formula in D4 to D5:D7.

4. Use the **Fill Down** command to copy the formula in D8 to D9. Compare your screen to Figure 10–2.

5. Save the spreadsheet as *Deli* and leave it open for the next exercise.

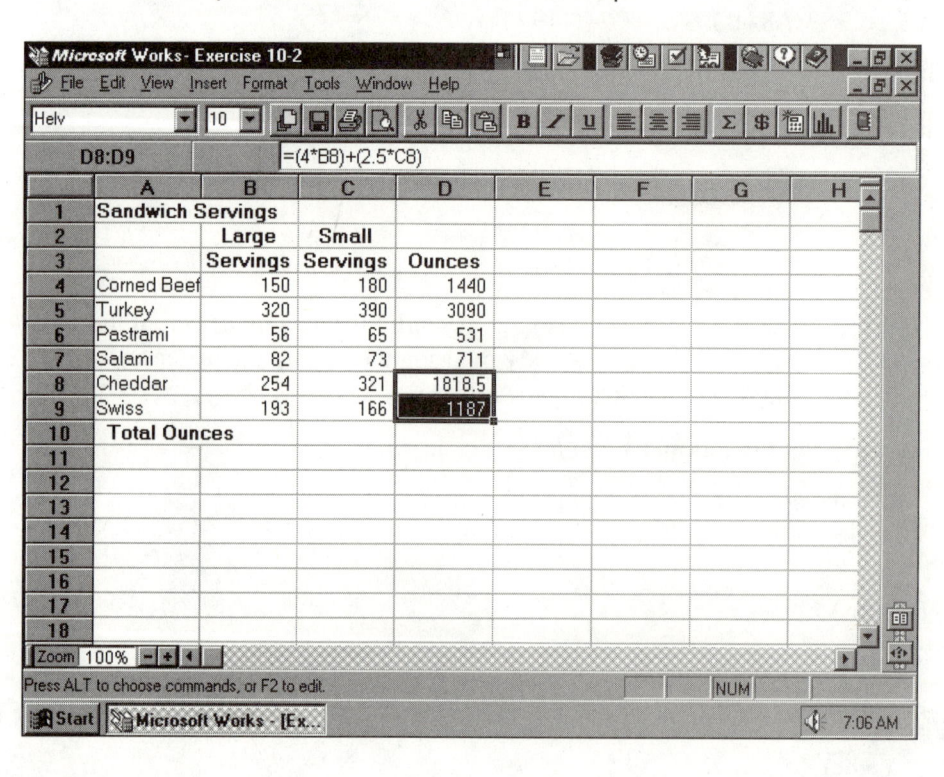

Figure 10–2
Spreadsheet formulas may be created quickly by moving the highlight to cell references.

> **note**
>
> The Autosum button has the Greek letter *sigma*, Σ, on it.

❖ THE AUTOSUM COMMAND

Spreadsheet users frequently need to sum long columns or rows of numbers. Works has a button on the toolbar, the Autosum button, that makes summing a simple operation.

To sum a column or row of numbers:

❖ Place the highlight at the bottom of a column or at the right of a row of filled cells.

❖ Click the **Autosum** button on the toolbar. Works scans the spreadsheet to determine the most logical column or row of numbers to sum and highlights the selected range. If you prefer a range other than the one Works selects, you may alter it by editing the range in the formula bar.

- Press **Enter**. The sum of the range will appear in the cell.

The sum of a range is indicated by a special formula called a function formula. Function formulas will be discussed in detail later in the next lesson.

## Exercise 10-3

In this exercise, you will perform the Autosum operation. *Deli* should be on your screen.

**Suppose the manager of the sandwich shop would like to determine the total ounces of meat and cheese sold during the month.**

1. Highlight **D10**.
2. Calculate the total ounces of meat and cheese sold this month by using **Autosum** to sum the range D4:D9. Cell D10 should display 8777.5.
3. Save the spreadsheet and leave it open for the next exercise.

### ❖ FORMULA HELPERS

The Formulas command and the manual calculation option can help you use formulas in the spreadsheet.

The Formulas command will replace the values shown on the screen with the formulas that created them. To view all the formulas in the spreadsheet simultaneously:

- Choose **Formulas** from the **View** menu.

When the Formulas command is selected, a cell that does not contain a formula will display the contents of the cell. A check mark will appear by the Formulas command in the View menu when the command is turned on. To display values determined by the formulas again, choose the Formulas command once more.

The manual calculation option will prevent spreadsheet formulas from calculating until you press the F9 key or choose Recalculate Now from the Tools menu. This can be useful when you are working with a large spreadsheet that will take longer than usual to calculate.

To delay calculation:

- Choose **Options** from the **Tools** menu.
- In the Data Entry section of the dialog box, choose the **Use manual calculation** option.
- Click **OK**. No calculation will occur until you press **F9**.

To return to automatic calculation, choose the Options command again and turn the Use manual calculation option off.

> **note**
> When there are values included in the spreadsheet that have not been calculated, the word CALC will appear at the bottom of the screen.

**lesson 10** *Using Formulas* 97

## Exercise 10-4

**In this exercise, you will use the Use manual calculation option in place of the automatic calculation option.** *Deli* **should be on your screen.**

1. Turn on the Formulas option.

2. If necessary, scroll to the right so Column D appears on the screen. Each value in the spreadsheet created by a formula has now been replaced by the formula that created the value.

3. Turn off the Formulas option.

4. Turn on manual calculation.

5. Change the following values in the spreadsheet.
   a. Key **190** in B4.
   b. Key **410** in C5.
   c. Key **96** in B7.

6. Press F9 while watching the screen. Calculations will be made as you press the key.

7. Print the range A1:D10.

8. Save and close the file.

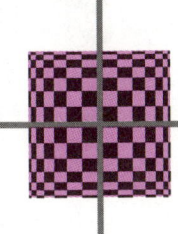

# activities

## ❖ TRUE/FALSE

In the blank space before each sentence, place a **T** if the statement is true and an **F** if it is false.

_____ 1. A formula is an equation that calculates a new value from existing values.

_____ 2. Works recognizes an entry as a formula when the first item in the cell is a cell reference.

_____ 3. An operator is a number or cell reference used in formulas.

_____ 4. In the order of evaluation, multiplication is evaluated before addition.

_____ 5. The Autosum command adds all the numbers on a spreadsheet.

## ❖ COMPLETION

Answer the questions below in the space provided.

1. What is the operation performed by the ^ operator?
   _____

2. In the order of evaluation, what is evaluated first?
   _____
   _____

3. What can you do to avoid keying entire formulas?
   _____
   _____

4. What command displays the formulas in a spreadsheet rather than the result of the equation?
   _____
   _____

5. What option is used to prevent spreadsheet formulas from automatically calculating?
   _____
   _____

**lesson 10** *activities* 99

# review 10-1

## Review Exercise 10-1

Match the letter of the spreadsheet formula to the description of the spreadsheet operation performed by the formula.

**Spreadsheet Operation**

1. Add the values in A3 and A4
2. Subtract the value in A4 from the value in A3
3. Multiply the value in A3 by 27
4. Divide the value in A3 by 27
5. Raise the value in A3 to the 27th power
6. Divide the value in A3 by 27, then add the value in A4
7. Divide the value in A3 by the result of 27 plus the value in A4
8. Multiply the value in A3 by 27, then divide the product by the value in A4
9. Divide 27 by the value in A4, then multiply the result by the value in A3
10. Raise the value in A3 to the 27th power, then divide the result by the value in A4

**Spreadsheet Formula**

a. =A3/(27+A4)
b. =A3^27
c. =A3^27/A4
d. =A3+A4
e. =A3/27
f. =A3/27+A4
g. =(A3*27)/A4
h. =A3-A4
i. =A3*(27/A4)
j. =A3*27

# Review Exercise 10-2

In this exercise, you will create formulas to perform calculations using numbers in the Review Exercise 10-2 spreadsheet.

Open the file *Review Exercise 10-2*. This is a spreadsheet containing several values. Enter formulas in the specified cells that will perform the requested operations. After you enter the formula, write the resulting value in the space provided. When you have completed the exercise, save the spreadsheet as *Formulas*, print the spreadsheet, and close the file.

| Resulting Value |     | Cell | Operation |
| --- | --- | --- | --- |
| _____ | 1. | C3 | Add the values in A3 and B3 |
| _____ | 2. | C4 | Subtract the value in B4 from the value in A4 |
| _____ | 3. | C5 | Multiply the value in A5 by the value in B5 |
| _____ | 4. | C6 | Divide the value in A6 by the value in B6 |
| _____ | 5. | B7 | Sum the values in the range B3:B6 |
| _____ | 6. | D3 | Add the values in A3 and A4, then multiply the sum by 3 |
| _____ | 7. | D4 | Add the values in A3 and A4, then multiply the sum by B3 |
| _____ | 8. | D5 | Raise the value in A5 to the 3rd power |
| _____ | 9. | D6 | Subtract the value in B6 from the value in A6, then divide by 2 |
| _____ | 10. | D7 | Divide the value in A6 by 2, then subtract the value in B6 |

# Review Exercise 10-3

In this exercise, you will create formulas to perform calculations using numbers in the Review Exercise 10-3 spreadsheet.

Your organization, the Entrepreneurs Club, has decided to have a holiday sale in which bags of oranges and grapefruit and tins of fruitcakes and hard candy will be sold at a profit. You have been asked to create a spreadsheet that will calculate the bills of individuals purchasing from your organization. You will be required to charge a sales tax of 4% on each sale. The file *Review Exercise 10-3* is a spreadsheet lacking the formulas required to calculate the bills. Complete the spreadsheet following these steps:

1. Open the file *Review Exercise 10-3*.
2. Enter formulas in D7, D8, D9, and D10 to calculate the cost of each food item when quantities are entered in Column C.

3. Enter a formula in D11 summing the totals in D7:D10.

4. Enter a formula in D12 to calculate a sales tax equal to 4% of the subtotal in D11.

5. Enter a formula in D13 to add the subtotal and sales tax.

6. Turn on manual calculation.

7. Format D7:D13 for currency with two decimals.

8. Save the file as *Entrepreneurs Club*. The saved data apply to all customers. The spreadsheet is now ready to accept data unique to the individual customer.

9. Suppose a customer purchases three bags of oranges, four bags of grapefruit, two fruitcakes, and one tin of hard candy. Enter the quantities in Column C and press **F9** to calculate.

10. Manually check the calculations made by the formulas to make sure you have entered the formulas correctly. If any of the formulas are incorrect, edit them and recalculate the spreadsheet.

11. When you are confident the spreadsheet is calculating as you intended, print the customer's bill.

12. Save and close the file.

# lesson 11

# Cell References and Function Formulas

## ❖ OBJECTIVES

Upon completion of this lesson, you will be able to:

1. Use relative, absolute, and mixed cell references.
2. Use function formulas.

**Estimated Time:** 1/2 hour

## ❖ CELL REFERENCES

Three types of cell references are used to create formulas: relative, absolute, and mixed. A *relative cell reference* adjusts to its new location when copied or moved. For example, in Figure 11–1, if the formula *=B2+A3* is copied or moved from B3 to C4, the formula will be changed to *=C3+B4*. In other words, this particular formula is instructing Works to add the cell directly above to the cell directly to the right. When the formula is copied or moved, the cell references change, but the instructions remain the same.

**Figure 11–1**
Relative cell references change when the formula is copied to another cell.

*Absolute cell references* contain row numbers and column letters preceded by a dollar sign ($). They do not adjust to the new cell location when copied or moved. For example, in Figure 11–2, if the formula *=$A$8+$B$7* is copied from B8 to C9, the formula will remain the same in the new location.

lesson 11  *Cell References and Function Formulas*  103

**Figure 11–2**
Absolute cell references do not change when the formula is copied to another cell.

| | A | B | C |
|---|---|---|---|
| 6 | | | |
| 7 | | 6.25 | |
| 8 | 7.35 | =$A$8+$B$7 | 1.85 |
| 9 | | 1.62 | =$A$8+$B$7 |
| 10 | | | |
| 11 | | | |

Cell references containing both relative and absolute references are called *mixed cell references*. When formulas with mixed cell references are copied or moved, the row or column references preceded by a dollar sign will not change; the row or column references not preceded by a dollar sign will adjust relative to the cell to which they are moved. For example, in Figure 11–3, when the formula *=B$12+$A13* is copied from B13 to C14, the formula changes to *=C$12+$A14*.

**Figure 11–3**
Relative and absolute references can be combined in the same formula.

| | A | B | C |
|---|---|---|---|
| 11 | | | |
| 12 | | 6.26 | |
| 13 | 3.86 | =B$12+$A13 | 9.33 |
| 14 | 6.92 | | =C$12+$A14 |
| 15 | | | |
| 16 | | | |

The use of relative and absolute cell references is important only when you are copying and moving data in a spreadsheet. If you want a moved or copied cell formula to use values in a specific part of the spreadsheet, you should use absolute cell references. If you want a moved or copied cell formula to use values that correspond to the new location of the data, you should use relative cell references.

## Exercise 11-1

In this exercise, you will enter formulas with relative and absolute cell references into a spreadsheet.

1. Open *Exercise 11–1*.
2. Replace the contents of cell A1 with your own name.

3. Place the highlight in D3. All cell references in the formula =(A3+B3)*20 (shown in the formula bar) are relative because neither the row nor the columns are preceded by a dollar sign.

4. Copy the formula in D3 to D4. The value in D4 should be 15440, and the formula in the formula bar should be =(A4+B4)*20. Because the cell references are relative, the row references in the operands were changed, down one row, to reflect change in the location of the formula.

5. Enter **=$A$3*($B$3-200)** in D5. The value in D5 should be 5499. The formula in the formula bar contains absolute cell references shown by the dollar signs that precede row and column references.

6. Copy the formula in D5 to D6. The value in D6 should be 5499, the same as in D5. Because the formula in D5 contains absolute cell references, the formula appearing in the formula bar should also be exactly the same as the formula for D5.

7. Print the range A1:E6.

8. Show formulas and print the range C3:E6. Display values again.

9. Save the spreadsheet as *Absolute* and close the file.

## ❖ FUNCTION FORMULAS

Function formulas are special formulas that perform complex calculations in specialized areas, such as mathematics, statistics, logic, trigonometry, accounting, and finance. Function formulas are also used to convert spreadsheet values to dates and times. There are 57 function formulas in Works. In this section, you will learn some of the more frequently used function formulas.

### PARTS OF FUNCTION FORMULAS

A function formula contains three components: an equals sign, a function name, and an argument.

- The *equals sign* tells Works a formula will be entered into the cell.

- The *function name* identifies the operation to be performed. A function name is usually two to seven characters.

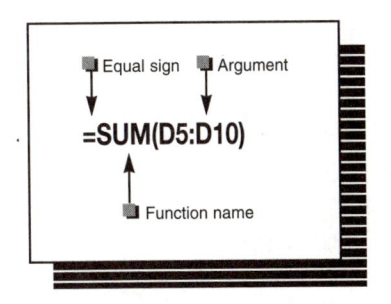

- The *argument* is a value, cell reference, range, or text that acts as an operand in a function formula. The argument is enclosed in parentheses after the function name. If a function formula contains more than one argument, the arguments are separated by commas. The range of cells that make up the argument is separated by a colon.

In the last lesson, you created a function formula, =SUM(D4:D9), using the Autosum command. In Cell D10, the Autosum command inserted an equals sign followed by the word SUM. The word SUM is the function name that identifies the operation. The argument is designated within parentheses; it is the range of cells to be summed.

## MATHEMATICAL AND TRIGONOMETRIC FUNCTIONS

Mathematical functions manipulate quantitative data in the spreadsheet. Three mathematical functions are described in Table 11–1. Notice that two arguments are required to perform the rounding operation.

| Function | Operation |
| --- | --- |
| ABS(x) | Returns the positive value of x. |
| SQRT(x) | Returns the square root of the value, x, identified in the argument. For example, =SQRT(C4) will display the square root of the value in C4. |
| ROUND(x,Places) | Displays the rounded value of x to the number of decimal places designated by the second argument. |

Table 11–1

## Exercise 11-2

**In this exercise, you will perform mathematical functions.**

1. Open the file *Exercise 11–2*.
2. In B9, calculate the square root of the value in B8 using the SQRT function.
3. In B10, round the square root calculated in B9 to the hundredths place using the ROUND function.
4. Save the spreadsheet as *Function* and compare your results to the screen shown in Figure 11–4.
5. Leave the file open for the next exercise.

Figure 11–4 Mathematical functions perform calculations such as determining square roots and rounding.

|    | A | B |
| --- | --- | --- |
| 1 | FUNCTION FORMULA WORKSHEET | |
| 2 | | |
| 3 | Mathematical Functions | |
| 4 | | 121 |
| 5 | | 684 |
| 6 | | 722 |
| 7 | | 394 |
| 8 | | 545 |
| 9 | The square root of B8 is | 23.345235 |
| 10 | B9 rounded to 2 decimal places is | 23.35 |
| 11 | | |

B10 =ROUND(B9,2)

## STATISTICAL FUNCTIONS

Statistical functions are used to describe large quantities of data. The SUM function that you have already seen is a statistical function. Table 11–2 shows some of the statistical functions available in Works.

| Function | Operation |
| --- | --- |
| AVG(Range) | Displays the average of the range identified in the argument. |
| COUNT(Range) | Displays the number of filled cells in the range identified in the argument. |
| MAX(Range) | Displays the largest number contained in the range identified in the argument. |
| MIN(Range) | Displays the smallest number contained in the range identified in the argument. |
| STD(Range) | Displays the standard deviation of the values contained in the range of the argument. |
| VAR(Range) | Displays the variance for the values contained in the range of the argument. |

> **note**
> All the statistical functions contain a range for the argument. The range is the body of numbers the statistics will describe.

Table 11–2

## Exercise 11-3

In this exercise, you will perform statistical functions. *Function* should be on your screen.

1. In the range B14:B20, enter statistical function formulas to satisfy the statements in column A. Compare your results to the screen shown in Figure 11–5.
2. Save the file and leave it on the screen for the next exercise.

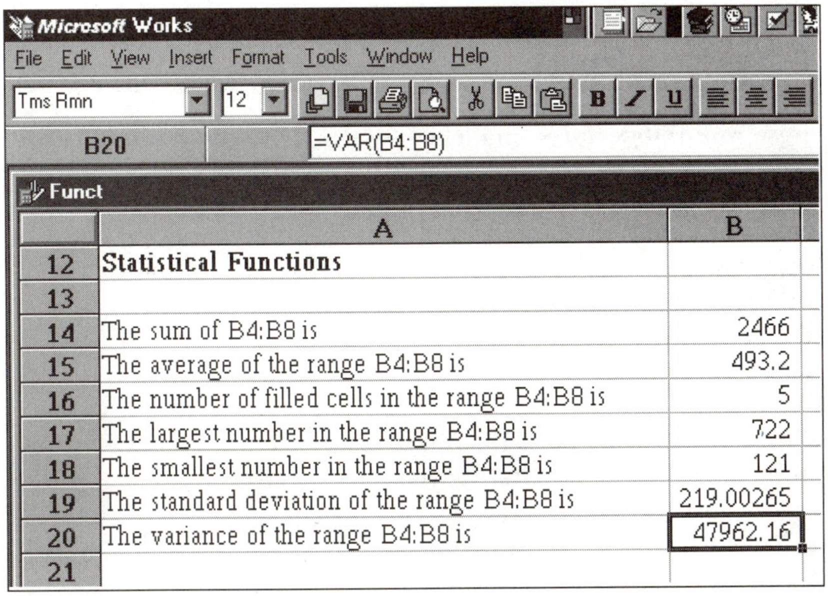

| | A | B |
| --- | --- | --- |
| 12 | Statistical Functions | |
| 13 | | |
| 14 | The sum of B4:B8 is | 2466 |
| 15 | The average of the range B4:B8 is | 493.2 |
| 16 | The number of filled cells in the range B4:B8 is | 5 |
| 17 | The largest number in the range B4:B8 is | 722 |
| 18 | The smallest number in the range B4:B8 is | 121 |
| 19 | The standard deviation of the range B4:B8 is | 219.00265 |
| 20 | The variance of the range B4:B8 is | 47962.16 |
| 21 | | |

B20 = =VAR(B4:B8)

Figure 11–5
Statistical functions are used to describe large quantities of data.

**lesson 11** *Cell References and Function Formulas* 107

### FINANCIAL FUNCTIONS

Financial functions are used to analyze loans and investments. The primary financial functions are future value, present value, and payment, which are described in Table 11–3.

| Function | Operation |
| --- | --- |
| FV(Payment, Rate, Term) | Displays the future value of a series of equal payments (first argument), at a fixed rate (second argument), over a specified period of time (third argument). For example, =FV(100,0.08,5) will determine the value of five $100 payments at the end of five years if you can earn a rate of 8%. |
| PV(Payment, Rate, Term) | Displays the present value of a series of equal payments (first argument), at a fixed rate (second argument), over a specified period of time (third argument). For example, =PV(500,0.1,5) will display current value of five payments of $500 at a 10% rate. |
| PMT(Principal, Rate, Term) | Displays the payment per period needed to repay a loan (first argument), at a specified interest (second argument), for a specified period of time (third argument). For example, =PMT(10000, 0.01, 36) will display the monthly payment needed to repay a $10,000 loan at a 12% annual rate (0.01 times 12 months), for three years (36 months divided by 12*). |

*Rate and term functions should be compatible. In other words, if payments are monthly rather than annual, the annual rate should be divided by 12 to determine the monthly rate.

Table 11–3

## Exercise 11–4

In this exercise, you will perform financial functions. *Function* should be on your screen.

1. You plan to make six yearly payments of $150 into an account that earns 9.5% annually. Use the FV function to determine the value of the account at the end of six years:
   a. Enter **150** in B25.
   b. Enter **.095** in B26.
   c. Enter **6** in B27.
   d. Enter **=FV(B25,B26,B27)** in B28. The savings account will have grown to the amount shown in B28 after six years.

2. Compare your results to the screen shown in Figure 11–6.

3. You have a choice of receiving $1,200 now or eight annual payments of $210. A typical rate for a savings account in your local bank is 6%. Use the PV function to determine which is the most profitable alternative:
   a. Enter **210** in B30.
   b. Enter **.06** in B31.
   c. Enter **8** in B32.
   d. Enter **=PV(B30,B31,B32)** in B33. The best decision is to take the delayed payments because the present value, $1,304.06, is greater than $1,200.

4. You need to borrow $5,000. Your banker has offered you an annual rate of 12% interest for a five-year loan. Use the PMT function to determine what your monthly payments on the loan would be:
   a. Enter **5000** in B35.
   b. Enter **.01** in B36. [A 1% monthly rate (12% divided by 12 months) is used because the problem requests monthly, rather than annual, payments.]
   c. Enter **60** in B37. [A period of 60 months (5 years times 12 months) is used because the problem requests monthly, rather than annual, payments.]
   d. Enter **=PMT(B35,B36,B37)** in B38. The value $111.22 will be in the cell. You will have to pay a total of $1,673.20 [($111.22 * 60 months) - $5,000 principal] in interest over the life of the loan.

5. Save and close the file.

| | A | B |
|---|---|---|
| 22 | Financial Functions | |
| 23 | | |
| 24 | Scenario 1 | |
| 25 | Payment | $150.00 |
| 26 | Rate | 9.50% |
| 27 | Term | 6 |
| 28 | Future Value | $1,142.83 |
| 29 | Scenario 2 | |

**Figure 11–6**
The Financial functions perform operations such as finding present and future values.

Works has many more function formulas available to help you with number problems. Consult the appendix in the Works User's Guide for a complete list.

lesson 11 Cell References and Function Formulas 109

# activities

❖ TRUE/FALSE

In the blank space before each sentence, place a **T** if the statement is true and an **F** if it is false.

_F_ 1. A cell reference that adjusts to its new location when copied or moved is called an absolute cell reference.

_F_ 2. Relative cell references contain row numbers and column letters preceded by a dollar sign.

_T_ 3. Whether a cell reference is relative or absolute is important only if the cell contents are copied or moved.

_T_ 4. A value, cell reference, range, or text that acts as an operand in a function formula is called an argument.

____ 5. The function formula that displays the sum of a range is the ADD function.

❖ COMPLETION

Answer the questions below in the space provided.

1. What is a mixed cell reference?

2. What does the SQRT function do?

3. Write a function formula to average the values in the range B3:B18.
   =AVG(B3:B18)

4. What category of functions is used to describe large quantities of data?
   Statistical

5. What category of functions is used to analyze loans and investments?
   Financial

# review

## Review Exercise 11-1

Write the appropriate function formula to perform each of the described operations. You may refer to Tables 11–1 through 11–3 to help you prepare the function formulas.

1. Determine the smallest value in A4:A90  
   *=MIN(A4:A90)*
2. Determine the standard deviation of the values in K6:K35  
   *=STD(K6:K35)*
3. Determine the average of the values in B9:B45  
   *=AVG(B9:B45)*
4. Determine the yearly payments on a $5,000 loan at 8% for 10 years  
   *=PMT(5000, .08, 10)*
5. Determine the value of a savings account at the end of 5 years after making $400 yearly payments; the account earns 8%  
   *=FV(400, .08, 5)*
6. Round the value in C3 to the tenths place  
   *=ROUND(C3, 10)*
7. Determine the present value of a pension plan that will pay you 20 yearly payments of $4,000; the current rate of return is 7.5%  
   *=PV(4000, .075, 20)*
8. Determine the square root of 225  
   *=SQRT(225)*
9. Determine the variance of the values in F9:F35  
   *=VAR(F9:F35)*
10. Add all the values in D4:D19  
    *=SUM(D4:D19)*
11. Determine how many cells in H7:H21 are filled with data  
    *=COUNT(H7:H21)*
12. Determine the largest value in E45:E92  
    *=MAX(E45:E92)*

## Review Exercise 11-2

In this exercise, you will calculate statistics on the grades given in Review Exercise 11–2.

The file *Review Exercise 11–2* contains a spreadsheet of student grades for one examination. Calculate statistics on the grades following these steps.

1. Open the file *Review Exercise 11–2*.
2. Enter function formulas in the range B26:B30 to satisfy the statements in Column A.
3. Save the file as *Exam*. Print and close the file.

## Review Exercise 11-3

**In this exercise, you will review financial functions.**

Generic National Bank makes a profit by taking money deposited by customers and lending it to others at a higher rate. In order to encourage depositing and borrowing activity, you have helped them develop a spreadsheet that will inform depositors about the future value of their investment. Another portion of the spreadsheet informs borrowers of the yearly payments they must make on their loans. The incomplete spreadsheet is in file *Review Exercise 11–3*. Complete the spreadsheet following these steps. Refer to Table 11–3.

1. Enter a function formula in B11 that will inform borrowers of the yearly payment. Assume that the loan principal will be entered in B5, the lending rate will be entered in B7, and the term of the loan will be entered in B9. (*Hint:* See the description of the PMT function formula in Table 11–3. ERR, indicating an error, will appear in the cell because no data are in the argument cell references yet.)

2. A potential borrower inquires about the payments on a $5,500 loan for 4 years. The current lending rate is 11%. Determine the yearly payment on the loan.

3. Enter a function formula in B24 informing depositors of the future value of periodic payments. Assume the yearly payments will be entered in B18, the term of the payments will be entered in B20, and the interest rate will be entered in B22. (*Hint:* See the description of the FV function formula in Table 11–3. $0.00 will appear because no data are in the argument cell references yet.)

4. A potential depositor is starting a college fund for her son. She inquires about the value of yearly deposits of $450 at the end of 15 years. The current interest rate is 7.5%. Determine the future value of the deposits.

5. Save the spreadsheet as *Generic,* print it, and close the file.

## Review Exercise 11-4

**In this exercise, you will review statistical functions.**

The file *Review Exercise 11–4* contains a spreadsheet which provides statistics on the ten highest dams in the United States. The dams appear in alphabetical order.

1. Open the file *Review Exercise 11–4*.

2. Use function formulas to place the appropriate values in cells C15, C16, C17, and C18.

3. Save the file as *Dams.* Print and close the file.

# Review Exercise 11-5

In this exercise, you will calculate the hypotenuse of a right triangle using the formula provided.

The file *Review Exercise 11–5* contains an incomplete spreadsheet intended to calculate the hypotenuse of a right triangle. The user of the spreadsheet is to enter the length of the triangle's two legs. You will create a function formula to calculate the hypotenuse based on the formula below.

$$\text{hypotenuse} = \sqrt{a^2 + b^2}$$

1. Open *Review Exercise 11–5*.

2. Enter a function formula in cell C7 to calculate the hypotenuse of a right triangle based on the values provided in cells C4 and C5.

3. Enter **12** as the length of leg A and **16** as the length of leg B. The calculated hypotenuse should have a length of 20.

4. Save the file as *Hypotenuse*. Print and close the file.

# lesson 12

# Charts

## ❖ OBJECTIVES

Upon completing this lesson, you will be able to:

1. Create and save a chart.
2. Print a chart.

**Estimated Time:** 1/2 hour

## ❖ TYPES OF SPREADSHEET CHARTS

There are several types of spreadsheet charts available in Works. The four most commonly used charts are bar charts, line charts, pie charts, and scatter charts. Among these types are many variations, including three-dimensional charts.

Figure 12–1 shows four simple examples of spreadsheet charts. A bar chart uses rectangles of varying heights to illustrate values in a spreadsheet. A bar chart is well suited for showing relationships among categories of data. A line chart is similar to a bar chart, except bars are replaced by points connected by a line. A line chart is ideal for illustrating trends of data over time. Pie charts show the relationship of a part to a whole. Scatter charts show the relationship between two categories of data.

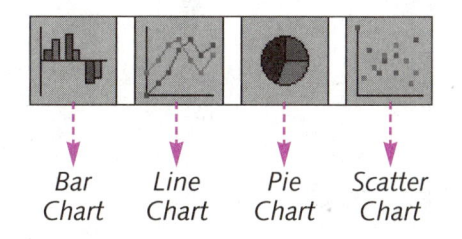

Bar Chart   Line Chart   Pie Chart   Scatter Chart

**Figure 12–1**
Several types of charts are available in Works.

## ❖ CREATING A CHART FROM A SPREADSHEET

To create a chart:

- Open or create a spreadsheet containing data you want to display in a chart.
- Highlight the data you want to include in the chart.
- Choose **Create New Chart** from the **Tools** menu. A dialog box appears allowing you to choose what type of chart you want. You can alter the chart to fit your specific requirements.

    -or-

    Click the **New Chart** button on the toolbar. A dialog box appears allowing you to choose what type of chart you want. You can alter the chart to fit your specific requirements.

- Click **OK**.

**note**

The New Chart button has a bar chart as an icon.

**lesson 12** *Charts* 115

# Exercise 12-1

In this exercise, you will create a three-dimensional bar chart illustrating the contents of a spreadsheet.

The file *Exercise 12–1* is a spreadsheet containing the median income of heads of households according to the educational level they have achieved. The words *High School* have been abbreviated as *HS* and *College* as *C*.

1. Open *Exercise 12–1*. Column A contains educational levels and Column B contains median incomes of those with the level of education.

2. Highlight the range **A5:B10**.

3. Choose **Create New Chart** from the Tools menu.

4. Choose the three-dimensional bar chart type, as shown in Figure 12–2.

5. Click **OK.** The bar chart appears, as shown in Figure 12–3. Leave the chart on the screen for the next exercise.

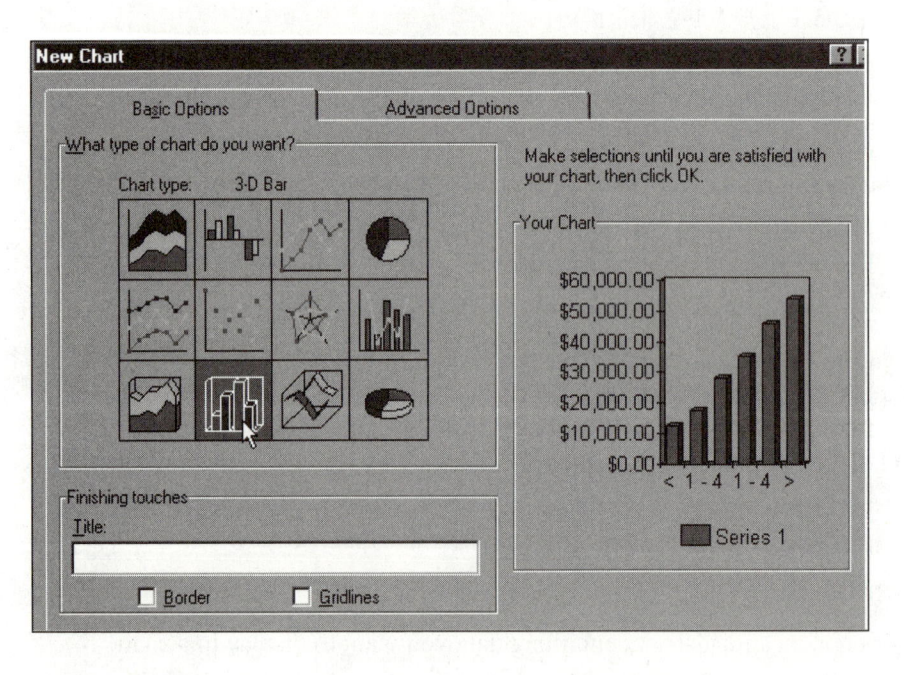

Figure 12–2
A sample of the highlighted chart type is shown in the dialog box.

### EDITING A CHART

A chart is closely related to the spreadsheet from which it was created. For example, if you change the data in a spreadsheet, these changes will be made automatically in the chart from the spreadsheet.

To edit a chart:

- Choose the spreadsheet name from the **Window** menu.
- Edit the spreadsheet.
- Choose the chart name from the **Window** menu.

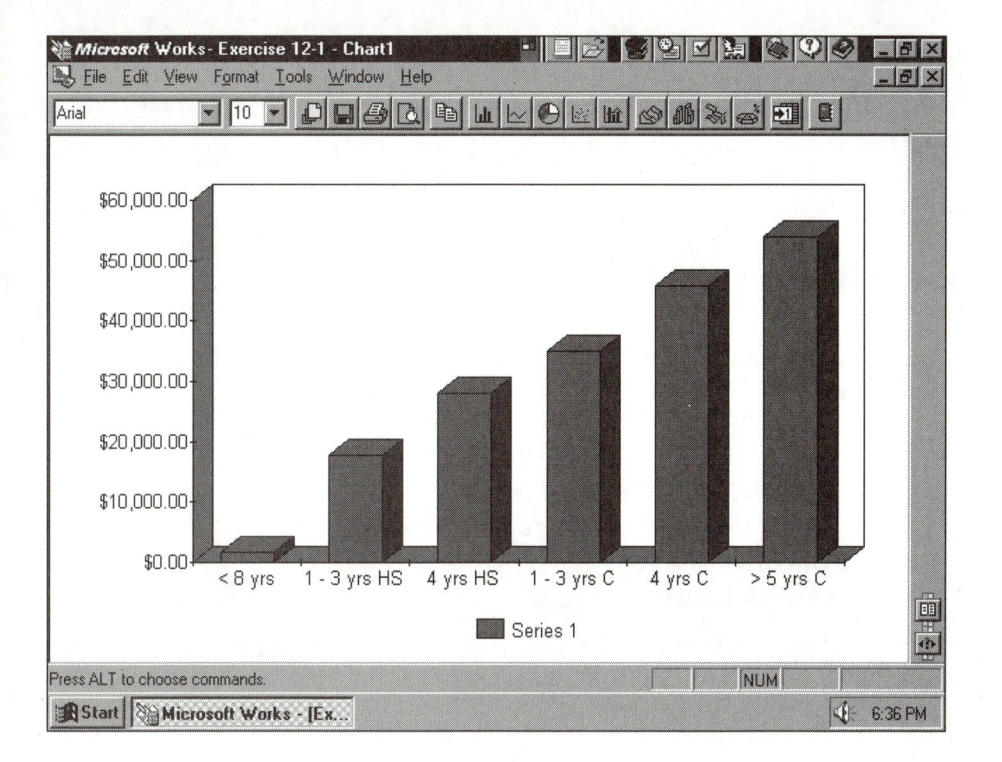

**Figure 12–3**
This chart illustrates the value of education in attaining higher income.

# Exercise 12-2

**In this exercise, you will edit a chart.** *Exercise 12–1* **should be on your screen.**

1. Notice the small bar showing income for less than eight years of education.

2. Change the contents of B5 from *$1,696.00* to the correct median income of *$12,696.00*.

3. Access the chart *Exercise 12–1 - Chart 1* again. The bar showing income for less than eight years of education should have increased in size.

4. Leave the chart on the screen for the next exercise.

## INSERTING CHART TITLES

Chart titles and headings make the chart easier to understand by describing the chart and the data.

To add titles:

- Choose **Titles** from the **Edit** menu. The Edit Titles dialog box will appear.

- Key the title in the Chart title box.

- If you want a subtitle to help clarify the title or give additional information, key the subtitle in the Subtitle box.

- In the Horizontal (X) Axis box, key the description of the axis that runs horizontally along the bottom of the chart.

**lesson 12** *Charts* 117

- In the Vertical (Y) Axis box, key the description of the axis that runs vertically along the left side of the chart.

- Click **OK**.

## Exercise 12-3

In this exercise, you will insert titles into a chart. *Exercise 12–1* should be on your screen.

1. Add the following titles to the chart:
   Chart title: **YOUR EDUCATION PAYS**
   Subtitle: **Incomes for Six Education Levels**
   X-axis: **Education Level**
   Y-axis: **Median Income**

2. The title will appear in the chart. Compare your screen to the one shown in Figure 12–4.

3. Leave the chart on the screen for the next exercise.

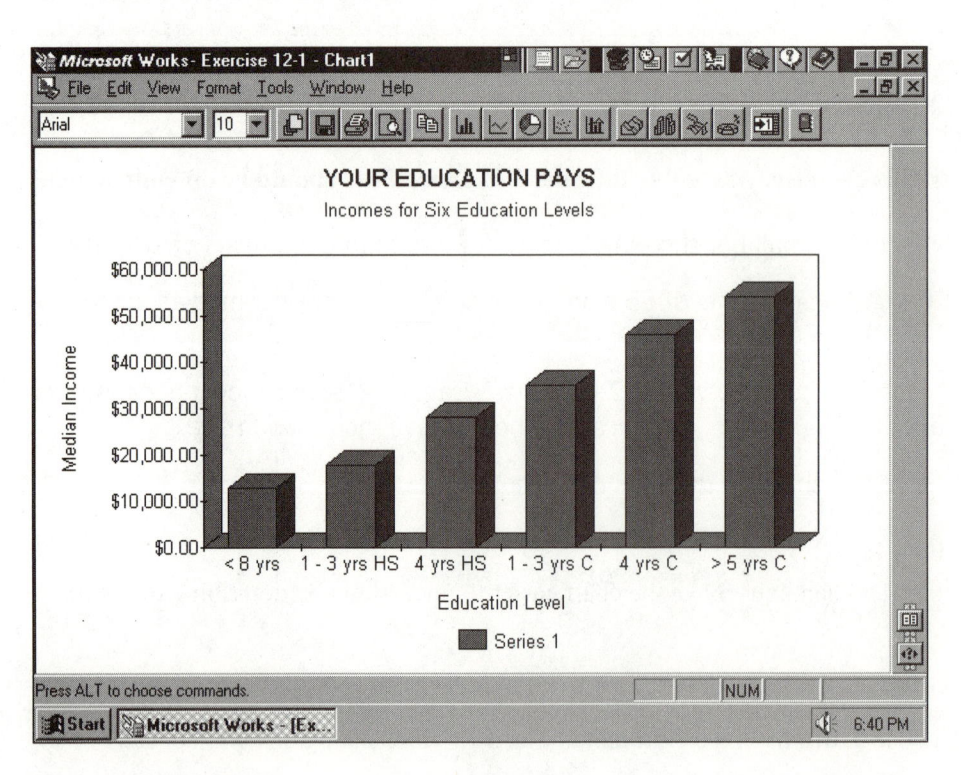

Figure 12–4
Chart titles make the chart easier to understand.

### RENAMING A CHART

Works will automatically name a chart the same name as the spreadsheet, followed by *Chart1*. If additional charts are created from the spreadsheet, they will become *Chart2*, *Chart3*, and so on.

Renaming a chart is particularly useful after you have prepared several charts from one spreadsheet. These charts may become difficult to distinguish by their chart numbers and would be easier to recognize with more descriptive names.

To name a chart:

- Choose **Rename Chart** from the **Tools** menu. The Rename Chart dialog box will appear, as shown in Figure 12–5.
- Highlight the chart in the Charts box that you want to rename.
- Key the chart name in the Type a name below box.
- Click **Rename.**
- Click **OK** to exit the dialog box. The new name(s) will appear in the Window menu.

**note**

A maximum of eight charts may be created from one spreadsheet.

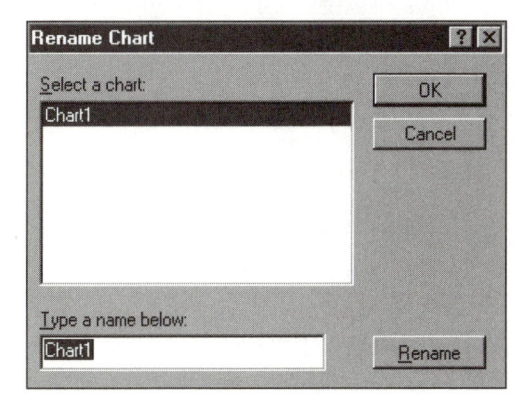

**Figure 12–5**
The Rename Chart dialog box allows you to rename he charts you have created.

## Exercise 12-4

In this exercise, you will rename a chart. *Exercise 12–1* should be on your screen. Rename *Chart1*, currently on your screen, to *Education Pays*. Confirm the name change by looking at the Window menu, and leave the chart on the screen for the next exercise.

❖ SAVING A CHART

A spreadsheet chart is considered part of a spreadsheet. When you save the spreadsheet, you will also save all the charts you have created from the spreadsheet. Save the spreadsheet and its associated charts by choosing Save from the File menu. The File menu may be accessed when viewing either the spreadsheet or a chart.

## Exercise 12-5

In this exercise, you will save a spreadsheet and chart. *Exercise 12–1* should be on your screen.

1. Save the spreadsheet and the chart.

lesson 12 *Charts* 119

2. Choose **Save** from the **File** menu.
3. Save as *Educate*.

### ❖ CHANGING THE TYPE OF CHART

To change the type of chart:

- Choose **Chart Type** from the **Format** menu. The Chart Type dialog box will appear.
  -or-
  Click the desired chart type in the toolbar. The Chart Type dialog box will appear.

- Click the desired type of chart.

- Click the **Variations** tab of the Chart Type dialog box to see the variations of the chart type that are available.

- Click the desired variation of the chart type.

- Click **OK**.

## Exercise 12-6

**In this exercise, you will change the bar chart in the spreadsheet to a line chart.** *Educate* **should be on your screen.**

1. Change the bar chart in the spreadsheet on your screen to a line chart. Choose the variation with horizontal gridlines.

### ❖ PRINTING CHARTS

Charts are printed in the same way word processing documents and spreadsheets are printed. The toolbar of the chart window has Print and Print Preview buttons that will print or preview the chart.

## Exercise 12-7

**In this exercise, you will print a line chart.** *Educate* **should be on your screen.**

1. Print the line chart.
2. After printing is complete, save and close the chart and spreadsheet files.

# activities

## ❖ TRUE/FALSE

In the blank space before each sentence, place a **T** if the statement is true and an **F** if it is false.

____ 1. There are several types of spreadsheet charts available in Works.

____ 2. A maximum of four charts may be created from one spreadsheet.

____ 3. If data in a spreadsheet change, you must recreate the chart to update them.

____ 4. Works automatically names a chart the same name as the spreadsheet, followed by *Chart 1*.

____ 5. All of a spreadsheet's charts are saved when the spreadsheet is saved.

## ❖ COMPLETION

Answer the questions below in the space provided.

1. Name four commonly used types of charts.
   _____
   _____

2. What command is chosen from the Edit menu to add labels to the X and Y axes?
   _____
   _____

3. How do you access a chart from a spreadsheet window?
   _____
   _____

4. When might you want to change the default name of a chart?
   _____
   _____

5. Describe the process used to change the type of chart to a line chart.
   _____
   _____
   _____

lesson 12 *activities* 121

# review

## Review Exercise 12–1

In this exercise, you will create a bar chart.

The file *Review Exercise 12–1* contains the populations of the world's largest cities. Create a bar chart indicating larger populations with a higher bar.

1. Open *Review Exercise 12–1*.
2. Create a bar chart from the data in A5:B11.
3. Title the bar chart **THE WORLD'S LARGEST CITIES**.
4. Subtitle the chart **Population in Millions**.
5. Title the vertical (Y) axis **Population**.
6. Rename the chart *Population*.
7. Save the spreadsheet and chart as *Cities 2*. Print the chart and close the file.

## Review Exercise 12–2

In this exercise, you will create a line chart.

You have been running each morning to stay in shape. Over the past ten weeks you have recorded running times along a specific route and entered times in the file *Review Exercise 12–2*. Create a line chart indicating the trend in running times over the ten-week period.

1. Open *Review Exercise 12–2*.
2. Create a bar chart for the data contained in A4:B12.
3. Change the chart from a bar chart to a line chart with gridlines.
4. Title the line chart **TEN-WEEK WORKOUT PROGRAM**.
5. Title the vertical axis **Time in Minutes**.
6. Rename the chart *Times*.
7. Save the spreadsheet and chart as *Workout*. Print the chart and close the file.

## Review Exercise 12-3

In this exercise, you will create a pie chart.

The file *Review Exercise 12–3* contains the number of McDonald's hamburger restaurants in different regions of the world. Create a pie chart in which each slice represents a region in Column A of the spreadsheet.

1. Open *Review Exercise 12–3*.
2. Create a pie chart with text labels for the data in A4:B8.
3. Title the pie chart **McDONALD'S RESTAURANTS**.
4. Subtitle the chart **Worldwide Locations**.
5. Rename the chart *Locations*.
6. Save the spreadsheet and chart as *McDonalds*. Print the chart and close the file.

## Review Exercise 12-4

In this exercise, you will edit a chart.

The file *Review Exercise 12–4* contains the populations of eight U.S. cities. You will chart the change in population of the first two cities: Atlanta and Boston.

1. Open *Review Exercise 12–4*.
2. Create a bar chart using data in the range A3:D5.
3. Title the chart **POPULATION CHANGE** and subtitle it **Atlanta and Boston**.
4. Title the horizontal axis **Year** and the vertical axis **Population in thousands**.
5. Rename the chart *Atlanta/Boston*.
6. Save the spreadsheet and chart as *Atlanta and Boston*.
7. Print the chart and close the file.

# lesson 13

# Databases: Opening a Database and Switching Views

❖ OBJECTIVES

Upon completion of this lesson, you will be able to:

1. Define a database.
2. Identify the parts of a database.
3. Switch between List and Form views.
4. Move the highlight in the database.

**Estimated Time:** 1/2 hour

❖ WHAT IS A DATABASE?

A *database* is an automated electronic filing system that stores and retrieves information. A database is similar to a filing cabinet that contains folders of information. Compared to a traditional paper filing system, however, a database can store, retrieve, and manipulate records quickly.

Like a spreadsheet, a database has columns and rows and a formula bar where information is entered. But databases and spreadsheets differ in the way they are used. A spreadsheet is used primarily for analysis of numerical data. By contrast, a database is used primarily to store and retrieve records. Databases are typically larger than spreadsheets because they are used for long-term storage of data. A database that keeps track of a club's membership, for example, expands as the names and addresses of new members are added. In a spreadsheet, you usually alter the existing information rather than add more data.

Database files are opened in the same way that word processor documents and spreadsheet files are opened.

# Exercise 13-1

**In this exercise, you will open a database.**

1. Open *Exercise 13–1*.

2. Your screen should appear similar to Figure 13–1.

3. Leave the database on your screen for the next exercise.

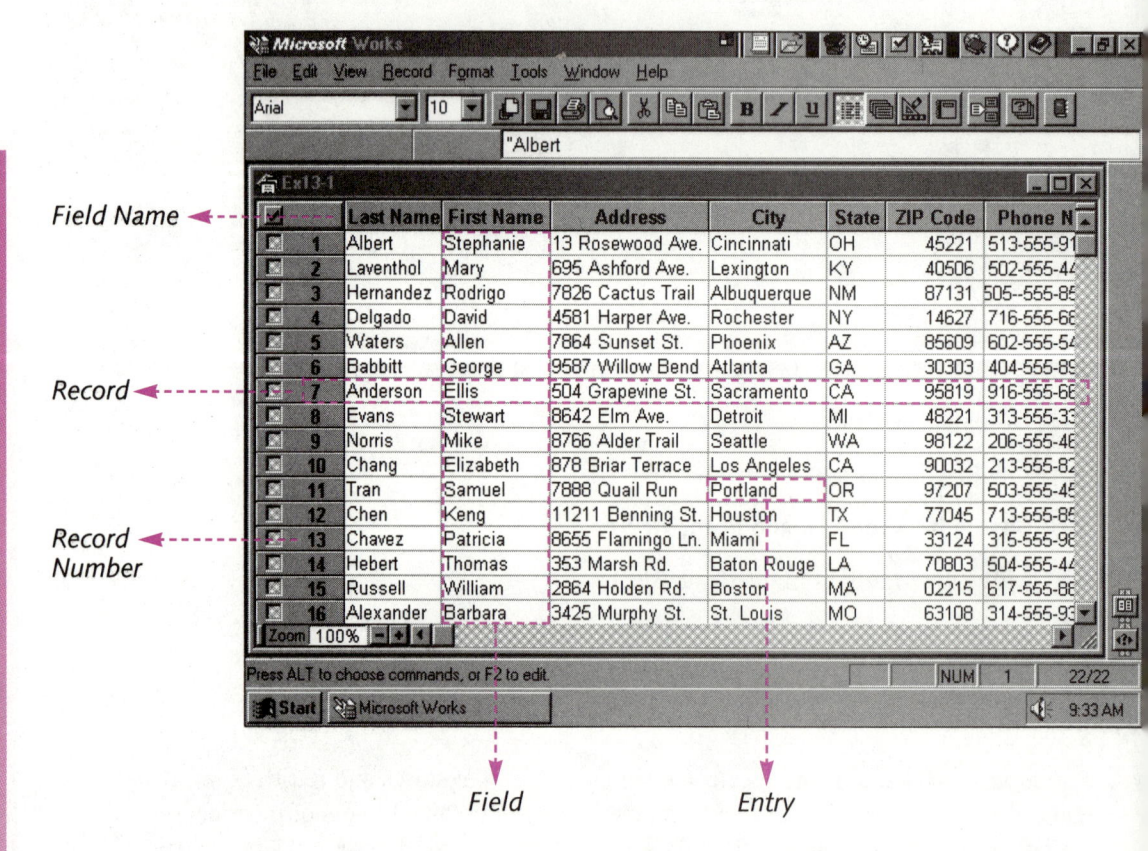

*Figure 13–1*
*The primary parts of the database are the entry, record, and field.*

**note**

A Works database can have up to 256 fields and 32,000 records.

## ❖ PARTS OF A DATABASE

In the database on your screen, the data is arranged so that each kind of information is grouped together. For example, all the last names are in one column and all the first names are in another. These categories of information are called *fields*. This database has seven fields of common information: last name, first name, address, city, state, ZIP code and phone number. The *field name* at the top of the column helps you to remember what kind of information will be stored in the column.

Each piece of information entered into a field is called an *entry*. In the database shown in Figure 13–1, for example, each name in the Last Name field is an entry.

One complete set of field entries is called a *record*. Each record has a *record number* displayed on the left side of the screen. In the database on your screen, Record 1 consists of the name, address, city, state, ZIP code, and phone number for Stephanie Albert.

126 *Microsoft Works 4.0 for Windows 95: QuickTorial*™

## ❖ VIEWING A DATABASE

As you become more familiar with databases, you will realize that they can become very large—too large for you to view all the records at once. Fortunately, Works allows several options for displaying the data you need on the screen.

### LIST AND FORM VIEW

A database may be displayed on the screen in List view or Form view. The database now on your screen is in *List view*, which is similar in appearance to the spreadsheet. List view is most appropriate when you want to display several records at once. *Form view*, on the other hand, displays one record at a time. It is most appropriate for entering or editing a specific record. Form view is shown in Figure 13–2.

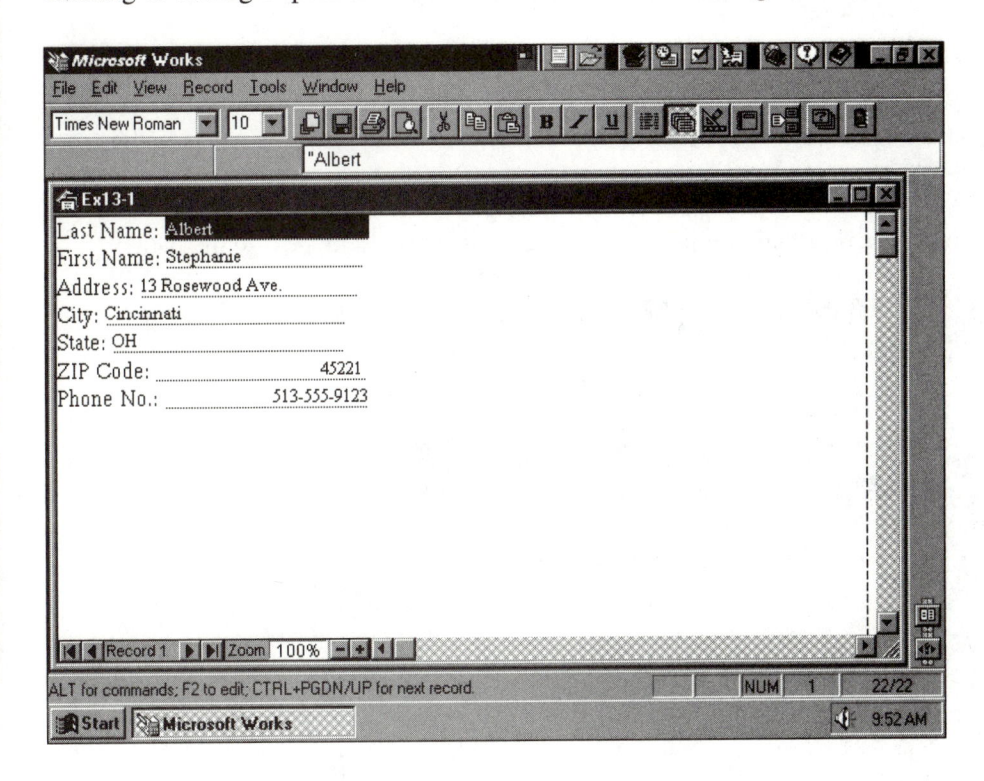

**Figure 13–2**
A database may be displayed in Form view.

To switch between List and Form views:

- Choose the **Form** or **List** command from the **View** menu.

    -or-

    Press **F9** to switch to **Form** view and **Shift** + **F9** to switch to **List** view.

    -or-

    Click the **List view** or **Form view** button on the toolbar, as shown in Figure 13–3.

*List View Button*

*Form View Button*

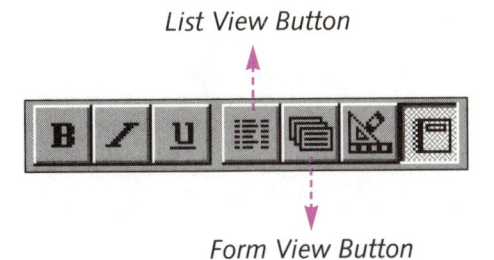

**Figure 13–3**
The List view and Form view buttons on the toolbar can be used to switch between views.

**lesson 13** *Databases: Opening a Database and Switching Views* 127

## Exercise 13-2

In this exercise, you will switch between List view and Form view. *Exercise 13-1* should be on your screen.

1. Practice switching between List view and Form view. Use the View menu, `F9`, and `Shift` + `F9`.

2. Practice switching views using the toolbar.

3. Leave the database on your screen in List view for the next exercise.

### SPLITTING THE DATABASE WINDOW

If a database is very large, you may want to view different parts of the database on the screen at the same time by splitting the database window. By creating panes in the window, you may view as many as four parts of the database at once. For example, the database in Figure 13-4 has been split into four panes. The split screen shows the City field, which was originally to the right side of the Address field, next to the names.

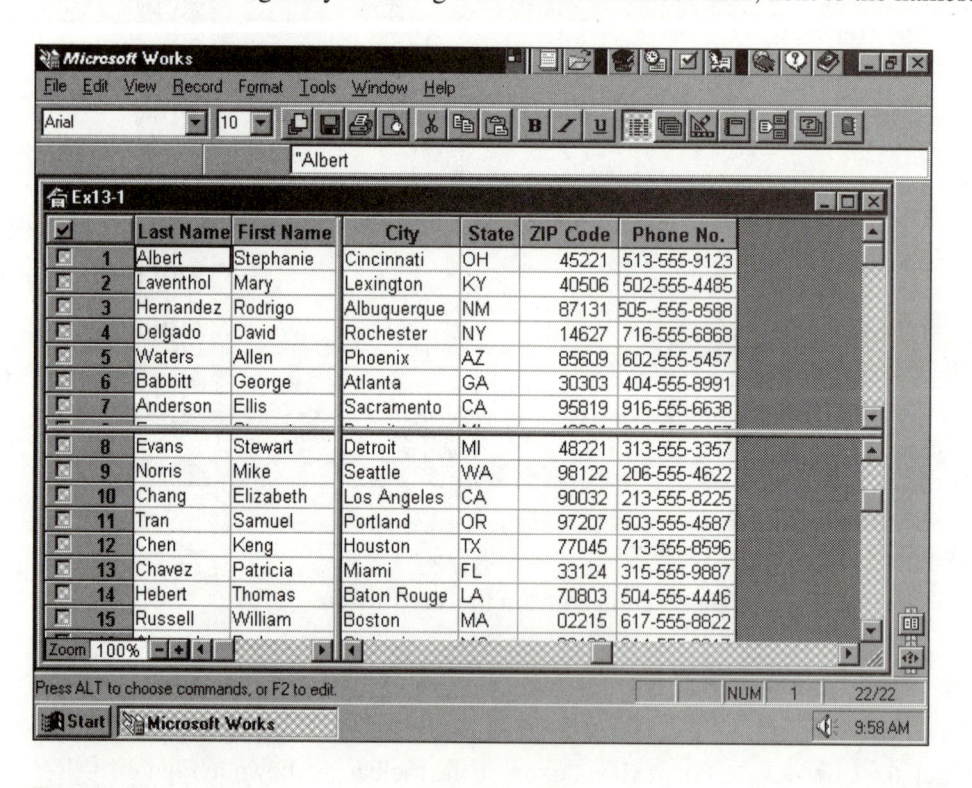

**Figure 13-4**
Splitting the database window enables you to view different parts of a database at the same time.

To split the screen:

- While the database is in List view, double-click the horizontal split box in the upper right corner of the document window, as shown in Figure 13-5.

- Double-click the vertical split box in the lower left corner of the window, as shown in Figure 13-5.

- Click and drag the split bars to the desired locations.

- Release the mouse button to complete the split.

128  *Microsoft Works 4.0 for Windows 95: QuickTorial*™

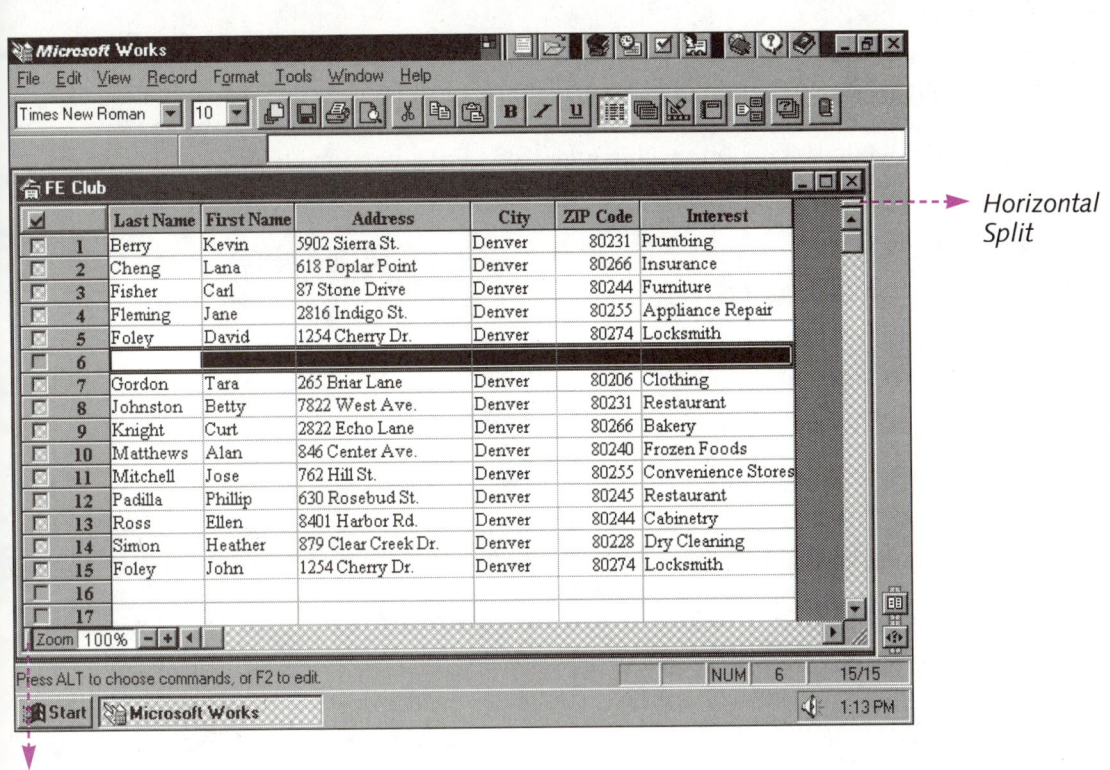

Figure 13-5
The horizontal and vertical split boxes enable you to split a database window.

*Horizontal Split* (label pointing to screen)

*Vertical Split* (label pointing to screen)

After you have split a database window, the F6 key will move your cursor from one pane to the next, or you can click the mouse in the pane where you want the cursor.

To return the screen to a single pane:

- Double-click on the split bars.

## Exercise 13-3

In this exercise, you will split a database window and scroll the panes. *Exercise 13–1* should be on your screen.

1. Split the window into four panes and practice moving the cursor from one pane to the next.

2. Practice scrolling the panes individually.

3. Return the screen to a single pane and leave the database on the screen for the next exercise.

### ❖ MOVING THE HIGHLIGHT IN THE DATABASE

In either Form view or List view, you can move the highlight with a mouse by clicking the area to which you want the highlight to move. You can also move the highlight using key commands. Keystroke commands to move the highlight are different in List view and Form view.

lesson 13  *Databases: Opening a Database and Switching Views*  129

### MOVING THE HIGHLIGHT IN FORM VIEW

In Form view, you may scroll only within the form of a single record. You will need to scroll only when the record exceeds the size of the screen. Table 13–1 shows the keystrokes for moving the highlight within a record in Form view and to other records if you prefer not to use the mouse.

| To Move in Form View | Press |
| --- | --- |
| Up one line | ↑ |
| Down one line | ↓ |
| Up one window | Page Up |
| Down one window | Page Down |
| To the next field | Tab |
| To the previous field | Shift + Tab |
| To the first field of the record | Home |
| To the last field of the record | End |
| To the first record | Ctrl + Home |
| To the last record | Ctrl + End |
| To the next record | Ctrl + Page Down |
| To the previous record | Ctrl + Page Up |

Table 13–1

### MOVING THE HIGHLIGHT IN LIST VIEW

Moving the highlight in List view is similar to moving it in a spreadsheet. You may scroll throughout the database using the mouse to drag the scroll bars. Table 13–2 shows how to move the highlight with keystrokes while in List view.

| To Move in List View | Press |
| --- | --- |
| Left one field | ← |
| Right one field | → |
| Up one record | ↑ |
| Down one record | ↓ |
| To the first field of a record | Home |
| To the last field of a record | End |
| To the first record | Ctrl + Home |
| To the last record | Ctrl + End |
| Up one window | Page Up |
| Down one window | Page Down |
| Left one window | Ctrl + Page Up |
| Right one window | Ctrl + Page Down |

Table 13–2

# Exercise 13-4

**In this exercise, you will move the highlight in List and Form views.** *Exercise 13-1* **should be on your screen.**

1. In List view, move the highlight to the first entry in the database.

2. Move to the last record in the database. The highlight will move to the lower right side of the database.

3. Move to the first field of the last record in the database. The highlight should appear in an entry with the name *Mitchell*.

4. Move the highlight up one record. The highlight will appear in an entry containing the name *Garner*.

5. Switch to Form view and move to the first record in the database. Move the highlight to the ZIP code entry containing *45221*.

6. Move to the previous field. The highlight will appear in an entry containing *OH*.

7. Close the database without saving.

# activities

### ❖ TRUE/FALSE

In the blank space before each sentence, place a **T** if the statement is true and an **F** if it is false.

___ 1. A database is an automated electronic filing system.

___ 2. A database has columns and rows.

___ 3. Each piece of information entered into a field is called a record.

___ 4. Form view is best for displaying several records at once.

___ 5. In Form view, the Tab key moves the cursor to the next record.

### ❖ COMPLETION

Answer the questions below in the space provided.

1. What view displays one record at a time?

2. How do you split a database window?

3. By splitting a database window, how many parts of the database may be viewed at once?

4. What key combination moves the highlight to the first record?

5. In List view, what key moves the cursor to the last field of a record?

# review

## Review Exercise 13-1

In the blank space, write the letter of the keystroke that matches the highlight movement in Form view of the database.

**Highlight Movement**

____ 1. Up one line

____ 2. Down one line

____ 3. Up one window

____ 4. Down one window

____ 5. To the next field

____ 6. To the previous field

____ 7. To the first field of the record

____ 8. To the last field of the record

____ 9. First record

____ 10. Last record

____ 11. Next record

____ 12. Previous record

**Keystroke**

a. Shift + Tab
b. ↑
c. Ctrl + End
d. ↓
e. Tab
f. Ctrl + Page Down
g. Page Up
h. Ctrl + Page Up
i. Ctrl + Home
j. End
k. Home
l. Page Down

# Review Exercise 13-2

In the blank space, write the letter of the keystroke that matches the highlight movement in List view of the database.

**Highlight Movement**

____ 1. Left one field

____ 2. Right one field

____ 3. Up one record

____ 4. Down one record

____ 5. To the first field of a record

____ 6. To the last field of a record

____ 7. To the first record

____ 8. To the last record

____ 9. Up one window

____10. Down one window

____11. Left one window

____12. Right one window

a. Ctrl + End
b. Ctrl + Page Down
c. ↓
d. ←
e. End
f. Home
g. Ctrl + Page Up
h. Page Up
i. →
j. Ctrl + Home
k. ↑
l. Page Down

# lesson 14

# Adding and Deleting Records and Printing

## ❖ OBJECTIVES

Upon completion of this lesson, you will be able to:

1. Add and delete records.
2. Save a database.
3. Copy data.
4. Insert records.
5. Cut and paste data.
6. Print a database.

**Estimated Time:** 1/2 hour

## ❖ ADDING AND DELETING RECORDS

Once a database has been created, it is simple to add new records to it or to delete records that you no longer need. New records may be entered in either Form or List view. Because Form view displays one record at a time, single records are usually entered in Form view.

To add a record in Form view, move to the blank record at the end of the database and key data into the record. To add a record in List view, scroll to the bottom of the database and key data in the first blank record below your existing data.

Records that are no longer useful may be deleted from the database.

To delete a record in Form view:

- Display the record to be deleted on the screen.
- Choose **Delete Record** from the **Record** menu.

To delete a record in List view:

- Select the entire record to be deleted.
- Choose **Delete Record** from the **Record** menu.

## Exercise 14–1

**In this exercise, you will add and delete records from a database.**

1. Open *Exercise 14–1*.
2. Switch to Form view.
3. Press **Ctrl** + **End** to move to the last record in the database. The last record will be blank and ready to receive new data. The Last Name field is highlighted.
4. Key **Chester**.
5. Press **Tab**. The highlight will move to the right of the colon beside the First Name field.
6. Key **Tom**.
7. Continue to tab to the remaining fields and enter the following data:

    Address: **3584 Daisy St.**
    City: **Washington**
    State: **DC**
    ZIP Code: **20549**
    Phone No: **202-555-8789**

8. Press **Enter**.
9. Press **Ctrl** + **Home**. The record for Stephanie Albert of Cincinnati will appear.
10. Delete the Stephanie Albert record. The record for Mary Laventhol of Lexington will appear in place of the deleted record.
11. Switch to List view.
12. Select the record for Keng Chen of Houston.
13. Delete the Keng Chen record.
14. Leave the database on your screen for the next exercise.

> **note**
>
> In List view, you can select a record with the mouse by clicking the record number at the left edge of the window.

### ❖ SAVING A DATABASE

You save a database file in the same way you save files in the word processor or the spreadsheet. Because you are currently working on a file that has already been named, you must choose Save As to save it to a new name and location.

## Exercise 14–2

**In this exercise, you will save and close a database.** *Exercise 14–1* should be on your screen.

1. Save the database on your screen as *Address*.
2. Choose **File** and select **Save As**.
3. Close the database.

136  Microsoft Works 4.0 for Windows 95: QuickTorial™

## ❖ COPYING DATA

Repetitive typing is unnecessary if you copy common data from one entry to another. Just as you learned in the spreadsheet chapters, you can copy data using either Copy, Fill Right, or Fill Down.

### THE COPY COMMAND

To copy data from one part of the database to another, click the Copy button on the toolbar (see Figure 14–1). Copying in the database is the same as copying in the word processor or the spreadsheet.

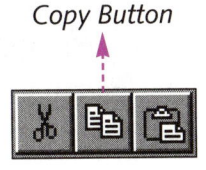

**Figure 14–1**
The Copy command can be accessed from the toolbar.

## Exercise 14-3

In this exercise, you will copy a record from one part of a database to another.

1. Open *Exercise 14-3*. The database contains the membership records for an organization called the Future Entrepreneurs club. David Foley's brother, John, recently joined the club. His address and interest are the same as his brother's.

2. Select **Record 5** (David Foley).

3. Use the Copy command to copy the record.

4. Select **Record 14** (the empty record at the bottom of the database).

5. Use the Paste command to replace the data. The record for David Foley will be copied into Record 14.

6. Highlight the entry of the First Name field of Record 14. (The field contains the name *David*.)

7. Enter **John** in the First Name field.

8. Save the database as *FE Club* and leave the database on the screen for the next exercise.

### FILLING

Filling down and filling right in the database work the same way as in the spreadsheet. Filling right is not often used in database files, however, because the fields are arranged in columns. It is rare that one needs to copy the same data across fields.

## Exercise 14-4

In this exercise, you will use the Fill Down command to copy in a database. *FE Club* should be on your screen.

1. Highlight the entry in the City field of Record 1.

2. Key **Denver** and press **Enter**.

**lesson 14** *Adding and Deleting Records and Printing*

3. Use Fill Down to enter *Denver* in the remaining cells in the City field.

4. Save the database and leave it on the screen for the next exercise.

## ❖ INSERTING A RECORD

You have learned how to enter a record at the bottom of a database. At times, however, you may want to insert a new record at a specific location in the database.

To insert a record in List view of the database:

✢ In List view, highlight the record that will be below the new record.

✢ Choose **Insert Record** from the **Record** menu. An empty record appears above the selected record.

### Exercise 14-5

In this exercise, you will insert a new record into a database. *FE CLUB* should be on your screen.

1. Select **Record 6** (Tara Gordon).

2. Insert a new record. An empty record will appear as Record 6. The record for Tara Gordon will be moved down to Record 7, as shown in Figure 14–2.

3. Enter the following data in the new record:

   **Ernie Galindo**
   **701 Rosebud St.**
   **Denver 80245**
   **Interest: Auto Mechanics**

4. Save the database and leave it on the screen for the next exercise.

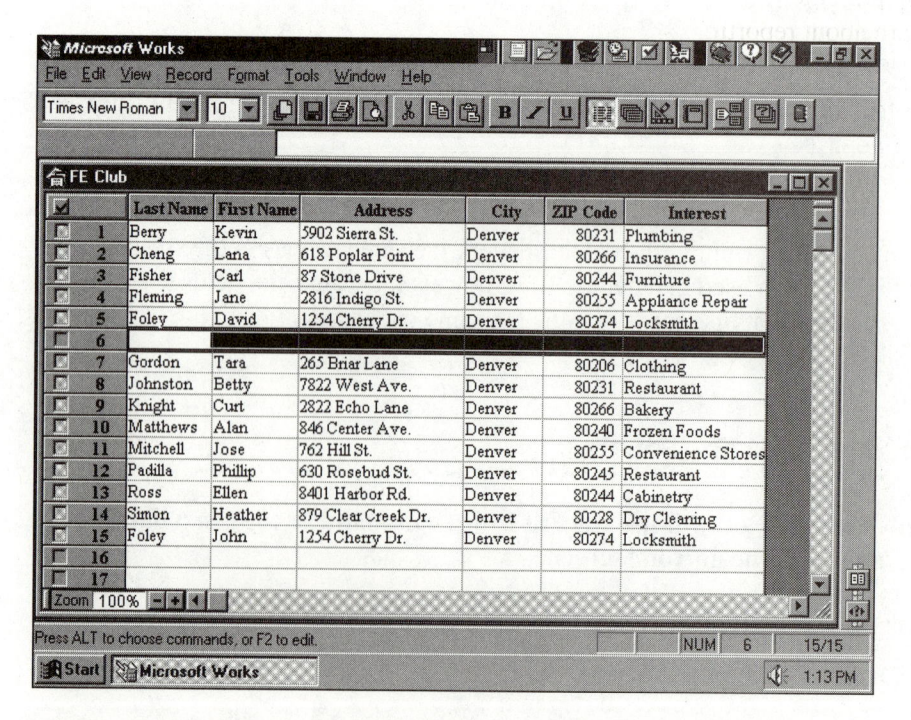

Figure 14–2
The Insert Record command places an empty record above the highlighted record.

| | Last Name | First Name | Address | City | ZIP Code | Interest |
|---|---|---|---|---|---|---|
| 1 | Berry | Kevin | 5902 Sierra St. | Denver | 80231 | Plumbing |
| 2 | Cheng | Lana | 618 Poplar Point | Denver | 80266 | Insurance |
| 3 | Fisher | Carl | 87 Stone Drive | Denver | 80244 | Furniture |
| 4 | Fleming | Jane | 2816 Indigo St. | Denver | 80255 | Appliance Repair |
| 5 | Foley | David | 1254 Cherry Dr. | Denver | 80274 | Locksmith |
| 6 | | | | | | |
| 7 | Gordon | Tara | 265 Briar Lane | Denver | 80206 | Clothing |
| 8 | Johnston | Betty | 7822 West Ave. | Denver | 80231 | Restaurant |
| 9 | Knight | Curt | 2822 Echo Lane | Denver | 80266 | Bakery |
| 10 | Matthews | Alan | 846 Center Ave. | Denver | 80240 | Frozen Foods |
| 11 | Mitchell | Jose | 762 Hill St. | Denver | 80255 | Convenience Stores |
| 12 | Padilla | Phillip | 630 Rosebud St. | Denver | 80245 | Restaurant |
| 13 | Ross | Ellen | 8401 Harbor Rd. | Denver | 80244 | Cabinetry |
| 14 | Simon | Heather | 879 Clear Creek Dr. | Denver | 80228 | Dry Cleaning |
| 15 | Foley | John | 1254 Cherry Dr. | Denver | 80274 | Locksmith |

138 *Microsoft Works 4.0 for Windows 95: QuickTorial*™

## ❖ MOVING DATA

To move data, click the Cut and Paste buttons on the toolbar (see Figure 14–3). The process is similar to the copy process except the Cut command removes data from its original position in the database.

*Cut Button    Paste Button*

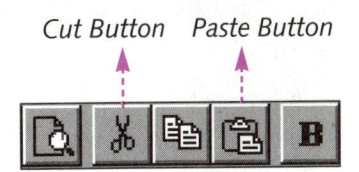

**Figure 14–3**
Using Cut and Paste removes data from its original position in the database.

### Exercise 14–6

In this exercise, you will cut and paste a record in a database. *FE Club* should be on your screen.

1. Select **Record 15** (John Foley).
2. Use the **Cut** command to remove the record.
3. Move the cursor to the Last Name field of Record 6 (Galindo).
4. Use the **Paste** command to insert the data. The record for John Foley appears in Record 6.
5. Save the database and leave it on the screen for the next exercise.

## ❖ PRINTING A DATABASE

Printing and closing a database are handled in much the same way as in the word processor and the spreadsheet.

It is possible that you will never need to print an entire database. Large databases can contain thousands of records—you can imagine how many pages it would take to print them all. Instead, large databases are usually summarized and printed in reports. (You will learn about reporting in Lesson 19.) You may, however, want to print a small database or an individual record in a database.

### PRINTING A SMALL DATABASE FROM LIST VIEW

Small databases may be printed as they appear in List view. In other words, rows of records will be printed in the order that they appear on the screen. To print a database from List view, choose the Print command from the File menu. If you desire, you can preview the printed database by choosing the Print Preview command from the File menu or by clicking the Print Preview button on the toolbar. If you want to adjust margins or page characteristics, choose the Page Setup command from the File menu.

### PRINTING RECORDS FROM FORM VIEW

You may also print records as they appear in Form view. Records will be printed, one per page, with fields in the same position as they appear on the screen. To print individual records from Form view, you must first click the Current record only option in the Print dialog box, which is shown in Figure 14–4. Otherwise, Works will print a page for every record in the database.

> **note**
>
> When printing from Form view, do not use the Print button from the toolbar unless you want a page printed for every record in the database.

**lesson 14** *Adding and Deleting Records and Printing* **139**

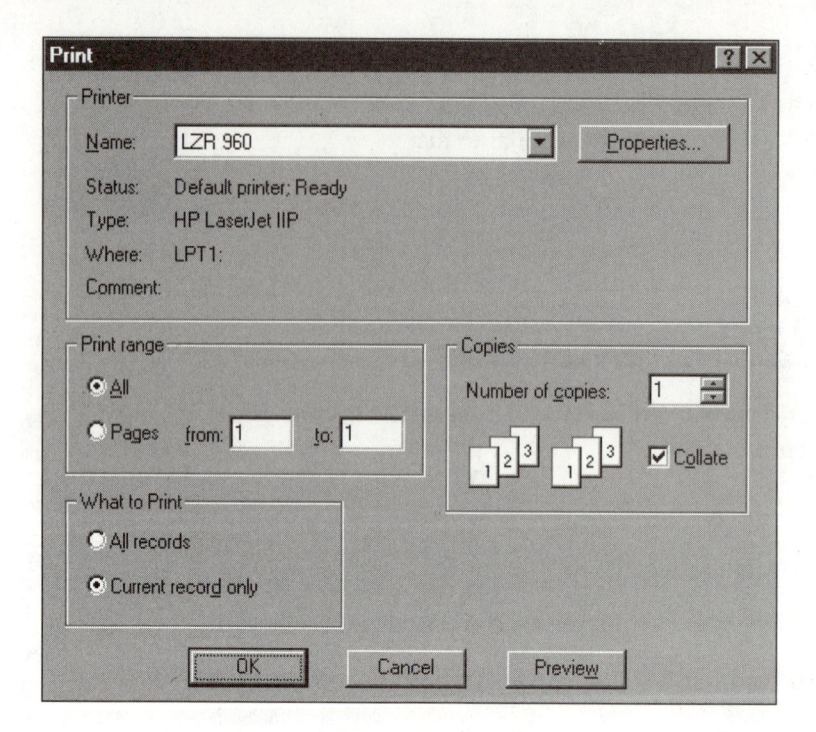

**Figure 14-4**
To print an individual record, click Current record only in the Print dialog box.

**note**

Depending on the selected font, the printout may be too wide for one page. If this is the case with your printout, two pages will be printed.

## Exercise 14-7

In this exercise, you will print a database and a single record from a database. *FE Club* should be on your screen.

1. Choose **Print Preview** from the **File** menu. The database appears on screen as it would be printed.

2. Click **Print** to print the database from Print Preview. The Print dialog box appears.

3. Click **OK.** The database will print.

4. Move the highlight to any field of the record for Ernie Galindo (Record 7).

5. Switch to Form view.

6. Choose **Print** from the **File** menu. The *All records* option is selected in the dialog box. Click the **Current record only** option.

7. Click **OK.** The current record prints.

8. Save and close the database.

140 Microsoft Works 4.0 for Windows 95: QuickTorial™

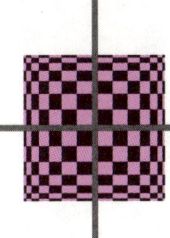

# activities

## ❖ TRUE/FALSE

In the blank space before each sentence, place a **T** if the statement is true and an **F** if it is false.

_____ 1. To delete a record in Form view, you must first display the record to be deleted on the screen.

_____ 2. The original data will be affected when the Copy command is chosen.

_____ 3. Fill Down is the Fill command that is not often used in a database.

_____ 4. When inserting a new record in List view, the empty record appears above the highlighted record.

_____ 5. You can print an individual record from Form view.

## ❖ COMPLETION

Answer the questions below in the space provided.

1. In what view are single records usually entered?
   _____
   _____

2. What command must be used to save a database to a new name or location?
   _____
   _____

3. How does the Cut command differ from the Copy command?
   _____
   _____

4. What two commands are used to move data in a database?
   _____
   _____

5. What does the *Current record only* option in the Form view Print dialog box do?
   _____
   _____

# review

## Review Exercise 14-1

In this exercise, you will add records to the database you saved as *Address*.

1. Open *Address*.
2. From Form view, add the following record at the end of the database:
   **Cindy Shobe**
   **8701 Elm Ave.**
   **Detroit, MI 48221**
   **313-555-3399**
3. From List view, insert the following record above the Barbara Alexander record:
   **Dalton Jackson**
   **5674 Saturn St.**
   **Seattle, WA 98122**
   **206-555-5946**
4. From Form view, print only the Cindy Shobe record.
5. Save the database as *Address 2* and close it.

## Review Exercise 14-2

In this exercise, you will insert and delete records from the database you saved as *FE Club*.

1. Open *FE Club*.
2. From List view, insert a record with your own name and address at the proper position in the database alphabetically.
3. Delete the Alan Matthews record.
4. Save the database as *FE Club 2*.
5. Print the database from List view and close it.

# lesson 15

# Creating a Database and Designing Fields

❖ OBJECTIVES

Upon completion of this lesson, you will be able to:

1. Create a new database.
2. Create fields.
3. Insert fields in an existing database.
4. Adjust field size.
5. Move fields in Form Design view.
6. Align data in a field.
7. Change font, style, and size.

**Estimated Time:** 1/2 hour

❖ CREATING A NEW DATABASE

To create a new database:

- Choose **New** from the **File** menu or press **Ctrl** + N. The Works Task Launcher appears.
- Click the **Works Tools** tab in the Works Task Launcher dialog box.
- Click the **Database** button. You may see a dialog box named First Time Help. Click one of the options in the dialog box if you want help or click **OK** to close the dialog box. The Create Database dialog box appears, as shown in Figure 15–1.

In order for a database to exist, it must have fields for the data. The Create Database dialog box is where you create the fields for a new database.

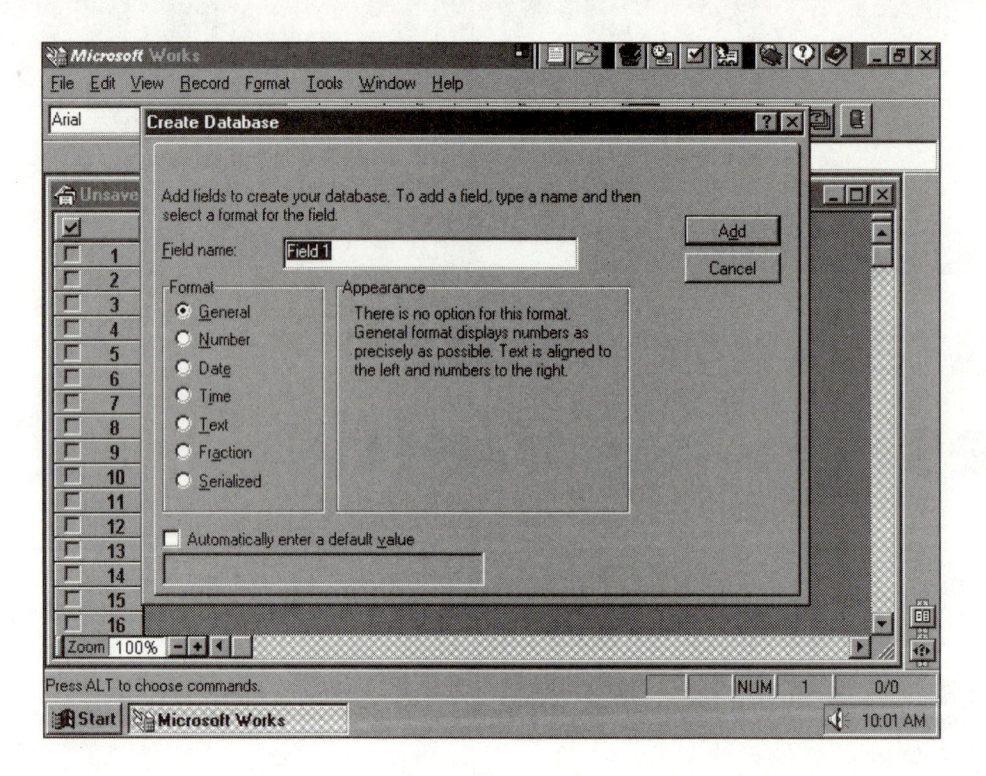

**Figure 15–1**
The Create Database dialog box is where the fields of a new database are created.

> **note**
>
> Notice that the Create Database dialog box includes options for the format of the data in the field. You will learn about field formats in the next lesson. For now, use the General format for all of your fields.

❖ **CREATING FIELDS**

The Create Database dialog box is not the only place you can create fields. You can create fields at any time using the Insert Field dialog box, which is almost identical to the Create Database dialog box.

To create a field using the Create Database dialog box:

❖ Key a name for the first field.

❖ Choose a format option.

❖ Click **Add.** The field is added and you are given the opportunity to enter another field.

❖ Continue to add fields following the steps outlined above until you have added all the necessary fields.

❖ Click **Done.** The new database appears in List view.

## Exercise 15–1

In this exercise, you will create a database that contains information on national parks in the United States.

1. Create a new database.

2. Create a field named *Park*.

3. Create two more fields named *State* and *Acres*.

144 Microsoft Works 4.0 for Windows 95: QuickTorial™

4. Click **Done.** Your screen should appear in List view and look similar to Figure 15–2.

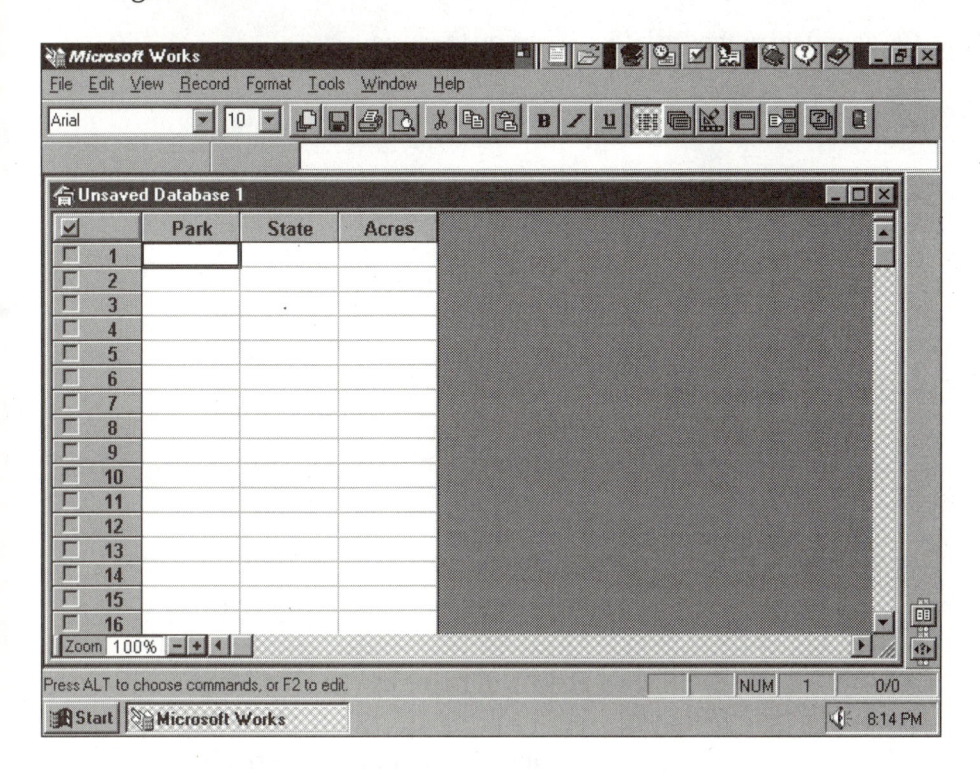

Figure 15–2
The fields of a new database appear in List view.

5. Save the database as *Parks* and leave the database on the screen for the next exercise.

## ❖ INSERTING FIELDS IN AN EXISTING DATABASE

You can insert fields in an existing database in List view or Form Design view. Form Design view is the view that allows you to make changes to a form that you use in Form view.

To insert a field in List view:

- Place the cursor in the field before or after the location where you want the new field inserted.

- Pull down the **Record** menu.

- Access the **Insert Field** submenu.

- Choose either **Before** or **After** to specify where you want the field inserted. The Insert Field dialog box appears, which functions like the Create Database dialog box.

- Insert one or more fields and click **Done.**

To insert a field in Form Design view:

- Choose **Form Design** from the **View** menu or click the **Form Design** button on the toolbar (see Figure 15–3).

- Choose **Field** from the **Insert** menu. The Insert Field dialog box appears.

> **note**
> Fields inserted in one view are automatically added to the other views.

lesson 15 *Creating a Database and Designing Fields* 145

✦ Name the field, choose a format option, and click **OK**. The new field appears on the form.

✦ Drag the new field to the desired position on the form.

*Figure 15–3*
*The Form Design button quickly accesses Form Design view.*

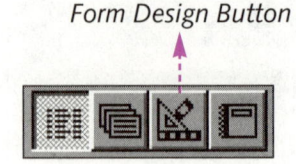

Form Design Button

## Exercise 15-2

In this exercise, you will add a field to a database. *Parks* should be on your screen.

1. From List view, add a field named **Estab.** between the State and Acres fields.

2. Enter the following data in the database. In List view, the fields will be about 10 characters wide. Go ahead and enter the data in the columns. You will adjust the widths in a later exercise.

   | Park | State | Estab. | Acres* |
   |---|---|---|---|
   | Acadia | Maine | 1919 | 39 |
   | Badlands | South Dakota | 1978 | 244 |
   | Big Bend | Texas | 1944 | 740 |
   | Carlsbad Caverns | New Mexico | 1930 | 47 |
   | Denali | Alaska | 1917 | 4700 |
   | Everglades | Florida | 1947 | 1401 |
   | Glacier | Montana | 1910 | 1014 |
   | Grand Canyon | Arizona | 1919 | 1218 |
   | Haleakala | Hawaii | 1961 | 29 |
   | Hot Springs | Arkansas | 1921 | 5 |
   | Isle Royale | Michigan | 1940 | 539 |
   | Mammoth Cave | Kentucky | 1941 | 52 |
   | Olympic | Washington | 1938 | 908 |
   | Rocky Mountain | Colorado | 1915 | 267 |
   | Shenandoah | Virginia | 1935 | 194 |
   | Yellowstone | Wyoming | 1872 | 2222 |
   | Yosemite | California | 1890 | 761 |
   | Zion | Utah | 1919 | 147 |

   *in thousands
   Source: Michael Frome, *The Leading National Park Guide* (Chicago: Rand McNally, 1987); and National Park Service, *National Park System Map and Guide* (Washington, D.C.: U.S. Department of the Interior, 1989).

3. Save the database and leave it open for the next exercise.

## ❖ ADJUSTING FIELD SIZE

In List view, you can adjust the field size by placing the mouse pointer on the boundary of the right edge of the field name. The pointer will turn into two vertical bars with arrows pointing right and left. Widen the column by dragging to the right until the column is wide enough to show all the data. You can also highlight the field and choose Field Width from the Format menu. The Field Width dialog box, shown in Figure 15–4, gives you the option of keying a new width or choosing the Best Fit option, which sets the width to the smallest width that will still hold the widest entry. In the Field Width dialog box, you can also click the Standard button to set the width to the original default width.

> **note**
> The Best Fit option is available only in List view.

Figure 15–4
In List view, field size can be adjusted by keying a width or choosing the Best Fit option.

In Form Design view, you can adjust the field size by clicking the field and pointing to one of the resizing handles. When the pointer turns into a double-headed arrow with the word RESIZE below it, drag it to the field size you desire. You can also highlight the field and choose Field Size from the Format menu. The Field Size dialog box, shown in Figure 15–5, allows you to enter a height and width. Usually, height will be one line.

Figure 15–5
In Form view, field size can be adjusted by keying a height and width.

### Exercise 15–3

In this exercise, you will adjust all the fields in a database using the Best Fit option. *Parks* should be on your screen.

1. From List view, choose **Field Width** from the **Format** menu.
2. Select **Best Fit** from the **Field Width** dialog box to adjust the width of all the fields.
3. Leave the database open for the next exercise.

## ❖ MOVING A FIELD IN FORM DESIGN VIEW

A field in Form Design view may be moved to any part of the form. To change the location of a field:

*lesson 15  Creating a Database and Designing Fields*

> **note**
>
> Changing the location of the field in Form Design view will not affect the location of the field in List view.

* Click the field name and the word *DRAG* will appear below the pointer.
* Drag the field to the location you desire.

In Form Design view, the position of a field is indicated in the formula bar. The number after the X indicates where the field appears horizontally, and the number after the Y indicates where the field appears vertically (see Figure 15–6).

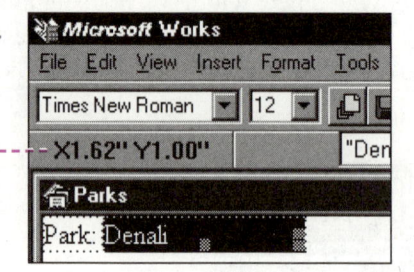

*Field Location Indicators*

**Figure 15–6
The position of a field is indicated in the formula bar.**

## Exercise 15-4

In this exercise, you will practice moving fields. *Parks* should be on your screen. Switch to the Form Design view before performing the following steps.

1. Move the Park field to location X1.33" Y1.00".
2. Move the State field to location X1.33" Y1.33".
3. Move the Estab. field to location X1.33" Y1.83".
4. Move the Acres field to location X1.33" Y2.17".
5. Leave the database on your screen in Form Design view for the next activity.

❖ FIELD ALIGNMENT

Works will automatically align alphabetical characters to the left side of the field and numerical characters to the right side of a field. You may, however, change the alignment of field data.

* Highlight the field (or a field entry).
* To change alignment, choose **Alignment** from the **Format** menu.

> **note**
>
> When an alignment is chosen, all the data in the field will be aligned. The alignment will occur in both Form and List views.

## Exercise 15-5

In this exercise, you will change the alignment of a field and print the entire database. *Parks* should be on your screen.

1. Switch to List view.
2. Center the Estab. field.

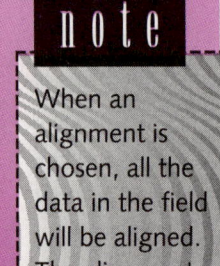

3. Print the entire database from List view.

4. Save and close the database.

## ❖ FONT, STYLE, AND SIZE

The font, style, and size of entries may be changed. To change the font, style, or size of a field, highlight the field (or a field entry) and choose Font and Style from the Format menu.

When a style is changed, all the data in the field will be for that view. You can choose different fonts for List and Form views.

To change the font of a field, click the Font Name box arrow on the toolbar and choose the name of the font you want. Use the same procedure to specify the font size by clicking the Font size box arrow.

The font and font size can affect the readability of a database when it is printed. Be especially careful with fields containing numbers. Some fonts produce numerals that are difficult to read.

> **note**
> To change type style, you can click one of the style options on the toolbar. The keyboard shortcuts you learned in the word processor tool can also be used.

**lesson 15** *Creating a Database and Designing Fields* 149

# activities

### ❖ TRUE/FALSE

In the blank space before each sentence, place a **T** if the statement is true and an **F** if it is false.

_____ 1. To create a new database, choose the Create New Database command from the File menu.

_____ 2. Fields created in Form Design view will also appear in List view.

_____ 3. In List view, you can widen columns by dragging the right-edge boundary of the column.

_____ 4. Changing the location of a field in Form Design view changes the location in List view.

_____ 5. When the font style of a field is changed, all the data in the field will be changed in both Form and List views.

### ❖ COMPLETION

Answer the questions below in the space provided.

1. What dialog box appears when a database is first created?

2. Where do the coordinates of fields in Form Design view appear?

3. How can you adjust field size in Form Design view?

4. By default, what alignment does Works use for alphabetic characters?

5. How can you change the font used in a field?

# review

## Review Exercise 15–1

In this exercise, you will change the fields of a database. The file *Review Exercise 15–1* is a database of population statistics for selected countries.

1. Open *Review Exercise 15–1*.
2. Switch to Form Design view.
3. Narrow the field size of entries in Form Design view to eliminate excess space.
4. Switch to List view and widen the fields to show all field names and entry contents.
5. Switch to Form Design view and insert a new field named *Life Expectancy* at X0.50" Y1.83" that is 6 characters wide, and enter the following data in the field:

| Country | Life Expectancy |
| --- | --- |
| Australia | 76 |
| Brazil | 66 |
| China | 70 |
| Cuba | 74 |
| Egypt | 63 |
| Ethiopia | 43 |
| France | 76 |
| India | 60 |
| Indonesia | 58 |
| Italy | 76 |
| Mexico | 70 |
| Nigeria | 52 |
| Poland | 71 |
| Turkey | 66 |
| United Kingdom | 76 |
| United States | 76 |
| USSR | 70 |
| West Germany | 75 |
| Zaire | 54 |

*Source:* United Nations Population Fund (UNFPA), The State of the World Population 1990 (1990).

6. Center the contents of the Birth Rate, Death Rate, and Life Expectancy fields.

7. Widen the Life Expectancy field in List view using the **Best Fit** option.
8. In List view, print the database using the **Print record and field labels** option using the **Other Options** command in the Page Setup dialog box.
9. Save the file as *Population* and close the file.

## Review Exercise 15-2

**In this exercise, you will enter additional records and delete obsolete records from the database you created in Review Exercise 15–1.**

1. Open the file *Population* from your data disk.
2. The countries of West Germany and the USSR no longer exist in their previous form. Delete these records from the database.
3. Add the following record for the unified Germany to the bottom of the database:

    | Country | Population | Birth Rate | Death Rate | Life Expectancy |
    |---------|------------|------------|------------|-----------------|
    | Germany | 77,188,000 | 10 | 11 | 75 |

4. Print the individual record for Germany from Form view.
5. Save the file as *Population 2* and close the file.

## Review Exercise 15-3

**In this exercise, you will create a database of the addresses and telephone numbers of some of your friends and relatives.**

1. Create a database containing the following fields: Last Name, First Name, Address, City, State, ZIP Code, Phone No.
2. Enter the names, addresses, and phone numbers of six of your friends or relatives.
3. Print the database.
4. Save the database as *Directory*.
5. Close the file.

# Lesson 16

# Formatting Database Fields and Calculating in the Database

## ❖ OBJECTIVES

Upon completion of this lesson, you will be able to:

1. Format database fields.
2. Calculate in the database.

**Estimated Time:** 1/2 hour

## ❖ FIELD FORMATS

*Field formats* determine how data is presented in a column of a database. The formats available are similar to those available in the spreadsheet. However, in the spreadsheet you were able to format individual cells; in a database, all entries within a field must have the same format.

### FORMATS IN THE DATABASE

Formats can be assigned to a new field or an existing field. Figure 16–1 shows the Format dialog box with the Field tab selected. The formats appear near the left edge of the dialog box.

The default format is called General format, which works with both text and numerical data. For more control over the format of data, you can specify other formats, such as a number, date, or time. Most of the formats allow you to choose an appearance to further customize the way the data is presented. For example, the Number format provides seven different appearances that allow you to display the numbers as currency, percentages, with commas, without commas, etc. You can also specify the number of decimal places you want displayed. Date and Time formats also allow you to choose how you want the date or time displayed.

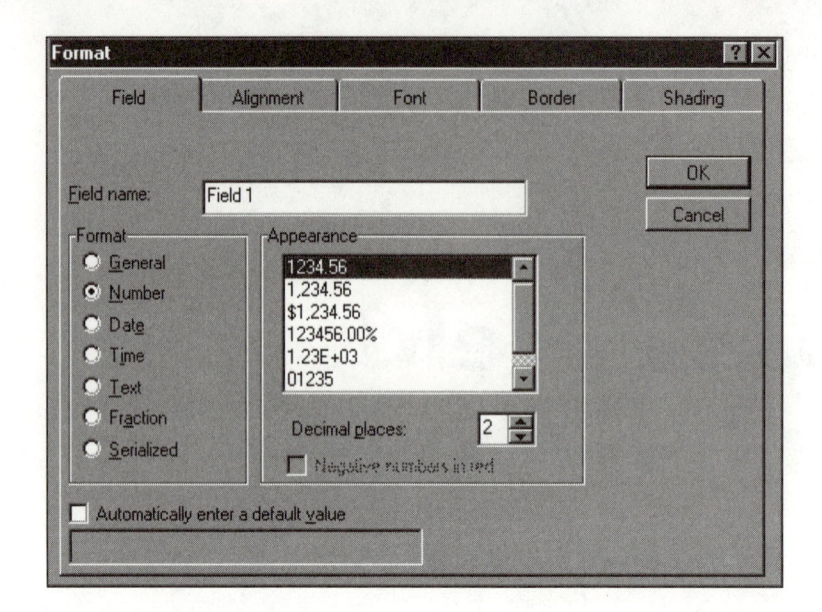

**Figure 16–1**
The Format dialog box allows you to choose a field format.

Use the Text format when you have text that the General format may not recognize as text. For example, a ZIP code will be considered a number and right-aligned by the General format, but will be interpreted as text by the Text format. The Fraction format displays numbers as fractions rather than decimals, and the Serialized format automatically assigns a number to records as they are added.

To format a new field, choose the format from the Insert Field dialog box or the Create Database dialog box. To format an existing field:

- Select an entry within the field you want to format.
- Choose **Field** from the **Format** menu.
- Choose a format.
- If necessary, choose an appearance and specify the number of decimal places.
- Click **OK**.

**note**
A field may be formatted in either Form or List view.

## Exercise 16–1

In this exercise, you will create new fields and format fields in a database.

1. Open *Exercise 16–1*.

2. Switch to Form Design view and create a field named **Dues Owed**. Choose the **Number** format and **$1,234.56** as the appearance to display the dues as currency.

3. Drag the new field to X0.50", Y2.83".

4. Create the following fields using the same currency format at the following locations:

   | Field | Location (or Approximate Location) in the Form |
   |---|---|
   | Dues Paid | X 0.50", Y 3.25" |
   | Balance | X 3.00", Y 3.25" |

154 *Microsoft Works 4.0 for Windows 95: QuickTorial*™

5. Switch to List view.

6. Scroll to the three new fields you created and adjust the column widths so that the entire headings can be seen on the screen.

7. Enter the following data in the Dues Owed and Dues Paid fields. You do not have to key the dollar sign ($). You can use Fill Down to speed data entry. You will enter data into the Balance field in another exercise.

| Record Number | Dues Owed | Dues Paid |
|---|---|---|
| 1 | $20.00 | $20.00 |
| 2 | $20.00 | $20.00 |
| 3 | $20.00 | $20.00 |
| 4 | $20.00 | $0.00 |
| 5 | $20.00 | $20.00 |
| 6 | $10.00 | $10.00 |
| 7 | $20.00 | $0.00 |
| 8 | $20.00 | $10.00 |
| 9 | $20.00 | $20.00 |
| 10 | $20.00 | $20.00 |
| 11 | $20.00 | $20.00 |
| 12 | $20.00 | $20.00 |
| 13 | $20.00 | $20.00 |
| 14 | $20.00 | $0.00 |
| 15 | $20.00 | $10.00 |

8. Save the database as *FE Club 3* and leave the database on the screen for the next exercise. Your screen should look similar to Figure 16–2.

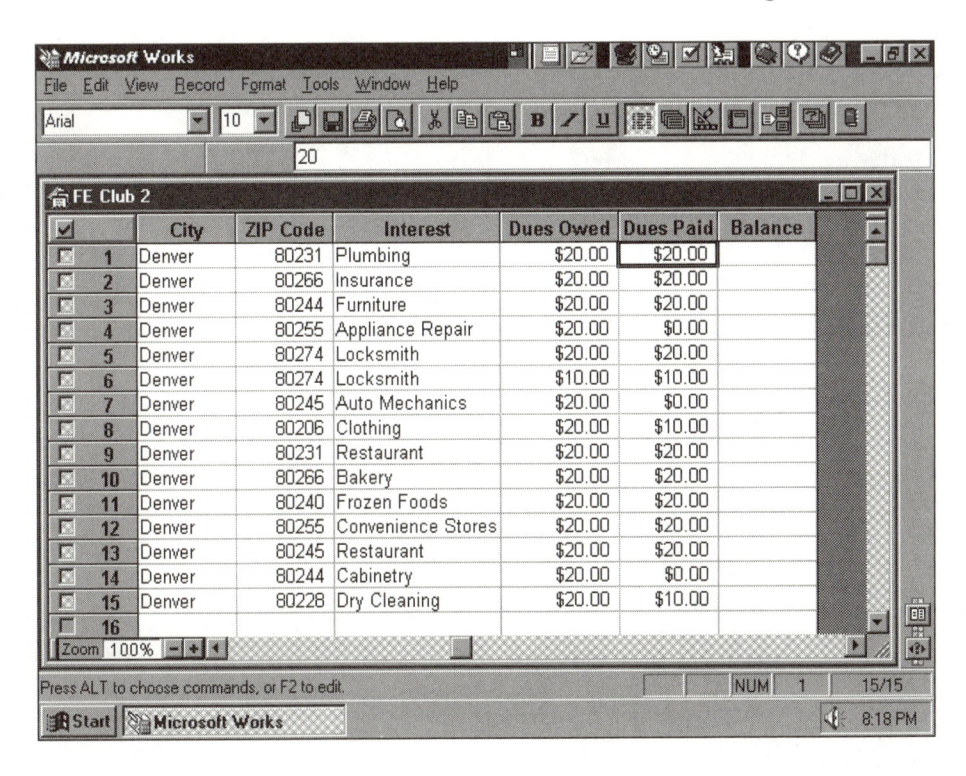

Figure 16–2
The Currency format automatically places a dollar sign on the entry.

lesson 16 Formatting Database Fields and Calculating in the Database 155

### TIME AND DATE FORMATS

Times and dates are sometimes entered as data in a database. Works has special formats for times and dates that permit them to be used in formulas and to be displayed in a variety of ways. Times can be displayed in 12- or 24-hour format, with or without seconds. Dates can be displayed in the formats shown in Table 16–1.

#### Date Formats

| | | |
|---|---|---|
| Short Formats | Month, day, year | 9/15/96 |
| | Month, day | 9/15 |
| | Month, year | 9/96 |
| Long Formats | Month, day, year | September 15, 1996 |
| | Month, year | September 1996 |
| | Month, day | September 15 |
| | Month only | September |

Table 16–1

## Exercise 16-2

In this exercise, you will create a field formatted for dates. *FE Club 3* should be on your screen.

1. Switch to Form Design view and create a field named **Date Joined** with the long month, day, year format.

2. Drag the field to X0.50", Y3.67".

3. Switch to List view and enter the following data in the Date Joined field. You may have to adjust the field width to make the field name or field contents visible.

   | Record | Date Joined | Record | Date Joined |
   |---|---|---|---|
   | 1 | 1/11/95 | 9 | 1/11/95 |
   | 2 | 2/15/95 | 10 | 1/11/95 |
   | 3 | 9/30/95 | 11 | 2/15/95 |
   | 4 | 1/11/95 | 12 | 1/11/95 |
   | 5 | 7/18/95 | 13 | 3/25/95 |
   | 6 | 2/1/96 | 14 | 1/11/95 |
   | 7 | 3/14/96 | 15 | 11/4/95 |
   | 8 | 9/2/95 | | |

4. Delete the day from the format by following these steps:
   a. With the highlight in the Date Joined field, choose **Field** from the **Format** menu. The Format dialog box will appear.

b. Choose the date format that shows only the month and year in long format.

c. Click **OK**. The field is formatted for month and year.

5. Save the database and leave it on the screen for the next exercise.

## CURRENT TIMES AND DATES

A computer contains an internal clock that keeps track of the current time and date. Works will insert the current time or date in your database or spreadsheet. To do this, select an entry or cell and use the following keystrokes:

| To Enter the Current | Press |
|---|---|
| Time | Ctrl+Shift; |
| Date | Ctrl+; |

## ❖ CALCULATING IN THE DATABASE

The database is not used as extensively for calculation as the spreadsheet is. However, the same mathematical and function formulas available for use in the spreadsheet are also available in the database.

Because the database does not use cell references, formulas in the database use field names to calculate values. For example, Figure 16–3 shows a database containing product prices, sales volumes, and the amount of total sales. Total sales were calculated by a formula that multiplied the price and volume (=Price*Volume). The formula is displayed in the formula bar. The formula results are displayed in the Sales field. Note that an equals sign is entered first, just as in the spreadsheet, to tell Works to expect a formula.

**Figure 16–3**
The values in the Sales field were determined by a formula that multiplied values in the Price and Volume fields.

A database formula consists of two types of characters: operands and operators. An *operand* is the field name used in formulas. An *operator* tells Works what to do with the operands. The operators used in formulas are shown in Table 16–2. The sequence in which a formula will perform calculations is the same as the order followed for formulas in the spreadsheet.

**lesson 16** *Formatting Database Fields and Calculating in the Database* 157

Table 16–2

| Operator | Operation |
|---|---|
| + | Addition |
| - | Subtraction |
| * | Multiplication |
| / | Division |
| ^ | Exponentiation |

## Exercise 16-3

In this exercise, you will enter a field formula to calculate the balance of the dues owed by each member to the club. *FE Club 3* should be on your screen.

1. Place the highlight in any entry of the Balance field.

2. Key **=Dues Owed-Dues Paid** and press **Enter**. The calculated values will appear in the Balance field, as shown in Figure 16–4.

3. Print the database in landscape orientation from List view and include record and field labels and gridlines.

4. Save and close the database.

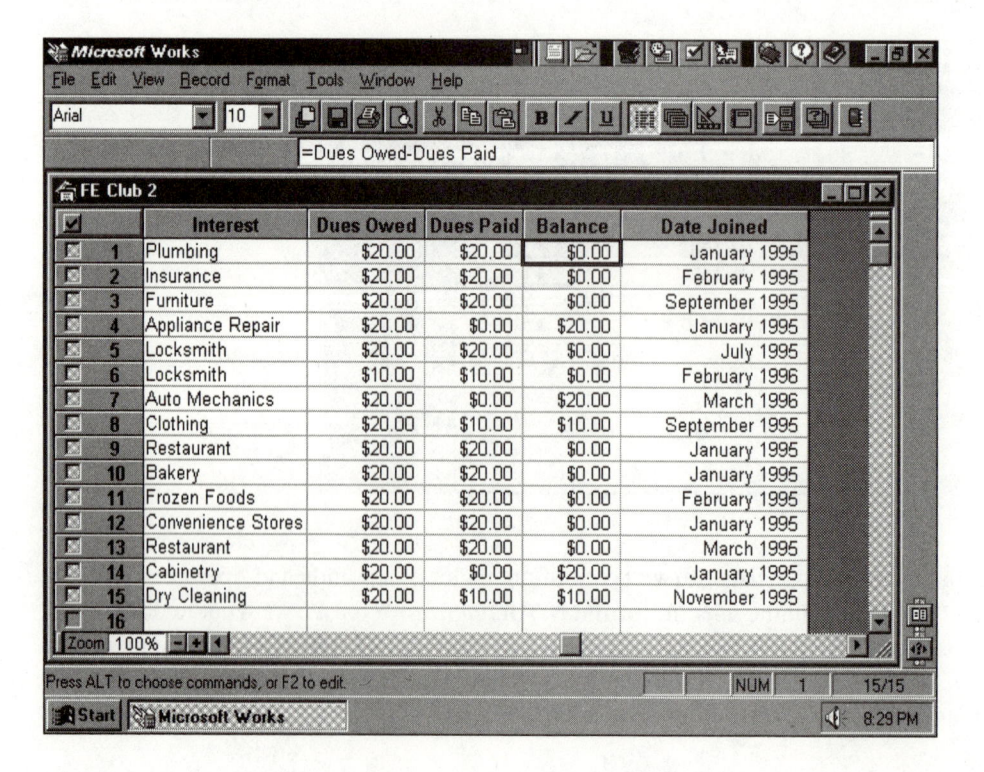

Figure 16–4
The formula calculated the amounts due in the Balance field.

158 *Microsoft Works 4.0 for Windows 95: QuickTorial*™

# activities

## ❖ TRUE/FALSE

In the blank space before each sentence, place a **T** if the statement is true and an **F** if it is false.

_____ 1. Field formats determine how data is presented in a database.

_____ 2. More than one field format can be used in the same field.

_____ 3. Fields may be formatted only in List view.

_____ 4. Pressing Ctrl+Shift+; will insert the current time in a database entry.

_____ 5. The spreadsheet function formulas are also available in the database.

## ❖ COMPLETION

Answer the questions below in the space provided.

1. What is the default database field format?

2. What field format is used to display dollar amounts?

3. What key combination inserts the current date in an entry in a database?

4. When calculating values, what does the database use instead of cell references?

5. What is an operator?

# review

## Review Exercise 16-1

In this exercise, you will plan a database to keep track of the CDs you own.

You have been collecting compact discs (CDs) for your stereo for the last year. The CDs have ranged in cost from $4.99 to $15.87. Each CD may have as many as 21 tracks (songs). Your interest in music includes rock 'n' roll, country, classical, and other types of music. Your database should contain at least five fields that will distinguish your CDs from one another.

1. In the Field Name column, identify fields you would include in the database.
2. In the Field Format column, designate which field format you would use. If a specific appearance is needed, show the appearance in parentheses following the field format.

| Field Name | Field Format |
| --- | --- |
| _____ | _____ |
| _____ | _____ |
| _____ | _____ |
| _____ | _____ |
| _____ | _____ |

## Review Exercise 16-2

In this exercise, you will create a database using the data in Figure 16-3.

1. Recreate the database you saw in Figure 16-3. Create all four fields and format them appropriately.
2. Enter the formula **=Price*Volume** in the Sales field.
3. Enter the data shown in Figure 16-3.
4. From List view, insert the following record above the Sunglasses record:
   Products: **Sun Visor**     Price: **$2.49**     Volume: **38**

5. Save the database as *Sales*.
6. Print the database from List view with record and field labels and close it.

## Review Exercise 16-3

In this exercise, you will insert and format fields and insert a new record into a database.

1. Retrieve the file *Review Exercise 16–3*.
2. Format the Assets, Sales, and Expenses fields for currency. Choose **0** for the number of decimals.
3. Insert a field named **Income** to the right of the Expenses field.
4. Create a field formula to determine Income. Income is determined by the difference between Sales and Expenses.
5. Format the Income field for currency with 0 decimals.
6. Add a record for the most current year, 1995:

    Assets      **24,231**
    Sales       **61,377**
    Expenses    **54,845**

7. Insert a record for the missing year, 1992:

    Assets      **15,464**
    Sales       **43,861**
    Expenses    **40,858**

8. Print the database from List view with record and field labels.
9. Save the file as *Income*.
10. Close the file.

# lesson 17

# Hiding Fields, Hiding Records, and Searching

## ❖ OBJECTIVES

Upon completion of this lesson, you will be able to:

1. Hide fields and field names.
2. Hide records.
3. Search a database.

**Estimated Time:** 1/2 hour

## ❖ HIDING FIELDS AND FIELD NAMES

In List view, fields can be hidden so that they neither display nor print. Hiding a field in List view can allow you to view fields side-by-side.

To hide a field in List view:

- Choose **Field Width** from the **Format** menu.
- Key **0** as the field width.

To redisplay a field that has been hidden:

- Choose **Go To** from the **Edit** menu.
  -or-
  Press **F5**.
- Choose the name of the hidden field.
- Choose the **Field Width** command and increase the field width (which is currently 0).

In Form Design view, you can hide field names. This feature can be used to replace the actual field name with a more descriptive label.

To hide a field name in Form Design view:

- Highlight the field name you want to hide.
- Choose **Show Field Name** from the **Format** menu. The command hides the field name.

To show the field name again:

- Highlight the field with the hidden field name.
- Choose the **Show Field Name** command again.

## Exercise 17-1

**In this exercise, you will hide a field name in a database.**

1. Open *Exercise 17-1*.
2. Switch to Form Design view.
3. Move the Interest field to X2.08", Y2.00".
4. Hide the Interest field name.
5. Move the cursor to X1.00", Y2.00".
6. Key **Career Interest**. Press **Enter**. Do not key a colon after the text or Works will create a new field. Your screen should look like Figure 17-1.

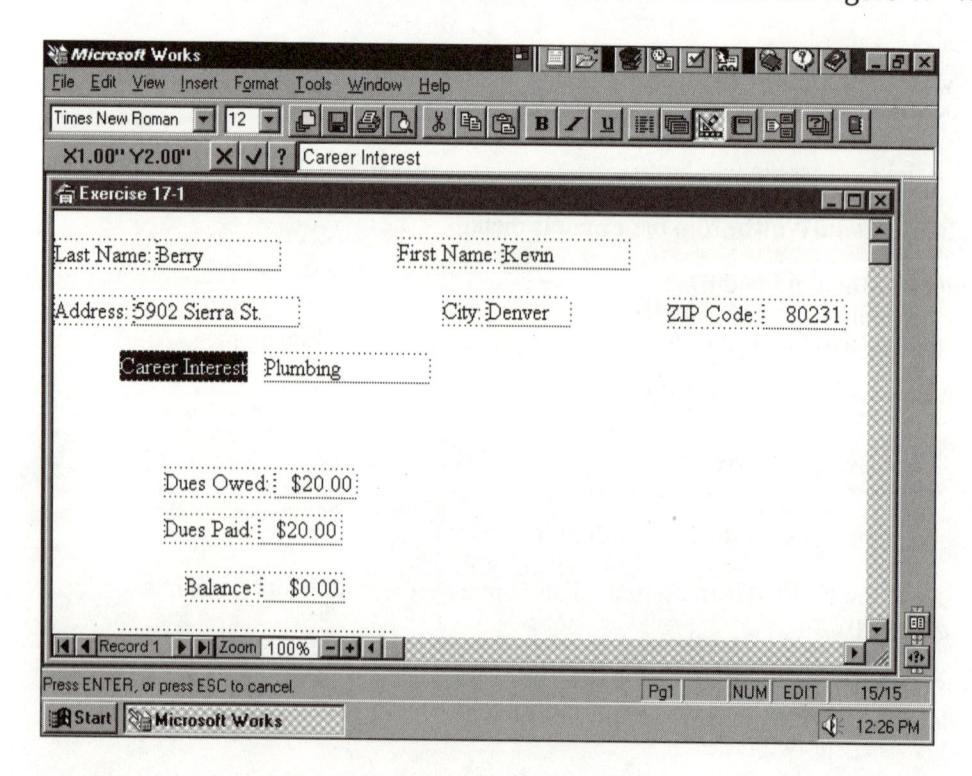

Figure 17-1
The Interest field name has been replaced with a more descriptive label, Career Interest.

164 *Microsoft Works 4.0 for Windows 95: QuickTorial*™

7. Switch to Form view and print the first record.

8. Save the database as *Hide Name* and leave the database on the screen for the next exercise.

## ❖ HIDING RECORDS

Records may be hidden from List view or Form view. Hidden records will not print, will not appear in reports, and cannot be accidentally deleted.

To hide records in List view:

- Select the record or records you want to hide.
- Choose **Hide Record** from the **Record** menu.

In Form view, you may only hide records one at a time. To hide the record currently on the screen:

- Choose **Hide Record** from the **View** menu.

To redisplay hidden records:

- Choose **All Records** from the **Show** submenu on the **Record** menu.

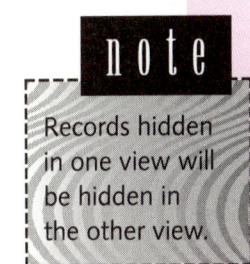

> **note**
> Records hidden in one view will be hidden in the other view.

## Exercise 17-2

In this exercise, you will practice hiding and redisplaying a database record. *Hide Name* should be on your screen.

1. Make certain you are in List view.
2. Hide **Record 8** (Tara Gordon). Redisplay the record.
3. Close the database.

## ❖ SEARCHING A DATABASE

*Searching* locates specific data in a database. For example, in a directory of names and addresses, you may want to search for someone whose last name is Johnson. Search criteria are specified in the Find dialog box, shown in Figure 17–2, and accessed by choosing the Find command from the Edit menu.

**Figure 17–2**
Search criteria are specified in the Find dialog box.

Works will perform two types of searches in a database. A *Next Record search* finds the first record after the highlight in which the specified data is present. An *All Records search* displays on the screen only those records containing the specified data.

**lesson 17** *Hiding Fields, Hiding Records, and Searching*

> **note**
>
> To search the entire database, you should begin the search by placing the highlight in the first entry of the database.

### SEARCHING NEXT RECORDS

A Next Record search looks for entries that match data specified in the Find What box of the Find dialog box. Works looks for the first occurrence of the data after the highlight.

To perform a Next Record search:

- Choose **Find** from the Edit menu or press **Ctrl** + F. The Find dialog box appears.
- In the Find What box, key the text you want to search for.
- Click the **Next record** button if it is not already selected.
- Click **OK**. The highlight will move to the next occurrence of the text.

You may repeat a Next Record search by pressing Shift + F4. The Find dialog box will not appear because Works assumes you are searching for the same data keyed in the Find What box in the previous search.

## Exercise 17-3

In this exercise, you will search for occurrences of the word *Ultra* in a database.

1. Open *Exercise 17–3*.
2. Find the first computer with the brand name *Ultra*.
3. Press **Shift** + **F4** (the Repeat key). The highlight will appear in the Brand field of Record 23, the second occurrence of the word *Ultra* in the database.
4. Press **Shift** + **F4** again. The highlight will appear in the Brand field of Record 24, the third occurrence of the word *Ultra* in the database, as shown in Figure 17–3.
5. Leave the database on your screen for the next exercise.

**Figure 17–3** Pressing Shift + F4 repeats a Next Record search.

166 *Microsoft Works 4.0 for Windows 95: QuickTorial*™

## SEARCHING ALL RECORDS

An All Records search will display all records containing data specified in the Find What box. Records that do not contain the specified data will be hidden. After you have completed the search, you can see what portion of the records is displayed by looking at the status line. The fraction at the right side of the status line indicates the number of records displayed and the total number of records in the database.

To perform an All Records search:

- Choose **Find** from the **Edit** menu. The Find dialog box will appear.
- In the Find What box, key the text you want to search for.
- Click the **All Records** button.
- Click **OK.** Only the records containing the specified text will appear.

## REDISPLAYING RECORDS

To redisplay records, pull down the Record menu, access the Show submenu, and choose All Records.

### Exercise 17-4

In this exercise, you will search all records of the database for computers with a 450-S CPU. *Exercise 17–3* should be on your screen.

1. Use an All Records search to display only those records of computers with a 450-S CPU.
2. Show all records.
3. Leave the database on your screen for the next exercise.

## SEARCHING WITH WILDCARDS

Suppose you want to find a particular record in your database but cannot remember enough information to use the Search command. For example, you know the last name of the person is either Jenson or Jonson. Rather than perform two searches to try to find the record, you can use a *wildcard* character to help you retrieve the record you want.

Works has two wildcard characters: the question mark (?) and the asterisk (*). The question mark represents a single character, either a letter or a number. In the example above, J?nson would find Jenson or Jonson.

The asterisk (*) can represent one or several characters and may be placed in any part of a word for a search. To find the record mentioned above, you would key J*nson in the Find What box. Works will find all names that begin with *J* and end with *nson*. It will find not only Jenson and Jonson but also Johanson and Johnson. Table 17–1 shows examples of how the wildcard character may be used to search for data.

**lesson 17** *Hiding Fields, Hiding Records, and Searching*

| These Wildcard Searches | Will Find |
|---|---|
| Will* | William, Will, Willy, Willard |
| *ness | kindness, selfishness |
| b*p | bump, bishop, blimp |
| n*t | not, net, nut, nest, next, night |
| n?t | not, net, nut |
| 450-? | 450-D, 450-S |
| *-D | 450-D, 600-D |

Table 17–1

## Exercise 17-5

In this exercise, you will perform a Wildcard search. *Exercise 17–3* should be on your screen.

1. Perform an All Records search for **$2***. All records containing computers in the price range of $2,000 to $2,999 appear on the screen.

2. Show all records.

3. Perform an All Records search for **450-?**.

4. Show all records.

5. Close the database without saving.

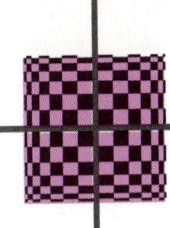

# activities

## ❖ TRUE/FALSE

*In the blank space before each sentence, place a **T** if the statement is true and an **F** if it is false.*

____ 1. Fields hidden in List view will print but will not display.

____ 2. Field names can be hidden in Form view.

____ 3. Records can be hidden in List view only.

____ 4. A hidden record cannot be accidentally deleted.

____ 5. The two wildcard characters are * and $.

## ❖ COMPLETION

*Answer the questions below in the space provided.*

1. How do you hide a field in List view?

2. When might you want to hide field names?

3. What key repeats a Next Record search?

4. What kind of search displays only those records containing specified data?

5. What Wildcard search could be used to find any word that ends with *ed*?

lesson 17  activities  169

# review

## Review Exercise 17-1

**In this exercise, you will hide and display records in a database.**

1. Retrieve the file *Review Exercise 17-1*.
2. From List view, hide the City field.
3. Hide records 6 and 14.
4. Print the database from List view and save the database as *Hidden*. (Do not print database with gridlines or record and field labels showing.)
5. Show the City field and hidden records again.
6. Use the Find command to display members in the 80244 ZIP code.
7. Show all records.
8. Find a member with an interest in *clothing*.
9. Display members with *restaurant* as an interest.
10. Show all records and close without saving.

# lesson 18

# Sorting and Using Filters

## ❖ OBJECTIVES

Upon completion of this lesson, you will be able to:

1. Sort records in a database.
2. Use filters to find records that meet a specific criteria.

**Estimated Time:** 1/2 hour

## ❖ SORTING A DATABASE

*Sorting* arranges records in a specific sequence. For example, a directory of names, addresses, and phone numbers is usually sorted in alphabetical order according to last names.

A database can be sorted by up to three fields at a time. This is useful if more than one record contains the same data in the first field. For example, if you would like to sort a directory geographically, you could sort first by the state. Because some records may contain the same state, a second-field sort will order by the city within each state. Table 18–1 shows the order in which records are sorted.

| Sort | Data | Direction of Sort |
|---|---|---|
| Ascending | Text | A to Z |
| | Times | Earlier to later |
| | Numbers | Smaller to larger |
| | Dates | Past to recent |
| Descending | Dates | Recent to past |
| | Numbers | Larger to smaller |
| | Times | Later to earlier |
| | Text | Z to A |

Table 18–1

To sort records in a database:

- Choose **Sort Records** from the **Record** menu. The Sort Records dialog box appears, as shown in Figure 18–1.

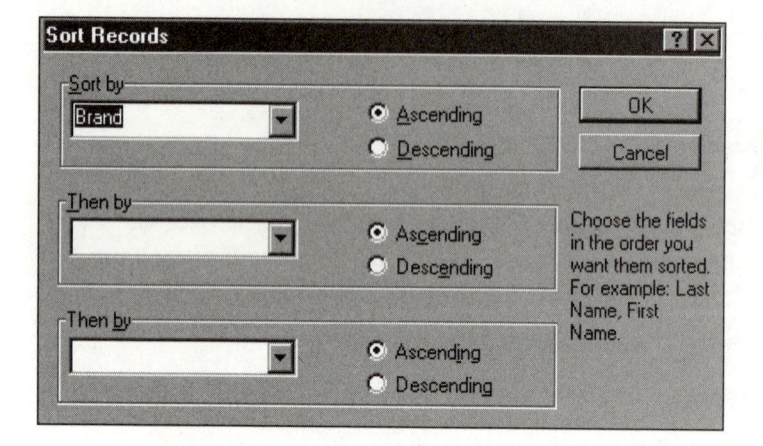

**Figure 18–1**
The sort field and sort order are designated in the Sort Records dialog box.

- In the box at the top of the dialog box, key the name of the first field by which you want to sort. You may also click the arrow at the edge of the box to choose the field from a list.

- Click the **Ascending** or **Descending** option next to the name of the field.

- If sorting by more than one field, key or choose a field name in the second and third boxes, as necessary, and choose **Ascending** or **Descending** for the fields.

- Click **OK.** The database will be sorted.

## Exercise 18–1

In this exercise, you will sort the records in certain orders based on the contents of certain fields to help you decide which computer to purchase.

1. Open *Exercise 18–1*.
2. Sort the records by price from least expensive to most expensive.
3. Sort the records by price from most expensive to least expensive.
4. Sort the records by the most to least hard disk storage.
5. Sort the records by brand name from A to Z and then by model number from smallest to largest.
6. Leave the database on your screen for the next exercise.

## USING FILTERS

Database *filters* display records meeting specific criteria. Filters differ from All Records searches in two ways. First, filters look for a match in a specific field, whereas searches look for matches in any part of the database. Second, filters can match records that fit into a range. For example, in a database of names and addresses, you may request all records with a ZIP code greater than 50000 or last names beginning with the letters G through K. Wildcards may be used in filters the same way they are used in searches.

To create and apply a filter:

- Choose **Filters** from the **Tools** menu. The Filter dialog box appears, as shown in Figure 18–2. If no filters yet exist, a smaller dialog box will appear over the Filter dialog box, asking you to name the new filter. If one or more filters exist, an existing filter will be displayed in the Filter dialog box. To create a new filter in this case, click the **New Filter** button.

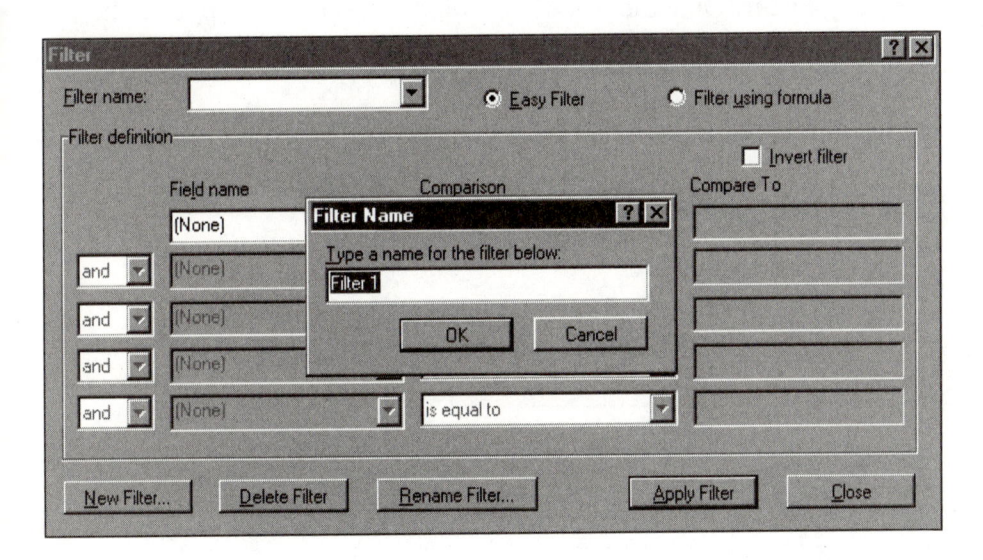

Figure 18–2
A filter is specified in the Filter dialog box.

**note**

When naming a filter, use a name that describes the filter's purpose.

- Key a name for the filter and click **OK.**
- Choose a field to compare in the Field Name box nearest the top of the dialog box.
- Choose a phrase in the Comparison box.
- Key a value in the Compare To box.
- Click **Apply Filter.** Only the records meeting the criteria of the filter will be shown.

A filter can include up to five criteria. When setting up filter criteria, you specify a field that the comparison will affect, the kind of comparison, and the value to which the field will be compared. Clicking the Apply Filter button displays the records that match the criteria of the filter.

### FILTERS BASED ON A SINGLE CRITERION

The easiest kind of filter is based on a single criterion. In other words, the filter considers the values in only one field.

**lesson 18** *Sorting and Using Filters* 173

## Exercise 18-2

In this exercise, you will display only the records of computers with a speed of 33 MHz. *Exercise 18–1* should be on your screen.

1. Choose **Filters** from the **Tools** menu. Because no filters yet exist, you are prompted for a name for the filter.

2. Key **Speed 33** as the name of the filter and click **OK.**

3. Choose **Speed** in the Field Name box.

4. The Comparison should already read *is equal to*. Key **33** in the Compare To box. Your dialog box should appear similar to Figure 18–3.

5. Click **Apply Filter.** Only the records showing a speed of 33 appear. The fraction at the bottom of the page in the status line should be 12/29, indicating that 12 of 29 records have a speed of 33.

6. Leave the database on your screen for the next exercise.

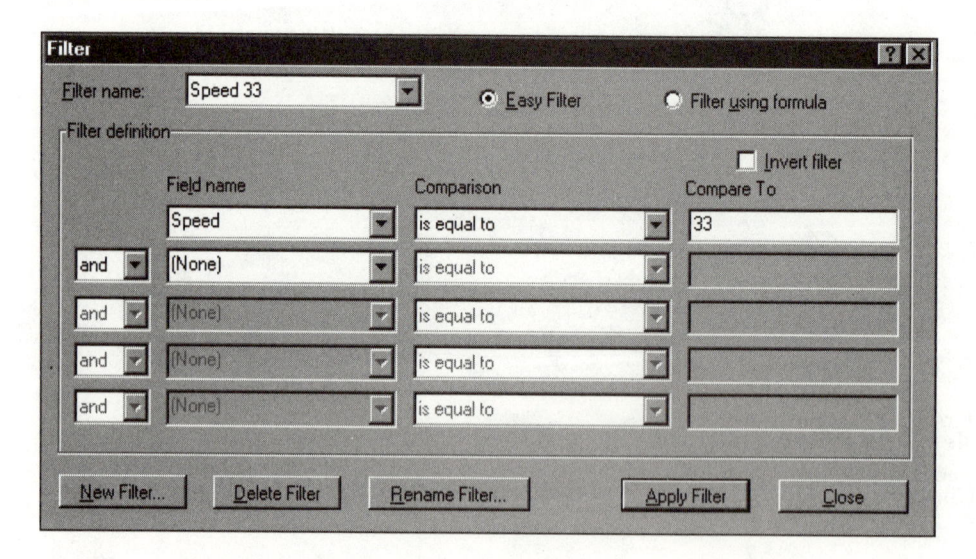

**Figure 18-3**
This filter considers only one field in the comparison.

### NUMERICAL FILTERS

Numerical filters may request data occurring within a range. For example, you may request records with data less than or greater than a certain value.

## Exercise 18-3

In this exercise, you will apply a numerical filter. *Exercise 18–1* should be on your screen.

1. Choose **Filters** from the **Tools** menu.

2. Click the **New Filter** button.

174 Microsoft Works 4.0 for Windows 95: QuickTorial™

3. Name the new filter **Price<1500** and click **OK.**
4. Choose *Price* as the field to compare.
5. Choose *is less than* in the Comparison box.
6. Key **1500** in the Compare To box. (Do not include the dollar sign.)
7. Click **Apply Filter.** Only the records for the computers costing less than $1,500 appear. The fraction at the bottom of the page in the status line should be 16/29, indicating that 16 of 29 computers cost less than $1,500.
8. Leave the database on your screen for the next exercise.

## FILTERS BASED ON MULTIPLE CRITERIA

A filter can make several comparisons simultaneously in the database. These comparisons are linked with the operators AND or OR. For example, you might create a filter that displays computers that cost less than $1,500 and have a speed of at least 33 MHz.

## Exercise 18-4

In this exercise, you will display records meeting multiple criteria. *Exercise 18–1* should be on your screen.

Suppose you have decided you would like to buy a computer with the following characteristics:

- The computer should have at least 8 megabytes of RAM.
- The computer should cost less than $1,200.
- The hard disk should have at least 100 megabytes of storage.

Display the records of computers meeting these criteria by following these steps:

1. Create a new filter named **My Computer**.
2. Make your selections and key values into the Filter dialog box so that it matches Figure 18–4. The *And* option is already chosen to link the criteria together.

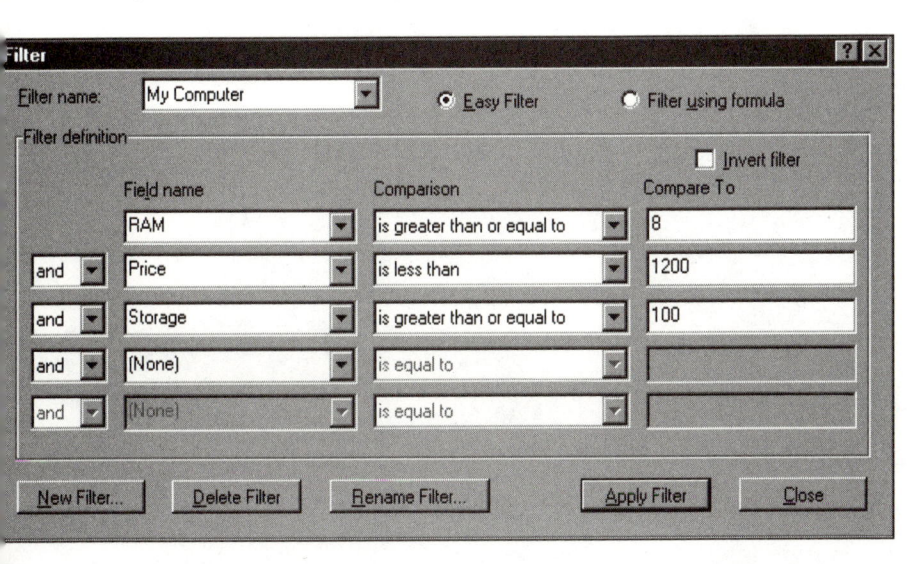

**Figure 18–4**
The Filter dialog box allows you to create a filter with up to five criteria.

**lesson 18** *Sorting and Using Filters* **175**

3. Click **Apply Filter.** Only the records with computers with at least eight megabytes of RAM, at least 100 megabytes of storage, and costing less than $1,200 appear. The fraction in the status line should be 10/29, indicating that 10 of 29 computers meet your needs.

4. From List view, print the database with the filter applied. Include record and field labels and gridlines in the printout.

5. Save the database as *Filters* and close the file.

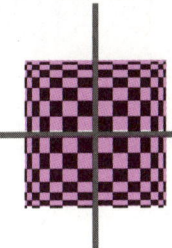

# activities

## ❖ TRUE/FALSE

*In the blank space before each sentence, place a **T** if the statement is true and an **F** if it is false.*

____ 1. Sorting arranges records in a specific sequence.

____ 2. A database can be sorted by up to two fields at a time.

____ 3. A filter is specified in the Filter dialog box.

____ 4. Filters can display data that fit into a range.

____ 5. The ALSO and OR operators can be used to make more than one comparison at a time.

## ❖ COMPLETION

*Answer the questions below in the space provided.*

1. Would an ascending or descending sort arrange dates beginning with the most recent?

2. What two ways do filters differ from an All Records search?

3. If one or more filters already exist, what button must be clicked to create a filter?

4. What is the maximum number of comparisons that can be entered in the Filter dialog box?

5. What does the fraction 7/52 in the status line of List view indicate?

**lesson 18** *activities* 177

# review

## Review Exercise 18-1

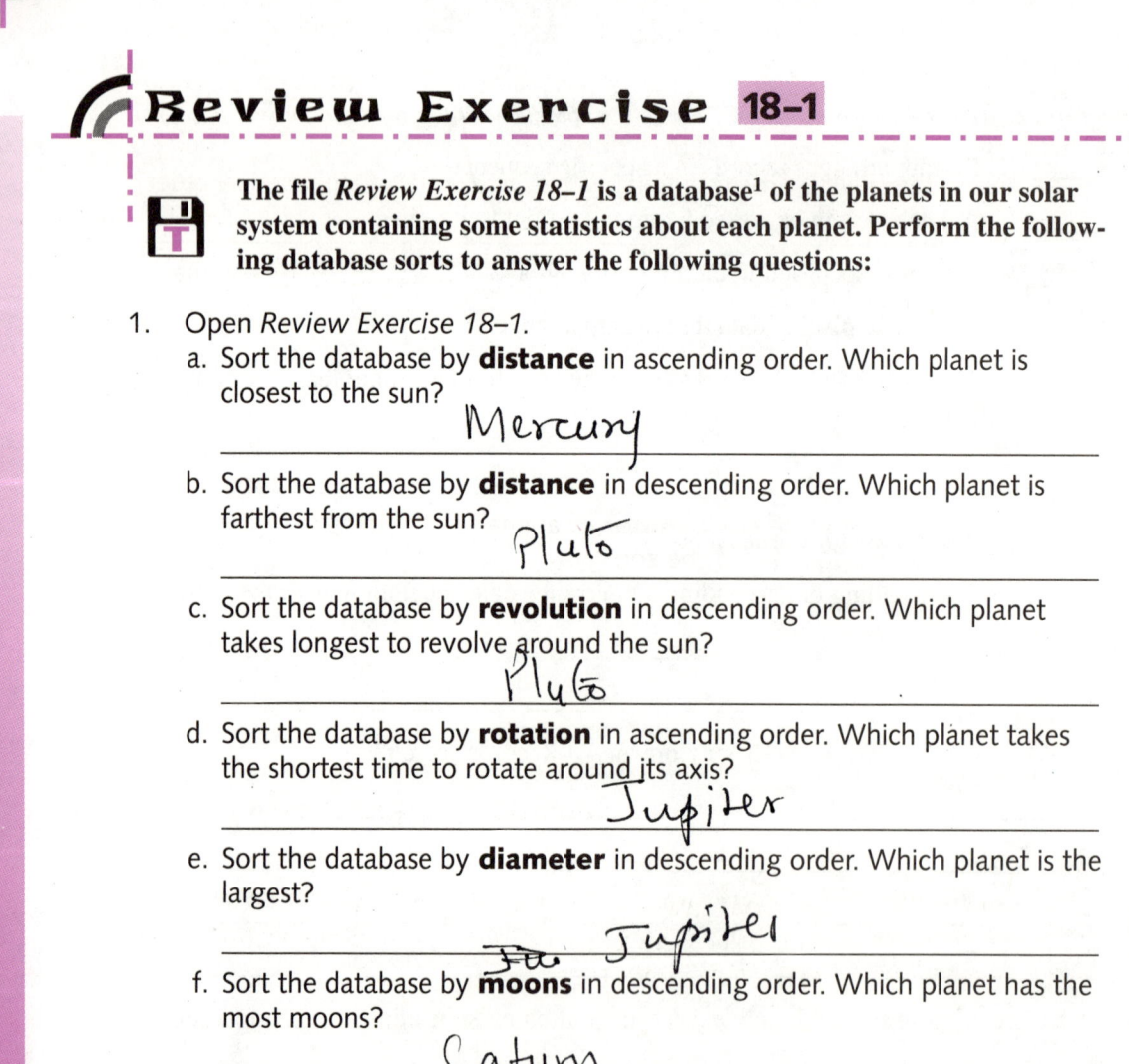

The file *Review Exercise 18-1* is a database[1] of the planets in our solar system containing some statistics about each planet. Perform the following database sorts to answer the following questions:

1. Open *Review Exercise 18-1*.
   a. Sort the database by **distance** in ascending order. Which planet is closest to the sun?
   
   *Mercury*
   
   b. Sort the database by **distance** in descending order. Which planet is farthest from the sun?
   
   *Pluto*
   
   c. Sort the database by **revolution** in descending order. Which planet takes longest to revolve around the sun?
   
   *Pluto*
   
   d. Sort the database by **rotation** in ascending order. Which planet takes the shortest time to rotate around its axis?
   
   *Jupiter*
   
   e. Sort the database by **diameter** in descending order. Which planet is the largest?
   
   *Jupiter*
   
   f. Sort the database by **moons** in descending order. Which planet has the most moons?
   
   *Saturn*

2. Close the file without saving.

[1] Source: *Hammond World Atlas* (Hammond, Inc., 1984), p. 352

# Review Exercise 18-2

The file *Review Exercise 18–2* is a database of zoo animals, their classification, and their continent of origin. The database also contains the location of the animals in the zoo (W is west, E is east, C is central, N is north, S is south) and the number of animals in the exhibit.

1. Open *Review Exercise 18–2*.

2. Sort the database in the following orders:
   a. Alphabetically by **animal**. What is the first animal in alphabetical order?

   b. Alphabetically by **classification**. What is the first classification to be listed in the database?

   c. Alphabetically by **zoo location**. What is the first zoo location to be listed?

   d. Decreasing order of the **number** of animals in the exhibit. What is the most common animal in the zoo?

   e. Increasing order of the **number** of animals in the exhibit. How many animals in the zoo occur in twos?

   f. Alphabetically by **zoo location** and alphabetically by **animal** within zoo locations. How many different animals are in the central location?

   g. Alphabetically by **continent,** then alphabetically by **classification** within continent and alphabetically by **animal** within classification. How many different animals are from Asia?

3. Close the file without saving.

lesson 18 *review* 179

# Review Exercise 18-3

The file *Review Exercise 18-3* is a database of restaurants in a city. The database has been developed by a hotel to aid guests in selecting a restaurant that meets their needs.

1. Open *Review Exercise 18-3*.

2. Create filters to identify the restaurants that satisfy the following guest requests:

    a. What are the names of restaurants that serve Chinese food?
    *Cuisine contains Chinese*

    b. What are the names of restaurants in the west part of town?
    *Location begins with W*

    c. Is Frank's open for dinner?
    *Res begins with F. Dinner is not blank*

    d. What are the names of restaurants that serve either barbecue or hamburgers?
    *Cuisine is equal to Hamburn*
    *Cuisine is = barbecue*

    e. Are there any inexpensive restaurants downtown?
    *Restaurants >= inexpensive*

    f. Which restaurant serves Italian cuisine at dinner and is not expensive?
    *Cuisine contains Italian*
    *Cost ≠ Expensive*
    *Dinner is not blank. (Dinner yes or Dinner no)*

3. Close the file without saving.

*Restaurant   Cuisine   Location   Lunch*
*Dinner*
*Cost*

*Restaurant begins with F } c*
*Dinner is not blank.*

# Review Exercise 18-4

The file *Review Exercise 18–4* is a database for a mail-order catalog business called The Night Shop. The store specializes in bedding and nightclothes. Many merchandise requests come over the telephone and require quick answers. Use search, sort, and filter techniques to respond to the following customer requests:

1. Open *Review Exercise 18–4*.
    a. How much does item 21-74-3 cost? (*Hint:* Do a Next Record search by Item No.)
        *$24.00*
    b. How many of Item No. 18-73-2 are available? (*Hint:* Do a Next Record search by Item No.)
        *1*
    c. What types of items are available in pink? (*Hint:* Do an All Records search for Pink.)
        *7*
    d. What are the least expensive items in the store? (*Hint:* Sort by Price ascending.)
        *Solid sheets*
    e. What sizes of sheets are available in a solid blue? (*Hint:* Filter the database for names equal to solid sheets and color equal to blue.)
        *Twin, full, King, Queen*
    f. What types of sheets are available in gray? (*Hint:* Filter the database for articles equal to sheets and color equal to gray.)
        *Solid, Stripped,*
    g. What sizes of terry robes are available in white? (*Hint:* Filter the database for articles equal to robe and color equal to white.)
        *Large, Medium, Small*
2. Close the file without saving.

# Review Exercise 18-5

In Review Exercise 15-3, you created a directory of friends and relatives and saved the database as *Directory*. In this exercise, you will sort the directory by last name and then first name.

1. Open *Directory*.
2. Sort the directory of friends and relatives by last name and then by first name.
3. Close the file without saving.

lesson 18  *review*  181

# lesson 19

# Database Reporting

## ❖ OBJECTIVES

Upon completion of this lesson, you will be able to:

1. Create a database report.
2. Change the appearance of a database report.
3. Save a database report.
4. Print a database report.

**Estimated Time:** 1/2 hour

## ❖ DATABASE REPORTS

Databases can become large as additional records are added. Because of its size, an entire database is rarely printed. By creating a *database report*, you may organize, summarize, and print a portion of the database. The report organizes by placing records, or portions of records, in a certain order or in groups. Reports can summarize data by inserting subtotals, totals, and statistics between groups or at the end of reports.

## ❖ USING THE REPORTCREATOR

Database reports are created using the ReportCreator. The ReportCreator is a dialog box which leads you through the steps of creating a report (see Figure 19–1).

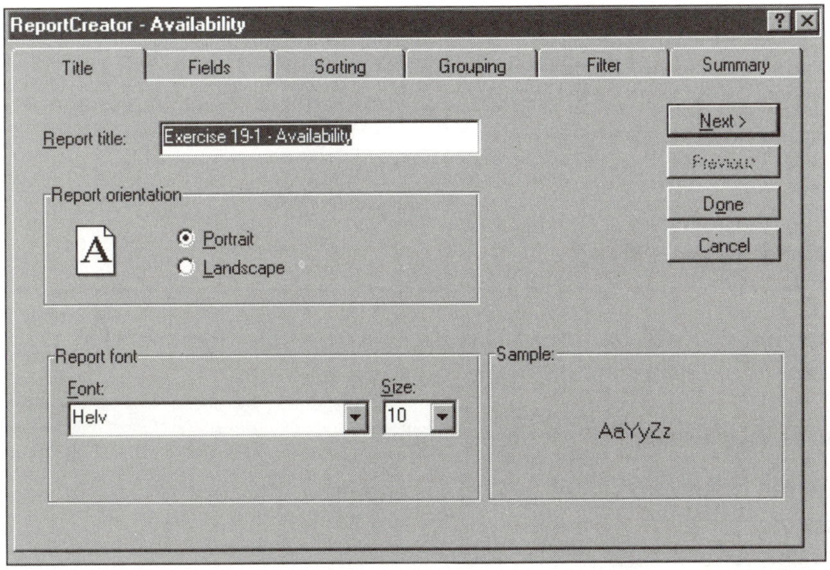

**Figure 19–1**
The ReportCreator dialog box guides you through the creation of a report.

lesson 19  *Database Reporting*  183

The dialog box is divided into sections. Each section is represented by a tab at the top of the dialog box. You can click a tab to move to another section of the dialog box. More often, however, you will begin with the first section, and click the Next button to move to the next section. When you have specified all of the information required for the report, click Done to create the report.

To access the ReportCreator, choose ReportCreator from the Tools menu. Before the ReportCreator dialog box appears, you are prompted for a name for the report, as shown in Figure 19–2.

Figure 19–2
The first step of creating a report is giving the report a name.

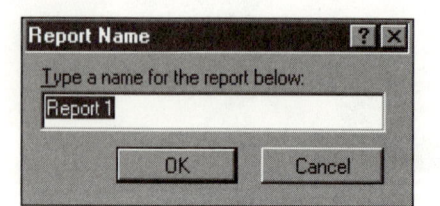

## Exercise 19–1

In this exercise and the exercises that follow, you will create an Availability Report to help the salespeople of a bicycle shop determine which bicycles are available for sale.

1. Open *Exercise 19–1*.

2. Choose **ReportCreator** from the **Tools** menu. You are prompted for a name for the report.

3. Name the report **Availability** and click **OK**. The ReportCreator dialog box appears.

4. Leave the ReportCreator dialog box on the screen for the next exercise.

❖ GIVING A TITLE TO A REPORT

The first section of the dialog box asks you to specify a title for the report. The title is the line that appears at the top of the printed report, not the name of the report you specified earlier. This section of the dialog box also allows you to select an orientation and font for the report.

## Exercise 19–2

In this exercise, you will continue to create an Availability Report. The ReportCenter dialog box should be on your screen.

1. Key **Availability Report** as the Report title.

2. Make sure the orientation is set to Portrait and leave the font set to the default setting.

184  *Microsoft Works 4.0 for Windows 95: QuickTorial*™

3. Click **Next.** The Fields section of the dialog box appears.

4. Leave the Fields section on the screen for the next exercise.

### ❖ SPECIFYING FIELDS FOR A REPORT

Fields are specified in the Fields section of the ReportCreator (see Figure 19–3). To specify the fields to be included in a new report:

- ❖ Select the first field to be included in the report from the Fields available list.
- ❖ Click **Add>.** The chosen field will appear in the Field order list.
- ❖ Add other fields by selecting them and clicking the **Add>** button.

> **note**
> Fields will appear in the report in the order they appear in the Field order list.

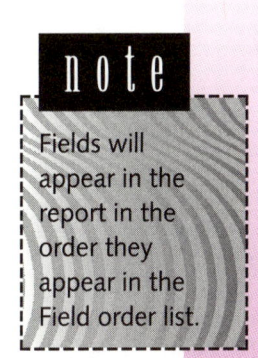

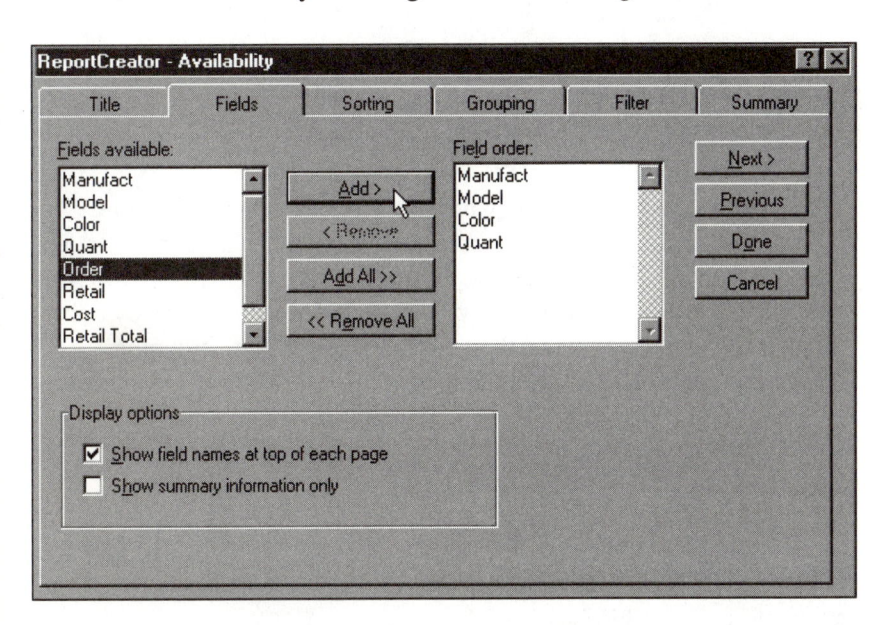

**Figure 19–3**
The Fields section of the ReportCreator allows you to choose fields for the report.

You can use the Add All button to quickly include all of the fields in your report. The Remove button will remove a field highlighted in the Field order list. The Remove All button clears the Field order list, allowing you to start over.

## Exercise 19–3

**In this exercise, you will add fields to your report. The Fields section of the ReportCreator should be on your screen.**

1. Add the *Manufact, Model, Color,* and *Quant* fields.
2. Click **Next** and leave the ReportCreator on the screen for the next exercise.

### ❖ SORTING AND GROUPING A REPORT

Sorting a report is similar to sorting a database outside of a report. The Sorting section of the ReportCreator dialog box (shown in Figure 19–4) allows sorting by up to three fields in ascending or descending order.

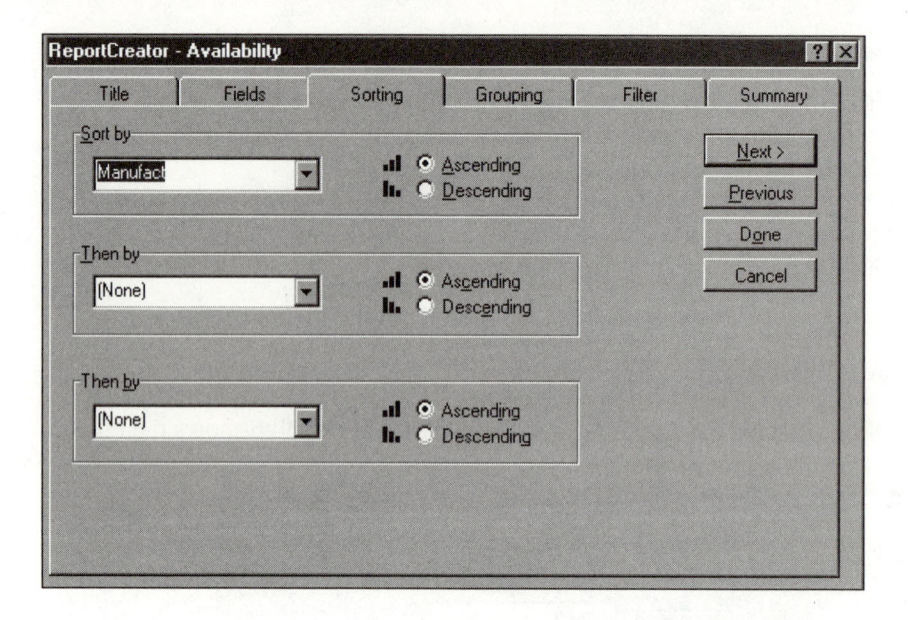

**Figure 19–4**
Sorting in a report is similar to sorting outside of reports.

You can group a report by the field or fields by which you sort. As shown in Figure 19–5, you can group by the sorted field each time the contents of the field change. You can also specify options such as whether to have a heading above each group and whether to start each group on a new page. In some cases, you may want to define your groups by only the first letter of the contents. For example, if the field by which you are grouping contains last names, you might wish to group by first letter.

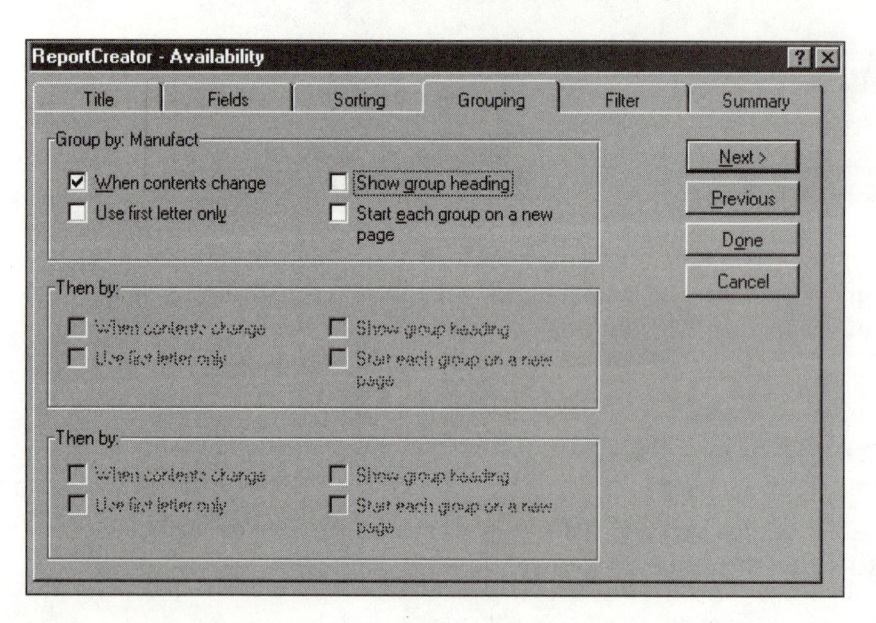

**Figure 19–5**
Reports can be grouped based on a sorted field.

## Exercise 19–4

In this exercise, you will practice sorting and grouping records. The ReportCreator should be on your screen.

1. Choose **Manufact** in the Sort by box. Be sure the Ascending option is selected.

186 *Microsoft Works 4.0 for Windows 95: QuickTorial*™

2. Click **Next.** The Grouping section of the ReportCreator appears.

3. Click the **When contents change** option at the top of the dialog box to group by the Manufact field.

4. Click **Next.** The Filter section of the ReportCreator appears.

5. Leave the ReportCreator on the screen for the next exercise.

## USING FILTERS IN A REPORT

You can apply existing filters to a report, or create filters from the ReportCreator. Filters in a report are like filters outside of reports. When a filter is applied, only the records which the filter selects will appear in the report. Figure 19–6 shows the Filter section of the ReportCreator dialog box.

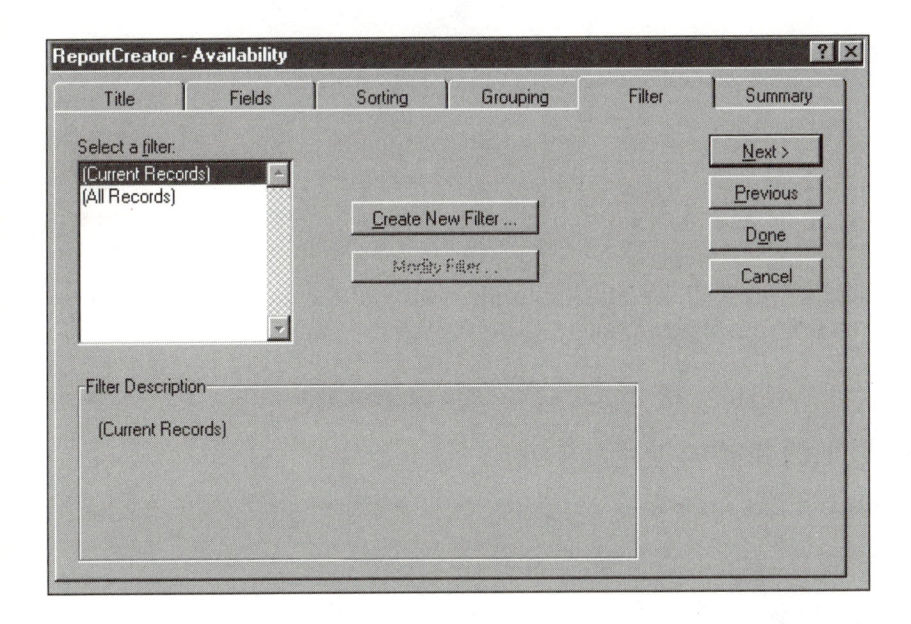

**Figure 19–6**
Filters can be used to select records for a report.

## USING SUMMARIES IN A REPORT

The Summary section of the ReportCreator dialog box, shown in Figure 19–7, is used to specify descriptive statistics for numerical data in the report. For example, at the bottom of a report containing the salaries of employees of a department, you may want to show the number of employees, the average salary, the largest salary, and the smallest salary.

There are seven types of summaries available. To specify a summary:

- Choose the first field you want to summarize.
- Click the box next to the summary you want.
- Repeat the steps above for any other fields you want to summarize.
- Choose whether you want the result to appear under each column or together in rows.

**lesson 19** *Database Reporting* **187**

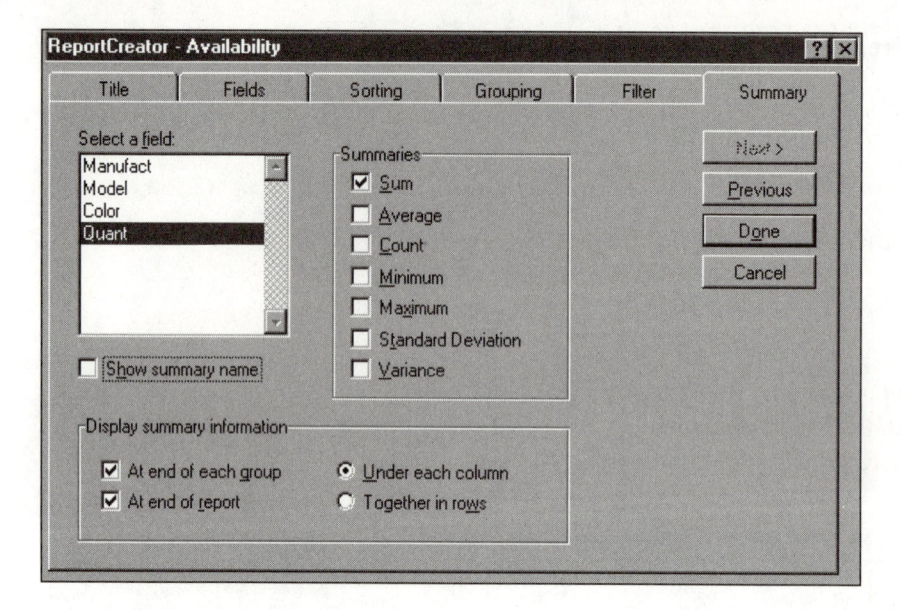

**Figure 19–7**
Summary information can produce totals, averages, and more.

## Exercise 19-5

In this exercise, you will prepare summary statistics for the following groups of data. The ReportCreator should be on your screen.

1. Click **Next.** The Summary section of the dialog box appears.

2. Highlight the **Manufact** field in the field list.

3. Click **Count** in the Summaries check boxes.

4. Highlight the **Quant** field in the field list.

5. Choose the **Sum** function to summarize the Quant field.

6. Choose to display the summary information at the end of each group and at the end of the report. Display the information under each column.

7. Click **Done.** You will be prompted to modify or preview the report.

8. Click **Preview.** The report appears on the screen, as shown in Figure 19–8. Zoom in to get a better view.

9. Cancel the preview and leave the database in Report view for the next exercise.

### ❖ CHANGING THE APPEARANCE OF A REPORT

You can alter the appearance of the database report by making changes in the Report view of the database. The Report view determines what information will be included in the report, how the information will be presented, and how the information will be printed.

Figure 19–8
Your report appears in print preview.

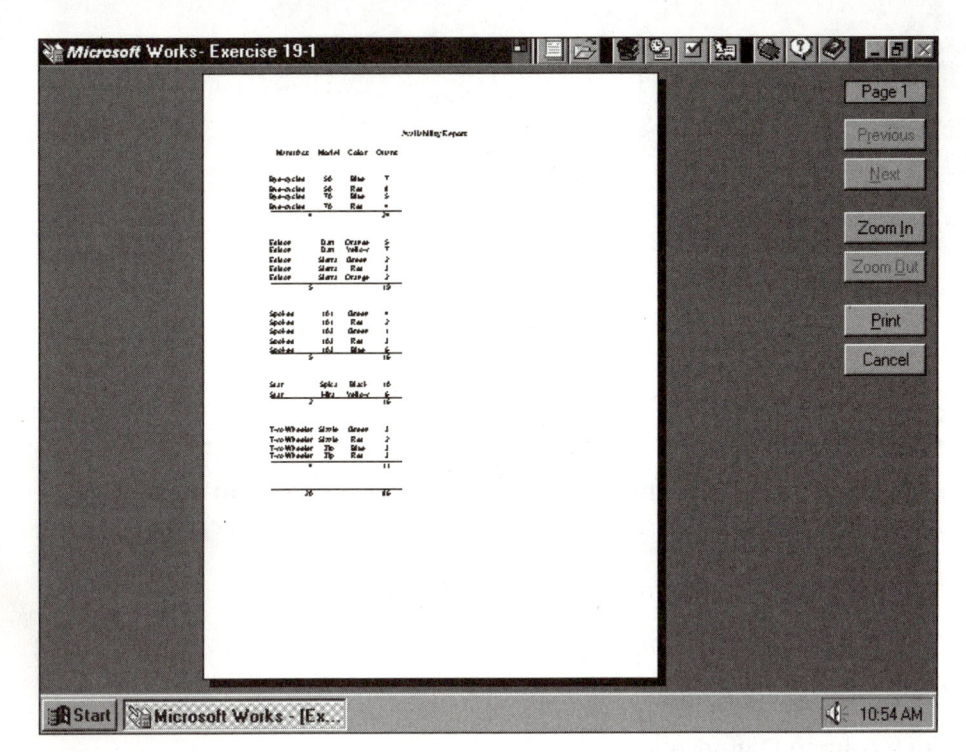

The *row labels* that appear on the left side of the Report view instruct Works on how the report will appear. The report you just created has row labels for the title, headings, records, and summaries. Table 19–1 describes the purpose of each row label available in Report view.

| Row Label | Function |
| --- | --- |
| Title | Prints a title on the first page of the report |
| Headings | Prints a heading at the top of each column |
| Record | Indicates which fields will be printed in the report |
| Summary | Indicates which statistic will be printed at the bottom of the report |
| Intr *field name* | Inserts a blank row or heading between groups of records in a sorted report |
| Summ *field name* | Indicates which statistics will be printed after each group of records in a sorted report |

Table 19–1

**note**

Report view can be accessed by clicking on the Report view icon in the toolbar.

You can insert rows to change the appearance of the report. When you choose Insert Row from the Insert menu, a special dialog box appears, as shown in Figure 19–9. Choose the type of row you want to insert.

### CHANGING HEADING NAMES

Heading names are contained in the rows with *Headings* row labels in Report view. The default heading will be the name of the field as it appears in the database. The field name is often abbreviated to fit the limited space in the database. If you prefer a different name, you must edit the field name as it appears in the row with the *Headings* row label.

**lesson 19** Database Reporting 189

**Figure 19–9**
The Insert Row dialog box allows you to specify the type of row to insert in a report.

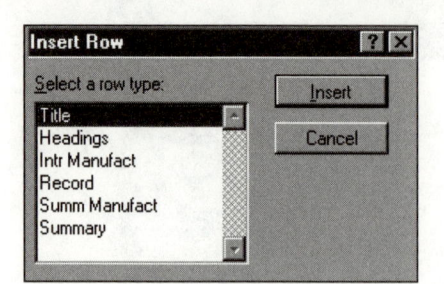

## Exercise 19-6

In this exercise, you will change headings, widen columns, and move copy in your report. The database should be in Report view on your screen.

1. Change the heading *Manufact* to *Manufacturer*.
2. Widen column A to accommodate the wider heading.
3. Change the heading *Quant* to *Quantity*.
4. Widen column D if necessary.
5. Use cut and paste to move the report title to column B.
6. Examine your changes by using Print Preview. When you finish, return to Report view.
7. Leave the database on your screen for the next exercise.

### INCLUDING ADDITIONAL FIELDS IN A REPORT

In most cases, fields to be included in a database report will be specified in the New Report dialog box when the report is created. However, if you want to add fields, you may add them in Record rows in Report view.

## Exercise 19-7

In this exercise, you will make formatting changes in your report. The database should be in Report view on your screen.

1. Enter **=Retail** in column E of the Record row.
2. Format the report data as currency with two decimals.
3. Enter **Price** in Column E of the first Headings label row.
4. Format the Price heading to be bold, underlined, and centered.
5. Use the Border command in the Format menu to add a top border to column E of the first Summ Manufact row and column E of the second Summary row.

6. Examine your changes by using Print Preview. When you finish, return to Report view.

7. Leave the database on your screen for the next exercise.

## ❖ SAVING REPORTS IN A DATABASE

When you save the database, you will save all of the database reports you have created from the database. You need not return to List or Form view to save.

## ❖ PRINTING A DATABASE REPORT

Printing a database report is like other printing you have done in Works.

## Exercise 19-8

**In this exercise, you will save and print your report.**

1. Save the database as *Mikes Bikes*.

2. Print the entire database report.

3. Close the database.

# activities

❖ TRUE/FALSE

In the blank space before each sentence, place a **T** if the statement is true and an **F** if it is false.

_____ 1. The ReportCreator guides you through the process of creating a report.

_____ 2. The procedure to sort records in a database report is similar to the way records are sorted in List view.

_____ 3. Row labels determine the type of information that will appear in a database report.

_____ 4. Database reports must be saved separately before you exit a database.

_____ 5. There is a special print command used to print reports.

❖ COMPLETION

Answer the questions below in the space provided.

1. Identify two summaries that may be used in a database report.

2. Which view is used to make changes to a database report?

3. What command allows you to insert a row in Report view?

4. What row label is used to print text at the top of a report?

5. Describe the process required to include an additional field in an existing report.

# review

## Review Exercise 19–1

The file *Review Exercise 19–1* contains a database of bicycles for Mike's Bikes (similar to the database used in the chapter). In this application, you will prepare a database report that answers the questions of the accountant for Mike's Bikes. Specifically, the accountant would like to know the number of bicycles in inventory and the value of the inventory at cost.

1. Open *Review Exercise 19–1*.

2. Create a report named *Inventory*.

3. Title the report *Year End Inventory*.

4. Include the Manufact, Model, Quant, Cost, and Cost Total fields.

5. In the Summary section of the dialog box, add the following summaries:
    a. SUM the Quant field.
    b. SUM the Cost Total field.
    c. Position the summaries under each column.

6. From Report view, perform the following steps:
    a. Change the *Manufact* heading to *Manufacturer*.
    b. Change the *Quant* heading to *Quantity*.
    c. Widen the columns to fit the expanded headings.
    d. Center the title over the report contents. (*Hint:* Move the title to Column B.)

7. Print the report.

8. Save the database as *Inventory Report*.

9. Close the database.

10. Using the information on your printed report, answer the following questions asked by the accountant:
    a. How many bicycles are in the year-end inventory? *24 (7854)*
    b. What is the value of the inventory at cost? *$14,295.10*

## Review Exercise 19-2

The file *Review Exercise 19-2* contains a database of bicycles for Mike's Bikes (similar to the database used in the chapter). In this exercise, you will prepare a database report that will be provided to customers that shows the retail prices for each bicycle model.

1. Open *Review Exercise 19-2* and prepare a database report with the following characteristics:
   a. Name the report *Price List*. Also title the report *Price List*.
   b. The fields to be included in the report include Manufact, Model, Color, and Retail.
   c. The records should be sorted by price (the Retail field), from the least expensive to the most expensive.
   d. The report should contain no summary data.
   e. The heading for *Manufact* should be changed to *Manufacturer*. Widen the column if necessary.
   f. The title of the Report should be centered over the report contents. (*Hint:* Move the title to Column B in Report view.)

2. Save the database as *Price List*.

3. Print the report.

4. Close the database.

## Review Exercise 19-3

The file *Review Exercise 19-3* contains grades recorded for three tests and a final examination by a course instructor. The database is currently sorted by grades made on the final examination.

1. Open *Review Exercise 19-3*. Prepare a report named *Stats* that indicates test averages, the highest grade for each test, and the lowest grade for each test. The database report should be titled EXAMINATION SUMMARY and appear similar to the following table.

| Name | Test 1 | Test 2 | Test 3 | Final Exam |
|---|---|---|---|---|
| Appleby | 85 | 86 | 90 | 91 |
| Barnett | 95 | 92 | 87 | 90 |
| Chandler | 77 | 74 | 73 | 70 |
| Dawson | 68 | 66 | 71 | 66 |
| Ellington | 75 | 74 | 78 | 72 |
| Fowler | 81 | 83 | 85 | 90 |
| Getz | 83 | 84 | 85 | 85 |
| Harrington | 74 | 78 | 76 | 79 |
| Ingram | 72 | 71 | 73 | 77 |
| Jones | 75 | 80 | 75 | 85 |
| Kinslow | 82 | 81 | 89 | 87 |

| Lowe | 74 | 75 | 76 | 79 |
| Martinez | 95 | 98 | 90 | 82 |
| Newsom | 83 | 88 | 90 | 82 |
| | AVG: 79.93 | AVG: 80.71 | AVG: 81.57 | AVG: 81.50 |
| | MIN: 68 | MIN: 66 | MIN: 71 | MIN: 66 |
| | MAX: 95 | MAX: 98 | MAX: 94 | MAX: 91 |

*Hints:*
- a. Make sure you position the report summaries under each column.
- b. Format the test averages as fixed with two decimals.
- c. Move the title of the report to Column B.
- d. Sort the database report alphabetically by name.

2. Save the database as *Exam*.

3. Print the database report.

4. Close the database.

## Review Exercise 19-4

In this exercise, you will create a report from the database *Directory*, which you created in *Review Exercise 15-3* and *Review Exercise 18-5*. Feel free to add more names, addresses, and phone numbers if you want.

1. Open *Directory*.

2. Create a database report named *Phone* that acts as a phone list of your friends and relatives. The report will be titled *Phone Directory* and have the following characteristics:
   - a. The report should include the fields Last Name, First Name, and Phone No.
   - b. The list should be sorted alphabetically by Last Name.

3. Create a database report that lists the names and addresses of your friends and relatives by geographical area. The report should be named *Addresses* and have the following characteristics:
   - a. The report should include the fields Last Name, First Name, Address, City, and ZIP Code.
   - b. The list should be sorted by ZIP code.

4. Save *Directory*, print both reports, and close the database.

# lesson 20

# Integration Basics

### ❖ OBJECTIVES

Upon completion of this lesson, you will be able to:

1. Understand the concept of integration.
2. Copy among documents.
3. Use linking to integrate documents.
4. Create a form letter.

**Estimated Time:** 1/2 hour

### ❖ INTRODUCTION TO INTEGRATION

*Integration* refers to using more than one Works tool to create a document. This means that you can use information created in a spreadsheet to complete a report in the word processor. Or you can use information from a database to create form letters in the word processor. Tables from the word processor can become spreadsheet data.

### ❖ MOVING AND COPYING DATA BETWEEN DOCUMENTS

The process of copying data among different tools varies, depending on what tools are involved. Word processor, spreadsheet, and database documents have unique formats. For example, data from a spreadsheet is arranged in cells, information in a database is collected in fields, and text in a word processor document does not follow any particular format. Table 20–1 shows how Works changes the format of the information you are copying among tools so that it may be used in the destination document.

| Copying from | Format Change |
|---|---|
| Spreadsheet to Word Processor | Tabs are used to separate the spreadsheet information into columns. |
| Word Processor to Spreadsheet | If the text from the word processor is set up as a table, with data separated by tabs, the spreadsheet will separate the text into separate cells in the spreadsheet. If the text is in a single block, all of the text will be copied into the currently highlighted cell of the spreadsheet. |
| Word Processor to Database | If the text from the word processor is set up as a table, with data separated by tabs, the database will separate the text into fields. Each line will be entered as a separate record. If the text is in a single block, all of the text will be copied into the currently highlighted field. |
| Spreadsheet to Database | The cells cut or copied from the spreadsheet will appear in the database, beginning with the highlighted entry. |
| Database to Spreadsheet | The field entries will be pasted into the spreadsheet columns, and the records will be pasted into the rows. |
| Database to Word Processor | The data is formatted with tabs when it enters the word processor. |

Table 20–1

## Exercise 20–1

In this exercise, you will copy spreadsheet data from a spreadsheet into the letter. By integrating the documents, Stephen can send one instead of two pages to Gabriel.

1. Open *Exercise 20–1a* and *Exercise20–1b*. *Exercise 20–1b* should be the active document.
2. Highlight the data in the spreadsheet from cell A1 to cell C14.
3. Click the **Copy** button on the toolbar.
4. Switch to *Exercise 20–1a*.
5. Place the cursor in the blank space between the first and second paragraphs.

6. Click the **Paste** button on the toolbar. The data from the spreadsheet appears in the letter. Insert one blank line before and after the spreadsheet data.

7. Save *Exercise 20–1a* as *Ski Letter* and *Exercise 20–1b* as *Ski Data*.

8. Print *Ski Letter*. Close *Ski Letter*. Leave *Ski Data* open for the next exercise.

## ❖ LINKING

Copying data from one document to another can be useful. There will be times, however, when the data you are copying may change periodically. Suppose your job as treasurer of an organization is to file a monthly financial report. Your report is basically the same each month except for the month's cash flow numbers. You keep the cash flow data up to date in a spreadsheet. Using the copying and pasting techniques discussed above, you would have to copy the latest spreadsheet numbers and paste them into your word processor document each month.

There is an easier way. Instead of pasting the data manually each time, the Paste Special command can be used to link the two documents. *Linking* will automatically paste the latest figures from your spreadsheet into your report. Each time the word processor document is opened, you have the opportunity to update the document with the latest spreadsheet data.

Figure 20–1 shows the Paste Special dialog box that appears when data from a Works spreadsheet is pasted into a word processor document. The Paste Link option places the spreadsheet data into the document and creates the link to the actual spreadsheet.

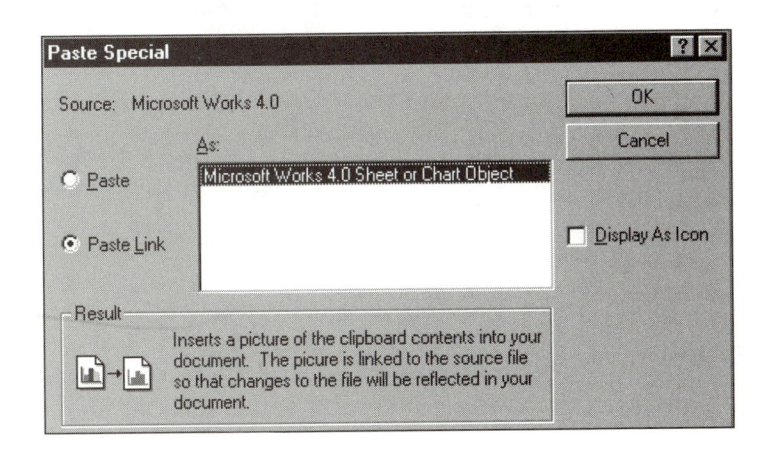

**Figure 20–1**
The Paste Special dialog box allows spreadsheet data to be pasted into a word processor document.

## Exercise 20-2

In this exercise, you will link data from the *Ski Data* spreadsheet into the *Ski Link* document. *Ski Data* should be on your screen.

1. Open *Exercise 20–1a*.

2. Switch to *Ski Data* and highlight cells A1 through C14, if they are not already highlighted. Copy the cells and switch back to *Exercise 20–1a*.

**lesson 20** *Integration Basics* 199

3. Place the cursor in the blank space between the first and second paragraphs.

4. Choose **Paste Special** from the **Edit** menu. The Paste Special dialog box appears.

5. Click **Paste Link.**

6. Click **OK.** The spreadsheet data appear in the document. The data are linked to *Ski Data*. Any changes made to *Ski Data* will be reflected in *Exercise 20–1a*.

7. Insert one blank line above and one blank line below the linked data.

8. Save *Exercise 20–1a* as *Ski Link*.

9. Save changes to *Ski Data*. Close *Ski Link* and *Ski Data*.

❖ UPDATING A LINKED DOCUMENT

Changes made in the *Ski Data* spreadsheet will become a part of the *Ski Link* letter when the letter is opened.

## Exercise 20-3

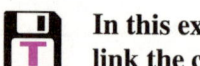

In this exercise, you will make changes to the *Ski Data* document and link the changes to *Ski Link*. *Ski Data* should be on your screen.

1. Open *Ski Data*.

2. Change the cost of transportation to **$95** for the two-day trip and **$35** for the four-day trip.

3. Save *Ski Data*.

4. Open *Ski Link*. You will be asked whether you want to update links.

5. Click **Yes.** *Ski Link* appears.

6. Scroll down until the transportation costs are in view. You can see that the data was updated.

7. Open *Ski Letter*. Scroll down until the transportation costs are in view. The data was not updated in *Ski Letter* because the data was not linked.

8. Save, print, and close *Ski Link*. Close *Ski Data* and *Ski Letter*.

❖ FORM LETTERS

Another way to integrate Works tools is to print form letters. A *form letter* is a word processor document that uses information from a database in specified areas to personalize a document.

For example, you might send a letter to all of the members of a club using a form letter. The information is the same in each letter, but the names will be different in each case. Each printed letter will carry the name of a different member of the club. One letter may begin "Dear Jennifer" and another "Dear Mike."

### ❖ CREATING A FORM LETTER

To create form letters, you integrate information from a database with a document from the word processor. Both the database and the word processor document must be open. You then insert the field names in the word processor document where you want to print information from the database. The field names you place in the word processing document are enclosed in brackets.

To insert a field from the database, choose the Database Field command from the Insert menu. The Insert Field dialog box will appear, as shown in Figure 20–2. The bottom of the dialog box allows you to choose the database from which the form letter will draw its information. The top of the dialog box allows you to choose which field from the database you want to insert.

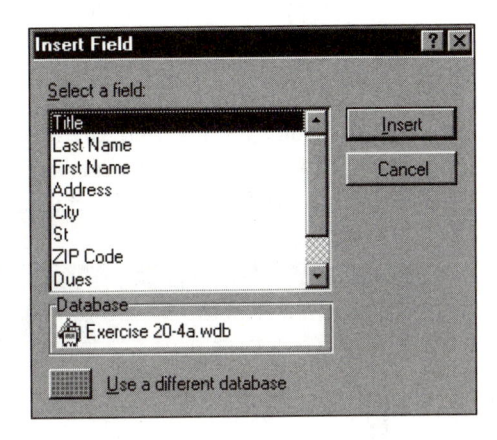

Figure 20–2
The Insert Field dialog box inserts database fields into a word processor document.

## Exercise 20-4

**In this exercise, you will create form letters.**

1. Open *Exercise 20–4a*.
2. Use the scroll bars to view all of the fields in the database.
3. Open *Exercise 20–4b*.
4. Position the cursor to the left of the *W* in the word *We* in the first sentence of the last paragraph in the letter.
5. Start a new paragraph before the last paragraph by keying **Dues this year are**. Key one space after the word *are*.
6. Choose **Database Field** from the **Insert** menu. The Insert Field dialog box appears. *Exercise 20–4a* is already selected as the database.
7. Click **Dues** in the Fields box. Click **Insert.** The field will appear in your document as {{Dues}}. Click **Close.**
8. Press (Backspace) to remove the space which was inserted after {{Dues}}.
9. Key a period to end the sentence. Key two spaces. Key **Our records indicate that you have paid**. Key one space after the word *paid*.
10. Insert the Paid field.
11. Key **and owe a balance of**. Key one space following the word *of*.

lesson 20 *Integration Basics* 201

12. Insert the Balance field.

13. Press **Backspace** to remove the space which was inserted after {{Balance}}.

14. Key a period after the Balance field. Key two spaces. Key the following sentence to complete the paragraph: **Please remit the balance to the address on this letterhead as soon as possible.**

15. Press **Enter** twice. Adjust the spacing around the paragraph if necessary. Save the document as *WUM* and leave the file open for the next exercise.

❖ PRINTING FORM LETTERS

After the fields are inserted, the form letters are ready to print. The Print dialog box has a check box called Print Merge, shown in Figure 20–3. When the Print Merge check box is chosen, data from the database are inserted into the document during printing.

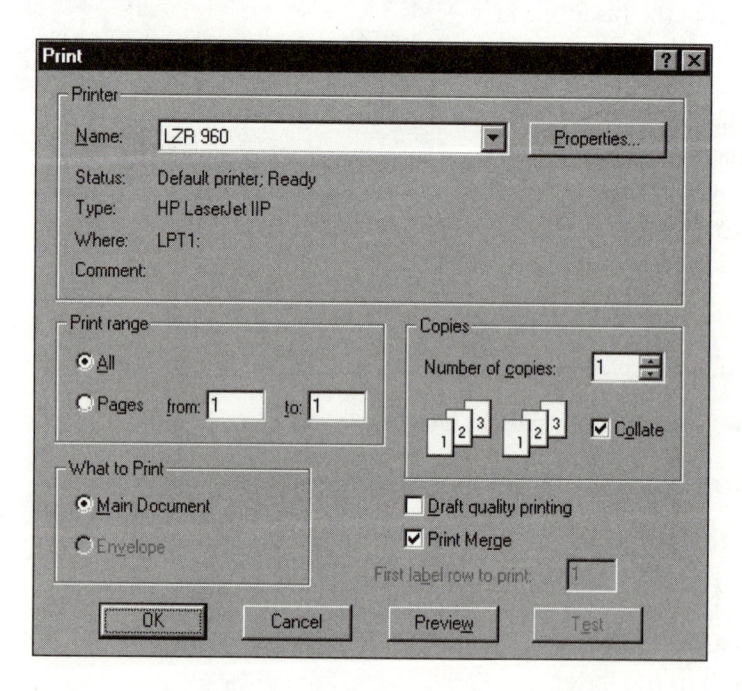

Figure 20–3
The Print dialog box's Print Merge check box is used when printing form letters.

## Exercise 20-5

**In this exercise, you will preview and print the form letters.**

1. Choose **Print** from the **File** menu.

2. Click the **Preview** button. A message box appears asking you if you want to preview all records.

3. Click **OK.** The first letter appears on the screen.

4. Click the **Zoom In** button twice. Your screen should look similar to Figure 20–4.

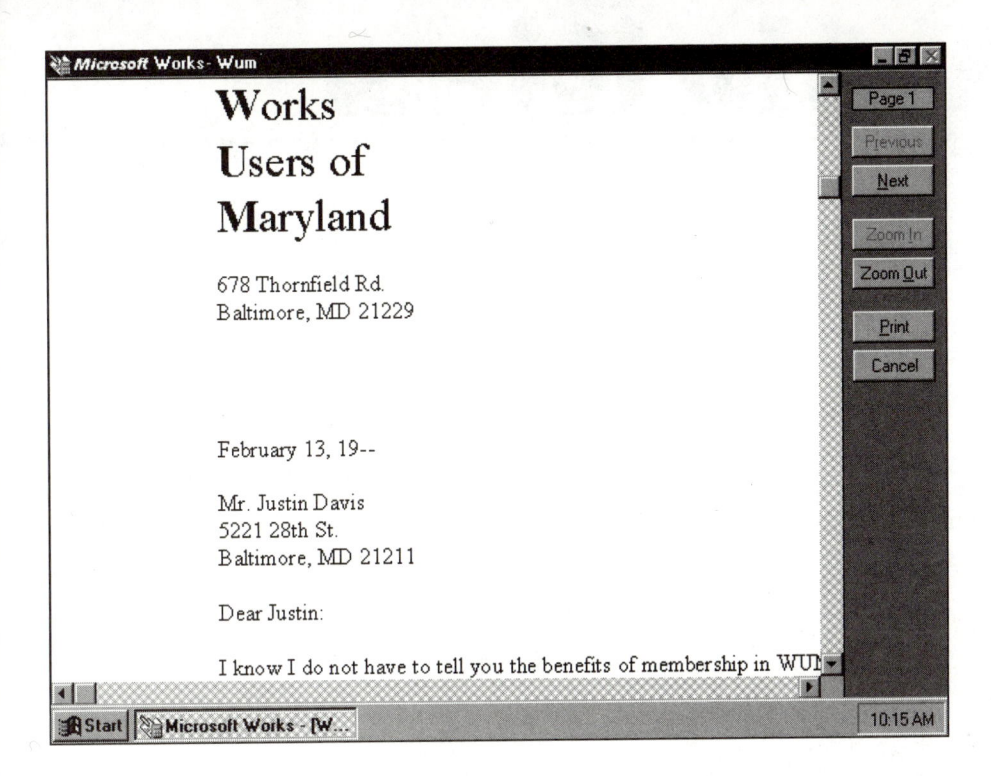

**Figure 20–4**
Form letters can be previewed before being printed.

5. Click the **Next** button to see the next letter. Notice that the name, address, and payment information change with each letter.

6. Click the **Next** button again to see the last letter.

7. Click **Print.** Click **OK.**

8. Close *WUM* and *Exercise 20–4a.*

# activities

### ❖ TRUE/FALSE

In the blank space before each sentence, place a **T** if the statement is true and an **F** if it is false.

_____ 1. Data can be copied among any of the Works tools.

_____ 2. Works does not change the format of data copied among the tools.

_____ 3. Linking spreadsheet cells is performed using the Paste Link option in the Paste Special dialog box.

_____ 4. In a word processing document, database fields appear in bold italics.

_____ 5. Form letters get their data from spreadsheets.

### ❖ COMPLETION

Answer the questions below in the space provided.

1. What is the term for using more than one Works tool to create a document?
   _____
   _____

2. What two commands are used to place data from a database into a spreadsheet?
   _____
   _____

3. What does Works do to spreadsheet data when it is copied into a word processor document?
   _____
   _____

4. Why is linking a better way than copying and pasting when you want to update data in a report you use every month?
   _____
   _____
   _____
   _____

5. What is a form letter?
   _____
   _____

# review

## Review Exercise 20–1

**In this exercise, you will use Copy and Paste to move and copy data among documents.**

1. Open *Review Exercise 20–1*.

2. Highlight the fields from First Name to ZIP Code for both Oscar Alvarado and Marcy Bell. Do not include their titles or prizes. Copy the data.

3. Create a new word processor document, and place the database data into the document. Notice how the fields are separated by tabs.

4. Create a new spreadsheet document. Copy the same database data into the new spreadsheet. Notice how each field is placed in a separate cell.

5. Close all three files. Do not save the files.

## Review Exercise 20–2

**In this exercise, you will use linking to create a report for the members of a science group that is raising funds for a trip.**

1. Open *Review Exercise 20–2a*. The number in cell D4 of the spreadsheet is the total amount of money raised for the science trip. The money is to be divided among the 11 students who are going on the trip. The spreadsheet takes the total funds raised and divides it by the number of students to calculate the portion of the trip paid for by the fund-raiser. Then the remaining balance is calculated to show the students how much of the cost they will be responsible for at the current level of funding. As the total funds raised grow, each student's portion of the cost decreases.

2. Open *Review Exercise 20–2b*.

3. Switch to *Review Exercise 20–2a*. Copy cells A3 through D7.

4. Save the spreadsheet as *Trip Fund*.

5. Switch to *Review Exercise 20–2b*. Position the cursor at the end of the document. Use the Paste Special and the Paste Link commands to link the data from the spreadsheet. Insert one blank line above the spreadsheet.

6. Save the word processor document as *Trip Report*. Print *Trip Report*. Save and close both files.

# Review Exercise 20-3

**In this exercise, you will draft a letter to notify customers that they won a prize in a promotional drawing.**

1. Open *Review Exercise 20–1*.

2. Add your own name, address, and the prize you would like to be awarded to the *Review Exercise 20–1* database.

3. Create a form letter that notifies the customers in the database of the prizes they have been awarded. Be sure to include:
   a. name of business awarding prizes
   b. address where prize can be claimed
   c. hours of business

   Make sure you insert the database fields in all appropriate places.

4. Print your form letters.

# index

? wildcard, 167–168
=, in formulas, 93, 105
* wildcard, 167–168
$, in cell references, 103–104

## A

absolute cell references, 103
active cells, 66
active document, 7, 11, 12
active windows, 11, 12
adding
   fields to reports, 185, 190
   headers and footers, 58
   records, 135
adjusting. See changing
aligning
   cells, 76–77
   fields, 148
   text, 35–36
All Characters command, 57
all records searches, 165, 167
applying filters, 173
arguments, 105
ascending sort, 171
asterisk (*) wildcard, 167–168
automatic page breaks, 48
Autosum, 96–97

## B

Backspace key, 13
bar charts, 115
bold text, 40–41
   in databases, 149
   in spreadsheets, 76
borders, cell, 78
buttons
   alignment, 36
   Autosum, 96–97
   copy, 22
   cut, 21

   in dialog boxes, 3
   font style, 40
   Form Design, 146
   Form view, 127
   List view, 127
   new chart, 115
   paste, 21
   print, 25
   print preview, 24
   spelling checker, 41
   on toolbar, 4

## C

calculations
   in databases, 157–158
   See also formulas
cell references, 66
   absolute, 103
   in formulas, 95
   mixed, 104
   relative, 103
cells, 66
   active, 66
   alignment, 76–77
   borders, 78
   changing appearance, 75–78
   clearing, 70
   copying, 83–85
   editing, 70
   fill down, 84
   fill right, 85
   fonts, 76
   formats, 77–78
   ranges, 75
   selecting, 75
center-aligned tabs, 45
changing
   appearance of cells, 75–78
   appearance of reports, 188–189
   column widths, 69
   data in spreadsheets, 70

   field formats, 154
   field sizes, 147
   fonts, 39–40
   fonts in databases, 149
   font sizes, 41
   fonts in spreadsheets, 76
   font styles, 40–41
   margins, 31
   spacing, 35
   type of charts, 120
characters
   special, 56–57
   viewing all, 57
   wildcards, 167–168
charts
   changing types, 120
   creating, 115
   editing, 116
   headings, 117–118
   names, 118–119
   printing, 120
   renaming, 118–119
   saving, 119
   titles, 117–118
   types, 115
check boxes, 3
choosing
   commands from menus, 5
   commands from toolbars, 4
   options in dialog boxes, 3
clearing cells, 70
close box, 4
closing
   documents, 8
   windows, 4
columns, 66
   Best Fit option, 69
   changing widths, 69
   deleting, 79
   freezing titles, 87
   inserting, 79
   sums, 96–97

*index* 207

# index

columns, database. *See* fields
Column Width dialog box, 69
complex formulas, 94
copy button, 22
copying
   in databases, 137
   between documents of different
      types, 197–198
   fill down, 84
   fill right, 85
   formats, 55–56
   spreadsheet data, 83–85,
      103–104
   styles, 55–56
   text, 22
   between word processing
      documents, 55
correcting errors
   with Backspace key, 13
   in formulas, 94
   misspelled words, 41–42
Create Database dialog box,
   143–144
creating
   charts, 115
   databases, 143–144
   documents, 11
   fields, 144–146
   filters, 173
   form letters, 201
   headers and footers, 58
   reports, 183–188
   spreadsheets, 65
cursor, 13
   moving, 19
cut button, 21
cutting and pasting, 21
   in databases, 139
   in spreadsheets, 86
   in word processor
      documents, 21

## D

databases, 125
   adding records, 135
   calculations, 157–158
   copying data to or from other
      documents, 198
   creating, 143–144
   deleting records, 135
   entries, 126
   fields, 126
   filters, 173–175
   form letters, 200–202
   formulas, 157–158
   Form view, 127
   List view, 127
   moving highlight in, 129–130
   opening, 125
   previewing, 139
   printing, 139
   records, 126
   reports, 183–191
   Report view, 188–189
   saving, 136
   searching, 165–168
   sorting, 171–172
   splitting window, 128–129
   uses, 125
   viewing, 127
date
   field formats, 153, 156
   inserting in databases, 157
   inserting in documents, 56
decimal-aligned tabs, 45
defaults
   field formats, 153
   spacing, 35
   tabs, 45
deleting
   columns and rows, 79
   data in spreadsheets, 70

   records, 135
   text, 13, 23
descending sort, 171
dialog boxes, 3
   buttons, 3
   option groups, 3
Directories box, 5
disk drives, opening files, 5–6
displaying
   all records, 167
   dates and times, 153, 156
   hidden field names, 164
   hidden fields, 163
   hidden records, 165
documents
   active, 7, 11, 12
   closing, 8
   copying between, 197–198
   creating, 11
   entering text, 13
   headers and footers, 58
   linking, 199
   margins, 31
   multiple, 7
   names, 14, 56
   Normal view, 58
   opening, 5–6
   page breaks, 48
   previewing, 24–25
   printing, 25
   saving, 14–16
   saving with new names, 16
   scrolling, 7
   searching, 49
document window, 13
   footer line, 58
   header line, 58
dollar sign ($), in cell references,
   103–104
dragging, 7
   and dropping, 23

208 *index*

# index

## E

Easy Formats, 34
editing
   charts, 116
   data in spreadsheets, 70
   formulas, 94
   *See also* changing
Enter button, 68
entering
   data in spreadsheets, 68
   formulas, 94
   text, 13
Enter key, 13
entries, 126
equal sign (=), 93, 105
errors, correcting
   with Backspace key, 13
   in formulas, 94
   misspelled words, 41–42
exiting Works, 8

## F

fields, 126
   adjusting sizes, 147
   aligning, 148
   Best Fit option, 147
   calculations, 157–158
   creating, 144–146
   filters using, 173
   fonts, 149
   formats, 153–154
   in form letters, 201
   hiding, 163
   hiding names, 163–164
   inserting, 145–146
   moving, 147–148
   names, 126
   in reports, 185–186, 190
   sorting by, 172, 185–186
   summarizing in reports, 187–188, 189
Field Size dialog box, 147
Field Width dialog box, 147
files
   closing, 8
   names, 14
   opening, 5
   saving, 14–16
fill down, 84
   in databases, 137
fill right, 85
   in databases, 137
Filter dialog box, 173
filters, 173
   creating, 173
   criteria, 173–175
   names, 173
   numerical, 174
   in reports, 187
financial functions, 108
Find dialog box, 49, 165
finding. *See* searching
first-line indents, 32–33, 34
F line, 58
folders, 5
font name box, 39
fonts, 39
   changing, 39–40
   copying styles, 55–56
   in databases, 149
   sizes, 41, 76
   in spreadsheets, 76
   styles, 40–41, 76
font size box, 39, 41
footers, 58
Format dialog box, 153–154
Format Paragraph dialog box, 33
formats
   cell, 77–78
   copying, 55–56
   of data copied between tools, 197–198
   Date, 153, 156
   field, 153–154
   Fraction, 154
   General, 153
   Number, 153
   Serialized, 154
   Text, 154
   Time, 153, 156
Format Tabs dialog box, 46
Form Design view
   adjusting field sizes, 147
   creating fields, 145–146
   field locations, 148
   hiding field names, 163–164
   moving fields, 147–148
form letters, 200–201
   creating, 201
   printing, 202
formula bar, 66, 93
   cell references in, 103–104
   complex, 94
   copying, 103–104
   correcting errors, 94
   database, 157–158
   editing, 94
   entering, 94
   entering data, 68
   formulas, 93
   function, 105
   highlighting cells, 95
   manual calculation option, 97
   moving, 103–104
   operands, 93–94, 157
   operators, 93–94, 157–158
   order of evaluation, 94
   structure, 93–94
   viewing, 97
Form view, 127
   adding records, 135
   deleting records, 135

index 209

# index

hiding records, 165
moving highlight in, 130
printing records, 139
Fraction format, 154
freezing titles, 87
function formulas, 105
functions
   financial, 108
   mathematical, 106
   names, 105
   statistical, 107
   trigonometric, 106

## G

General format, 153
Go To command, 67
grouping reports, 186

## H

hanging indents, 34
header pane, 13
headers, 58
headings
   charts, 117–118
   report, 189
hiding
   field names, 163–164
   fields, 163
   formatting characters, 57
   records, 165
highlighting
   cells, 75
   entire documents, 20
   records, 136
   text, 20
highlights
   moving in databases, 129–130
   moving in spreadsheets, 66–67
H line, 58

## I

indenting, 32
   from both margins, 34
   first-line, 32–33, 34
   hanging, 34
inserting
   columns and rows, 79
   date and time, 56, 157
   document names, 56
   fields, 145–146
   page breaks, 48
   page numbers, 56
   records, 138
   rows in reports, 189, 190
   special characters, 56–57
   text, 20
Insert Row dialog box, 190
Insert Special Character dialog box, 56–57
integration, 197
   copying data, 197–198
   form letters, 200–202
   linking, 199–200
   moving data, 197–198
italic text, 40–41
   in databases, 149
   in spreadsheets, 76

## J K

justifying text, 35–36

keyboard
   moving cursor with, 19
   moving highlights in databases, 130
   moving highlights in spreadsheets, 67

## L

leaders, tabs, 46
left-aligned tabs, 45
letters. *See* form letters
line charts, 115
line spacing, 35
linking, 199
List view, 127
   adding records, 135
   adjusting field sizes, 147
   creating fields, 145–146
   deleting records, 135
   hiding fields, 163
   hiding records, 165
   inserting records, 138
   moving highlight in, 130
   printing, 139
   selecting records, 136

## M

manual page breaks, 48
margins, changing, 31
mathematical functions, 106
menus, 4
   choosing commands from, 5
   opening, 5
Microsoft Works. *See* Works
mixed cell references, 104
mouse
   adjusting field sizes, 147
   changing column widths, 69
   dragging, 7
   dragging and dropping, 23
   highlighting text, 20
   moving cursor with, 19
   moving highlights in databases, 129
   moving highlights in spreadsheets, 67

# index

moving
  cursor, 19
  database data, 139
  data between documents of different types, 197–198
  fields, 147–148
  highlights in databases, 129–130
  highlights in spreadsheets, 66–67
  spreadsheet data, 86, 103–104
  text, 21, 23
  text between word processing documents, 55

## N

names
  charts, 118–119
  document, 14, 56
  fields, 126
  files, 14
  filters, 173
  functions, 105
  reports, 184
  windows, 4
New Chart button, 115
next record searches, 165–166
Normal view, 58
numbers
  field formats, 153–154
  in filters, 174
  in spreadsheets, 68
  summarizing in reports, 187–188, 189
  sums, 96–97

## O

Open dialog box, 5–6
opening
  databases, 125
  documents, 5–6
  menus, 5

multiple documents, 7
  spreadsheets, 65
operands, 93–94, 157
operators, 93–94, 157–158
option groups, in dialog boxes, 3

## P

page breaks, 48
page numbers, inserting, 56
pages, margins, 31
Page Setup dialog box, 31, 32
paragraphs
  copying formats, 55–56
  indenting, 32–34
  spacing, 35
paste button, 21
Paste Special command, 55–56, 199
Paste Special dialog box, 56, 199
pasting
  spreadsheet data, 83
  text, 21
pie charts, 115
previewing
  databases, 139
  documents, 24–25
print button, 25
Print dialog box, 25
printing
  charts, 120
  databases, 139
  documents, 25
  form letters, 202
  previewing, 24–25
  records, 139
  reports, 191
  spreadsheets, 88
print merge check box, 202
print preview button, 24

## Q

question mark (?) wildcard, 167–168
quitting. *See* exiting

## R

ranges, 75
records, 126
  adding, 135
  deleting, 135
  filters, 173–175
  hiding, 165
  inserting, 138
  numbers, 126
  printing, 139
  searching, 165–166
  selecting, 136
  sorting, 171–172
relative cell references, 103
removing
  fields from reports, 185
  font styles, 40
  tabs, 48
Rename Chart dialog box, 119
renaming charts, 118–119
Replace dialog box, 50
replacing
  data in spreadsheets, 70
  text, 50
ReportCreator, 183–188
reports, 183
  adding fields, 185, 190
  changing appearance, 188–189
  creating, 183–188
  filters, 187
  grouping, 186
  headings, 189
  inserting rows, 189, 190
  names, 184

# index

printing, 191
removing fields, 185
row labels, 189
saving, 191
sorting, 185–186
summaries, 187–188, 189
titles, 184, 189
Report view, 188–189
adding fields, 190
right-aligned tabs, 45
row labels, 189
rows, 66
deleting, 79
freezing titles, 87
inserting, 79
labels, 66
in reports, 189, 190
sums, 96–97
ruler, 13
setting tabs on, 47

## S

Save As dialog box, 14–15
saving
charts, 119
databases, 136
documents, 14–16
in new location, 16
with new name, 16
reports, 191
spreadsheets, 71
scatter charts, 115
scroll arrows, 7
scroll bars, 4, 7
scroll boxes, 7
scrolling, 7
searching
all records, 165, 167
databases, 165–168
documents, 49
with filters, 173–175

next record, 165–166
wildcards, 167–168
Select All command, 20
selecting. *See* highlighting
Serialized format, 154
Set Print Area command, 88
setting tabs, 46–47
showing. *See* displaying
sorting
databases, 171–172
reports, 185–186
Sort Records dialog box, 172
special characters, inserting, 56–57
spelling checker, 41–42
Spelling dialog box, 42
splitting database windows, 128–129
spreadsheets
borders, 78
cell formats, 77–78
cells, 66
changing column widths, 69
changing data, 70
columns, 66
copying data to or from other documents, 198
creating, 65
deleting columns and rows, 79
Enter button, 68
entering data, 68
fonts, 76
formula bar, 66
formulas, 93–94
freezing titles, 87
highlights in, 66–67
inserting columns and rows, 79
opening, 65
parts of, 65–66
printing, 88
ranges, 75
rows, 66
saving, 71

textual data, 68
*See also* charts
starting Works, 1–2
statistical functions, 107
status bar, 5, 13
sums
in reports, 187–188, 189
in spreadsheets, 96–97

## T

tabs, 45
center-aligned, 45
decimal-aligned, 45
leaders, 46
left-aligned, 45
removing, 48
right-aligned, 45
setting, 46–47
symbols, 45
text
aligning, 35–36
aligning in spreadsheets, 76–77
bold, 40–41
copying, 22
copying between documents, 55
cutting and pasting, 21
deleting, 13, 23
dragging and dropping, 23
entering, 13
finding, 49
highlighting, 20
inserting, 20
italic, 40–41
moving, 21, 23
moving between documents, 55
replacing, 50
spacing, 35
in spreadsheets, 68
underlining, 40–41
word wrap, 13
Text format, 154

# index

xtual data, 68
ne
   field formats, 153, 156
   inserting in databases, 157
   inserting in documents, 56
le bars, 4, 13
les
   chart, 117–118
   report, 184, 189
olbar, 4, 5
   alignment buttons, 36
   Autosum button, 96–97
   changing fonts, 39–40
   choosing commands from, 4
   copy button, 22
   cut button, 21
   font name box, 39
   font size box, 39, 41
   font style buttons, 40
   Form Design button, 146
   Form view button, 127
   List view button, 127
   New Chart button, 115
   paste button, 21
   print button, 25
   print preview button, 24
   spelling checker button, 41
trigonometric functions, 106
typefaces. *See* fonts

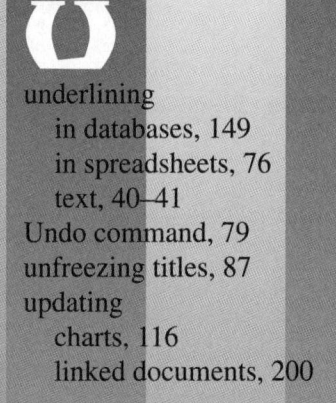

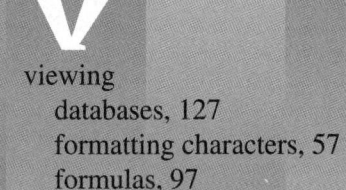

## U

underlining
   in databases, 149
   in spreadsheets, 76
   text, 40–41
Undo command, 79
unfreezing titles, 87
updating
   charts, 116
   linked documents, 200

## V

viewing
   databases, 127
   formatting characters, 57
   formulas, 97

## W

wildcards, 167–168
windows, 4
   active, 11, 12
   close box, 4
   closing, 4
   document, 13
   names, 4
   scroll bars, 4, 7
   splitting, 128–129
   status bar, 5, 13
   title bars, 4, 13
word processor
   copying data to or from other
      tools, 198
   document window, 13
   form letters, 200–202
   *See also* documents; text
word wrap, 13
Works, 1
   exiting, 8
   screen, 4
   starting, 1–2
Works Task Launcher, 2, 3

# notes